FOLKLORE / CINEMA

Popular Film as Vernacular Culture

FOLKLORE / CINEMA
Popular Film as Vernacular Culture

Edited by
Sharon R. Sherman and Mikel J.Koven

Utah State University Press
Logan, Utah

Copyright ©2007 Utah State University Press

Utah State University Press
Logan, Utah 84322–7200

Manufactured in the United States of America
Printed on recycled, acid-free paper

ISBN: 978–0–87421–673-8 (hardback)
ISBN: 978–0–87421–675-2 (e-book)

Library of Congress Cataloging-in-Publication Data

Folklore/cinema : popular film as vernacular culture / edited by Sharon R.
Sherman and Mikel J. Koven.
   p. cm.
  ISBN 978-0-87421-673-8 (hardback : alk. paper) -- ISBN 978-0-87421-675-2
(e-book)
  1. Motion pictures. 2. Folklore in motion pictures. 3. Culture in motion
pictures. I. Sherman, Sharon R., 1943- II. Koven, Mikel J.
  PN1994.F545 2007
  791.43--dc22
                       2007029969

Contents

III. Through Folklore's Lenses

IV. Disruption And Incorporation

Introduction

Popular Film as Vernacular Culture

W<small>E BOTH HAVE</small> been working in the areas of folklore and film studies for a number of years, and this current volume demonstrates that we are not alone in exploring the convergence of popular cinema and folklore. *Folklore/Cinema* first emerged out of our work on film and folklore for a special issue of *Western Folklore* (2005). When we edited that issue, we realized how much interest and work focused on this subject and that an audience awaited a book on it. Once we chose to move on to a book, we knew we would have no trouble finding high-quality essays to include. In fact, only one of the chapters comes from that issue of *Western Folklore*. It is reprinted here because of its particularly successful treatment of the convergence of film and folklore. Scholars are producing excellent work with direct interest for folklorists, film scholars, and those in disciplines that analyze the discourses of both film and folklore (for example, comparative literature, the arts, journalism, and European and other area studies).

The difficult balance we faced as editors was to ensure a double market/double audience for this book: these chapters needed to be sufficiently grounded in academic folkloristics and film studies to be of more than passing interest to readers in those fields. In many respects, this work seeks to broaden the dialogue between film and folklore studies in an environment where we can all learn from each other outside of the confines of our own disciplines. The eleven chapters in this collection are all concerned with exploring popular film and folklore, albeit from a number of different approaches and disciplines. This interdisciplinary approach allows us insight into a variety of academic perspectives; we are interested not only in seeing how folklorists see film but also how film scholars see folklore.

The title of the first section, "Filmic Folklore," reflects this convergence; the term comes from Juwen Zhang's contribution to our special issue of *Western Folklore*. Zhang coined the term as a response to Sherman's "folklore," folkloric," or "folkloristic" film, all of which she uses synonymously. Such films focus on folklore as their central interest and are produced by folklorists or filmmakers for those interested in folklore. As Sherman notes in *Documenting Ourselves,*

> Folklore films combine the goal of the documentary to record unstaged events with the goal of the ethnodocumentary to provide information about culture. The folkloric film focuses primarily on traditions, those expressive forms of human behavior which are communicated by interactions and whose formal features mark them as traditional. The folklore film covers a wide range of traditional behavior, from rituals, ceremonies, folk art and material culture to games, sayings, and songs and to the lore of various peoples bonded by ethnicity, age, gender, family, occupation, recreation, religion, and region. (1998,63)

These films may be fairly obscure, such as the Seegers' Folklore Research Film Series (1956–1966), or as widely circulated as Stacy Peralta's *Dogtown and Z-Boys* (2001), created for a large audience with interests not demarcated as folklore but nevertheless falling within the parameters of folkloristics.

Naturally, such usage presupposed that the term applied exclusively to a particular type of *documentary* film, despite Sherman's coverage of some fiction features and their reflection of folklore content (Sherman 1996, 265). Koven's work, from an exclusive focus on the fictional feature film, has explored both the way popular film can behave like folklore (e.g., 1999) and what new discourses on popular films open up when they are viewed through the methodological lenses of folkloristics (e.g., 2003). As Sherman already laid claim to the term folkloric or folkloristic film to refer explicitly to a kind of documentary cinema, Koven's work avoids such a designation to define the terrain he works in. Zhang's term filmic folklore offers a fusion of the folkloristic study of popular fictional cinema that may include elements of the documentary folkloric film. As Zhang defines it,

> Filmic folklore, by definition, is an imagined folklore that exists only in films, and is a folklore or folklore-like performance that is represented, created, or hybridized in fictional film. Taken out of the original (social, historic, geographic, and cultural) contexts, it functions in similar ways to that of folkloristic films. Filmic folklore imposes or reinforces certain stereotypes (ideologies), and signifies certain meanings identified and consumed (as "the truth") by a certain group of people. The folklore in filmic folklore may appear as a scene, an action, an event, or a storyline (plot), and in verbal or non-verbal form. (2005, 267)

If, for Sherman, folkloric film is film acting as a folklorist, then filmic folklore presupposes folklore mediated through the filmic and asks how folklore is created via film. Thus, the term filmic folklore, as coined by Juwen Zhang, refers to a kind of artificial folklore-like phenomenon that only exists cinematically, that is, in fictional films. Filmic folklore may behave *like* "proper" folklore does, but it is entirely a construct for the camera.

The opening chapters address the postmodern problematizing of what Regina Bendix characterizes as the authenticity of experience. Gillian Helfield, Julie LeBlanc, and Rebecca Prime explore filmmakers' search for the authentic in places where folklore once emerged but authenticity now seems lost. Thus, through the medium of popular culture, the folkloric experience becomes a postmodern one.

Gillian Helfield's chapter documents the Québec cinéma direct movement in the 1960s. Helfield argues, in filmic-folklore fashion, that the 1960s vogue for authenticity within cinéma vérité, the revival of folkways, and the newly established outlets for Québécois culture to express itself (and, more importantly, *to* itself) coalesced in a series of short romanticized documentaries about folkloristic topics, much as early folklorists might have documented them. Her explanation of differences between American and French cinéma vérité and Canadian cinéma direct points to the distinctions filmmakers signified among these forms through how they thought the camera represented reality.

Québécois culture is also the subject of Julie LeBlanc, who analyzes the filmic fictional figure of "Elvis" Gratton as both folk hero and anti-hero. While filmmakers, through three short and (to date) three feature films, created the character of Elvis Gratton as a satiric assault on Canadian Federalism within Québec, he has become a vernacular cult figure. LeBlanc's astute writing gives us insight into the highly political and discursive world of these films. Gratton is actually what Richard M. Dorson would call a "mass-culture hero" (1959, 200), except, unlike other such heroes, he is not situated in a mass culture. He is known primarily to a small group of people in Québec and has thus acquired a type of "folk" status. The films are in French and mirror the Québécois culture back to French Canadians in Québec (we know of no one else, even in neighboring provinces, who has heard of Gratton). Like all folk heroes, he is heroic to a particular group—in this case, Québécois viewers of a certain generation.

Like scholars before her, LeBlanc draws upon Lord Raglan's classic definition of a hero (1936) to further her argument. In this way, she also raises questions regarding the oral, literary, and filmic traditions of having a hero as the centerpiece of a plot. LeBlanc's heroizing of Elvis Gratton fits Zhang's definition of filmic folklore and puts a positive spin on what folklorists, such as Dorson, refer to as *fakelore:* behavior that is presented as traditional folklore although no traditional circulation exists.

The complicated search for the authentic continues in Rebecca Prime's chapter exploring the ideological role played by the German *Bergfilm* (mountain film) in both the Weimar and early Nazi periods, as a manufactured site for the authentic German *Volk.* This chapter not only reads these early films as ideological constructions but also situates their attempt to appropriate an identity as ethnography within the context of early cinema's pseudoanthropological desire to document the "other." These films are important on yet another level: that of Leni Riefenstahl as actress, a role that brought her to Hitler's attention. Taken collectively, the chapters by Helfield, Le Blanc, and Prime develop the implications of filmic folklore, identifying ways that these films seem to embody an "authentic" ethnographic experience.

The second section of this work focuses on transformation, which has long been a central theme of both folktales and popular films. In "PC Pinocchios," Holly Blackford looks at the structural connection between hero plots in science fiction and the genre's appropriation of the folkloric motif in *Märchen* of inanimate objects coming to life. In doing so, she draws upon Propp's *Morphology of the Folktale* (1968) as well as Stith Thompson's *Motif-Index of Folk Literature* (1955–58). She finds the motif ubiquitous as objects that stand for characters become "real" by developing their own consciousness of their "lives." Looking at the computer/ android as child across several science fiction films, including *AI: Artificial Intelligence, WarGames, Tron, The Computer Wore Tennis Shoes, Terminator 2: Judgment Day,* and *Star Trek: Insurrection,* Blackford identifies a metamorphosis motif where a child becomes computerlike and a computer/ android becomes more childlike. This comparison, the author argues, is not limited to contemporary science fiction cinema; she also identifies the motif within several children's books, including *The Velveteen Rabbit* and *Pinocchio.* Like those children's classics, the films use the metaphor of human/nonhuman relationships to express a strong humanist agenda. In Blackford's analysis, the relationship between fathers and sons in these films in particular depends upon the way coming-of-age journeys are depicted.

Mark Allen Peterson explores a wide range of films in his chapter to note the differences between Arab (mostly Egyptian) and Hollywood depictions of jinn and genies, especially in the transcultural *Arabian*

Nights collections that move intertextually into European and American film and television and back into Middle Eastern media. Peterson contextualizes this transformation from Islamic demon to cartoon character within ideological Orientalism in the nineteenth and twentieth centuries. Particularly noteworthy in this chapter are Peterson's descriptions of a whole cache of largely unfamiliar horror films made in Egypt about jinn. He thus provides insight into Egypt's vernacular cinema, the ways these films reflect the belief traditions of their countries of origin, and the powerful influence on these Egyptian films of Hollywood narratives (ones that generally use the figure of the genie). In such films, wealth and power through wishes (such as those given by Aladdin's genie) become the central plot. As these figures work their way back into their own cultures, their folklore is transformed by the popular culture of the West.

How do contemporary ghost films draw upon intermediaries, such as priests or mediums? James A. Miller explores several recent films—notably *Ghost, Field of Dreams, Stir of Echoes,* and *The Sixth Sense*—that employ such intermediaries, all of whom are able to see ghosts. Rather than parodying the supernatural, as in *Ghostbusters* or *Beetlejuice,* the films Miller discusses portray what he refers to as a "vocational crisis" for those who can see and interact with the revenants. As functional figures, mediums have a vocational calling to address the dead and bring them from the past into communication with the living in the present. The movies' principal characters are obliged to act as helpers. Ultimately, Miller asks the ontological question of what it means to see the dead as cultural Other and how past and present register for the hero. As a section, the chapters by Blackford, Peterson, and Miller, all describe a common folkloric theme of transformation—the doll-that-comes-alive, the jinn, and the medium—and these authors explore this folklore topic across a range of films.

Our third section asks what new insights are revealed when cinema is looked at through the eyes of a folklorist. The chapters by Margarete Landwehr, Tarshia Stanley, and Carol Henderson each focus on a single film and explore its range of folklore using what Clifford Geertz (1973) has called "thick description," going beneath the surface to interpret complexity in search of meaning. Landwehr's "*Märchen* as Trauma Narrative: Helma Sanders-Brahms's Film *Germany, Pale Mother*" keeps within the folk-narrative tradition and employs Propp's *Morphology* (1968) to examine the film's use of "The Robber Bridegroom" story. For Landwehr, this traditional *Märchen* ties in with the film's themes of post-Holocaust trauma, particularly within New German Cinema. Unlike the more historical chapter by Prime ("A Strange and Foreign World"),

Landwehr's analysis explores the avenues for discussion opened up by contextualizing the film's use of the tale within the cinematic movement and in relation to national identity.

Tarshia Stanley, on the other hand, elucidates the role of the conjure woman in African American folklore and explains how filmmaker Kasi Lemmons treats this image in her highly regarded film *Eve's Bayou* (critic Roger Ebert called it one of the best films of 1997). The conjure woman has the ability to see both past and future and affect memory, spirituality, and identity. The present-day Eve is named after the slave woman Eve and inherits her powers. Eve's Aunt Mozelle also shares this gift. Elzora is a third conjure woman. Together these three merge to create a force in the bayou. Premonitions and reflections constantly shift as the three faces of the conjurer become one. In *Eve's Bayou*, the African American woman reclaims herself, according to Stanley, and survives as a storyteller, keeper of memory, and expression of power for African American women in the present.

Carol Henderson also discusses African American folklore in her analysis of the horror film *Tales from the Hood*, a portmanteau film that fuses the HBO television series *Tales from the Crypt* with *Boyz 'n the Hood*. The film's use of the horror genre, according to Henderson, reworks the traumas of black men in America. As in Miller's analysis of film's treatment of the medium who crosses barriers in time (chapter 6), and Stanley's study of the conjure woman who transcends time (chapter 8), Henderson demonstrates the "twining of life in the here and hereafter." *Tales from the Hood* intertwines the African American experience during slavery with the present-day through its central character, an old man who weaves stories and "witnesses" to save today and the future. He acts as both conjurer and trickster. The filmmaker examines the cultural fears of contemporary African American urbanites while employing and harking back to more traditional belief traditions.

This collection ends with two essays that consider how film examines questions of cultural identity. In her chapter about a medieval Danish murder-revenge ballad (that bears certain similarities with "The Robber Bridegroom"), K.A. Laity engages in a close reading of two very different film versions of the same story: Ingmar Bergman's *The Virgin Spring* and Wes Craven's *The Last House on the Left*. Bergman looks at morality, whereas Craven, setting his tale in the early seventies, attacks the assumption of moral behavior as an essential ontology. As in *Märchen*, the forest is a place where anything can happen. Both of these filmmakers use the forest to disrupt society. Laity's chapter exemplifies what we hope to establish with this book: a well-considered analysis of a film with specific reference to its use of folklore and an eye on the cultural contexts of production and consumption which inform and are changed by human transmission and expression.

LuAnne Roth's chapter looks at the ways that foodways in three popular feature films—*American History X, Along Came Polly,* and *My Big Fat Greek Wedding*—confer a sense of exclusion or belonging, of otherness and self. She asks what happens when we are what we *don't* eat. Using Kristeva's theory of abjection, Roth strongly suggests that food symbolizes the negotiation of gender, culture, race, and family dynamics. Unlike other scholars' ideas about food serving to create *communitas,* food may act as an expression of power.

We believe *Folklore/Cinema* contributes to both film and folklore studies. It provides an awareness not only of popular cinema's indebtedness to traditional forms of human expressive behavior (beliefs, ballads, stories, and other traditional communication) but also of the ways folklore changes because of its mass-mediated variants and dissemination in a variety of situations and cultural contexts in addition to cinema.

Not all the films discussed here are fictional narratives, nor are all the chapters written by academic folklorists. In both of our experiences, when film scholars write about folklore, folklorists find fault with their inadequate use of folkloristics; likewise, when folklorists write about film, film scholars find they do not pay enough attention to the methodologies of film studies. In editing these chapters, we strove to ensure that we represented both their filmic and folkloristic dimensions while also speaking to scholars in other disciplines.

We intend this collection to be provocative: to provoke reactions either in support or rejection of our authors' arguments from both film and folklore scholars. We are asking what happens when we look at popular cinema through the lenses of folklore and folklore studies. What new areas of discourse open to us (as both film scholars and folklorists) when we consider these films folkloristically? And what happens when folklore is presented to us through the filmic? *Folklore/Cinema* asks scholars to propose new ways of addressing the visual and folkloristic and to begin to discuss and analyze the multitude of visual expressions that involve folklore.

Works Cited

Dorson, Richard. 1959. *American folklore.* Chicago: University of Chicago Press.

Geertz, Clifford. 1973. *The interpretation of cultures.* New York: Basic Books.

Koven, Mikel J. 1999. Feminist folkloristics and women's cinema: Towards a methodology. *Literature Film Quarterly* 27 (4): 292–300.

———. 2003. The terror tale: Urban legends and the slasher film. *Scope: An online journal of film studies,* April. http://www.scope.nottingham.ac.uk/

Propp, Vladimir. 1968. *Morphology of the folktale.* 2nd and rev. ed. Trans. Laurence Scott. Publications of the American Folklore Society, bibliographical and special series 9. Austin: University of Texas Press.

Raglan, Lord. 1936. *The hero: A study in tradition, myth and drama.* London: Methuen & Co.

Sherman, Sharon R. 1996. Film and folklore. In *American folklore: An encyclopedia,* ed. Jan Harold Brunvand, 263–65. New York: Garland Publishing, Inc.

———. 1998. *Documenting ourselves: Film, video, and culture.* Lexington: The University Press of Kentucky.

Thompson, Stith. 1955–58. *Motif-index of folk-literature: A classification of narrative elements in folk-tales, ballads, myths, fables, medieval romances, exempla, fabliaux, jest-books, and local legends.* 6 vols. Rev. ed. Bloomington: Indiana University Press.

Zhang, Juwen. 2005. Filmic folklore and Chinese cultural identity. *Western Folklore* 64 (3–4): 263–80.

I.

FILMIC FOLKLORE AND AUTHENTICITY

"I' y ava't un' fois" (Once Upon a Time)

Films as Folktales in Québécois Cinéma Direct

GILLIAN HELFIELD

THIS CHAPTER CONCERNS a small group of films produced at the National Film Board of Canada (NFB) in the late 1950s and early 1960s, the Golden Age of Canadian documentary. These short films, which aired on Radio-Canada TV as part of the television series *Temps présent* (1957–64), intended only to deliver direct reportages of their subject material without overt sociological or political agendas.[1] And yet, by making "visible the complex and changing face of French Canadians" (Morris 1984, 291), the films became an aesthetic and political turning point for Québécois cinema and Québécois cultural representation in general (Véronneau 1987, 37).

This group of films, led by *Les Raquetteurs* (1958), launched the *cinéma direct* movement in Québec, and was instrumental in initiating a new wave in French-language cinema and awakening a Québécois "national" consciousness (Coulombe and Jean 1991, 107).[2] The films also consolidated the Francophone documentary team at the NFB, thus providing a major source of original French-language film and television production. Significantly, this series was the first produced at the NFB to introduce original French-language segments, rather than *versionings* (French-language versions of English films using Francophone actors and/or commentators). Finally, the *Temps présent* series provided a vehicle for Francophone filmmakers to demonstrate their conscious, active engagement with social and political issues affecting Québécois society.

I am specifically concerned with a subset of the films aired on *Temps présent* which demonstrate the aesthetic and social aims and ideals of cinéma direct and most clearly illustrate two main themes: first, that Québécois cinema at this time demonstrated, through its combination of contemporary and traditional modes of representation, existing tensions within Québécois society; and secondly, that the traditional modes of representation used in the films took the narrative and structural forms of French Canadian folktales. Each of the films discussed addresses some aspect or element of Québécois daily life engaging French Canadians, ranging from popular pastimes and community celebrations to key social and economic issues such as urban decline and unemployment. Thus, *Les Raquetteurs* (Michel Brault, Gilles Groulx, Marcel Carrière, 1958) features an annual snowshoers' congress in Sherbrooke, Québec, while *La Lutte* (Michel Brault, Claude Fournier, Claude Jutra, Marcel Carrière, 1961), *Un jeu si simple* (Gilles Groulx, 1963), and *Golden Gloves* (Gilles Groulx, 1961) examine, respectively, wrestling, hockey and boxing in Québec, and *Margaret Mercier, ballerine* (George Kaczender, 1963) highlights the career of a principal dancer with Les Grands Ballets Canadiens.[3] On the urban/industrial front, *À Saint-Henri le cinq septembre* (Hubert Aquin, 1962) presents a day-in-the-life of a working-class neighborhood in serious decline. *Bûcherons de la Manouâne* (1962) and *De Montréal à Manicouagan* (1963), both made by Arthur Lamothe, and *Jour après jour* (Clément Perron, 1962) profile the operations of modern-day Québécois industry, while *Les Bachéliers de la cinquième* (Clément Perron, 1962) addresses the problems of unemployment.

As suggested by the series title, which translates both to "Present Times" and "Present Tense," the films focus on the "here and now," the current social reality of Québec, which is a distinct departure from the typically historical subject matter of most NFB documentaries. This focus is borne out by the films' cross section of subjects and themes related to contemporary Québécois society and culture. Additionally, the films are striking for their cinematic evocation of the rhythms of modern life. Unceasing activity in various urban loci, combined with the images and sounds of the hustle and bustle of vehicular and human traffic, convey a spirit of energy and vitality. Movement itself—the movement of the camera, of bodies in action within the frame, and movement between the frames via montage—becomes emblematic of change. Movement-as-change is also expressed through the association between technology, industrial labor, and the cinema: camera movement and montage, which replicate the patterns and rhythms of construction, stress that cinema itself is a form of technology that contributes to the transformations taking place.

The films' evocation of movement and change in the contemporary Québécois social milieu is highly germane to the time and context of their production at the dawn of the Quiet Revolution, a ten-year period of unprecedented social, economic, and cultural transformation in Québec. The revolution was initiated by wide-sweeping reforms legislated by the Liberal government that came to power in 1960. The provincial election that year, precipitated by the death of ultraconservative premier Maurice Duplessis, brought to an end the eighteen-year regime of his Union Nationale party. The Liberals' reforms aimed primarily to modernize the province and provide equal social and economic opportunities for its majority Francophone population, who, since the British Conquest of 1760, had represented an underclass relative to the socioeconomically dominant Anglophone minority. The Quiet Revolution also articulated a significant transformation taking place in Québec's national self-image. One of its most prominent and enduring symbols was the reformulation of Francophone national identity: this identity shifted from French Canadian, previously denoting "an indistinguishable minority from coast-to-coast" (Shek 1991, 45) to Québécois, which instead underscored both the Francophones' majority status in the province and their aim to become "masters in their own house."

The reformulation of national identity correspondingly manifested itself in Québécois literature, theater, and the visual arts. In literature, for example, the third-person, omniscient narration common to French Canadian novels gave way to the first-person, subjective mode or "insider" perspective, which also would become a principal characteristic of cinéma direct. Additionally, the new Québécois novel was more political in its choice of working-class urban protagonists and *joual*, the "truncated, highly anglicised speech of the uneducated masses of Québec" (Shek 1991, 57), to give its characters a truly "authentic" voice.

In the cinema, the revolution in the cultural sphere made itself equally felt at the NFB, which at this time was the center of Canadian film production and provided the only real training ground for aspiring young filmmakers. In response to the changes taking place both within Québécois society and documentary cinema elsewhere in the world, a group of Francophone filmmakers rejected the standard expository style associated with NFB documentary (instituted and formalized by its British founder and first commissioner, John Grierson) in favor of a more interactive, participatory approach. In conjunction with new lightweight cameras and equipment which afforded them greater mobility and flexibility (portable lights, faster film stock, and later, synch-sound recorders), the new "direct" documentary style permitted these filmmakers to capture events in the Québécois social milieu from the inside and then transmit the reality of those events to their viewers.

These developments enabled the filmmakers to "turn against the game" (*Parti pris* 1964, 4) they felt had been imposed upon them by the predominantly Anglophone NFB through its consistent underrepresentation of Francophone culture in its films, programming priorities, and structural organization. They were greatly assisted in this task by the NFB's 1956 move from Ottawa, the nation's capital and seat of the federal government, to Montréal, the center of French Canadian culture. The move plunged the filmmakers into the midst of a society in the throes of transition, exposing them to a cultural milieu infected with a new curiosity and critical spirit, as well as providing them with a local Québécois context and ready supply of Francophone performers for their material (Lever 1991, 32).

Also significant for French-language production at the NFB was the arrival of television in 1952. In addition to providing a new demand and outlet for French-language material, television determined a certain social vision that was in tune with the changing face of Québécois culture. The national broadcast of French-language films on television importantly reached Francophones across the province, including the rural milieu isolated from regular cinema circuits.

Yet, despite the films' overriding emphasis on the processes of movement and change, they frequently and paradoxically evoke Québec's traditional rural culture, specifically the visible and aural signs and practices of French Canadian folktales. Some historians have duly noted the presence of such elements in these films: Yves Lever remarks on their "mix of traditional form and Cinéma direct form" (Lever 1995, 160) and their display of traditions and ancestral rituals, mythic symbols and structures (Lever 1995, 194). David Clandfield further observes that the formal elements of folk ritual (e.g., rhythm, cycle, and repetition) are used in the films to reflect and express the effects of modernity (such as mechanization and technology) on the daily lives of the Québécois at this time (Clandfield 1978, 32).

I propose that beyond merely referring to or incorporating these elements of folk ritual, the films examined here, in their use of iconography, archetypes, narrative structural patterns, and modes of narration, function like folktales. I also suggest that this function is neither anomalous nor antithetical to the surrounding context of change and modernization, but rather entirely in keeping with it.

During the period when the Quiet Revolution and cinéma direct movement arose, a mass folk revival took place throughout North America. This decade, while marked on the one hand by the younger generation's social rebellion against the ideals and values of the existing establishment, also testified on the other hand to a longing for the comparative simplicity and purity of the past: this was manifested in the adoption of naturalist lifestyles and the concomitant rejection of capitalist/materialist values; of products and processes associated with modern technology, industry, science, and medicine; and of established formal religion (Rodnitzky 1976, xiv).

In Québec, the folk revival of the 1960s had deeper historical and political implications. There had been an earlier folk revival during the mid-nineteenth century, which had arisen in response to Francophone fears of cultural assimilation following the British Conquest and subsequent colonization of Québec. These fears produced a deeply conservative ideology, which aimed to preserve the principal elements of French Canadian national culture: the French language, the Catholic faith, and the rural agrarian way of life. Excluded from an economy controlled by English and American industrial interests, and with no recourse to other domains of economic activity, French Canadians were relegated to a "culture of the soil" (Brunet 1964, 119), which included renewed interest in local lore and legendry and the corresponding interest in earlier literary genres. For example, the *romans du terroir,* or "novels of the land," such as *Les anciens Canadiens* (1863) by Philippe Aubert de Gaspé *(père)* or *Le chercheur des trésors* (1837) by Aubert de Gaspé *(fils),* featured numerous country traditions, superstitions, and beliefs. By rekindling interest in the culture of the countryside, this earlier folk revival consolidated associations between the French Canadian people and the land, thereby also helping establish the rural milieu as the heartland of French Canada.

The 1960s folk revival to a considerable degree traded upon the mythical significance of traditional French Canadian culture as a touchstone of its national heritage. Despite the Quiet Revolution's overarching credo of reform and modernization, poets, folksingers, and filmmakers of the 1960s nonetheless incorporated folk traditions and conventions into their work. For example, Gaston Miron, the radical nationalist poet, relied extensively on folk traditions in some of his own poems, including "L'Ombre de l'ombre" (Miron 1996, 152), which attempts to recreate the rhythmic models of folk songs and dances.[4] The '60s also witnessed the revival of the *chansonniers*: itinerant folk singers, such as the legendary La Bolduc (aka Mary Travers), who traveled throughout rural Québec in the 1930s and '40s, performing traditional French Canadian folk songs in local halls and church basements, accompanied simply by one or two instruments such as guitar or piano. The new generation of chansonniers in the 1960s, including Gilles Vigneault, Pauline Julien, Monique Leyrac, and others, looked back to this tradition for inspiration (Carpenter 1979, 263), routinely adapting folk melodies from the past and modifying their lyrics to contextualize them to the contemporary Québécois social reality. For all these artists, use of these forms of traditional folk music helped foster the creation of a new popular and cultural imaginary. At the same time, in its fusion of traditional folk-song cadences and contemporary nationalist rhetoric, the new folk music also seemed to capture both the hope and the malaise of an entire society that suddenly felt Québécois.

At this critical juncture, documentary cinema was also undergoing a revolutionary revival. The emergence of new documentary movements during the 1960s announced the rise of a sensibility that was on the one hand modern and progressive, and on the other, conservative in its affirmation and reinforcement of "certain patterns of life and structures of feeling" (Hall and Whannel 1964, 46). In their aim to capture the elemental "truth" of an event, the new generation of documentary filmmakers evinced a desire to return to the basics of filmmaking, comprised of the original materials (man and movie camera) and the philosophical concerns with realism of early cinema. For the cinéma direct filmmakers, in particular, this return to origins also included using familiar conventions of folktales in their representations of the "new" Québécois nation and national identity.

These folktale conventions correspond to the signposts of the regional picturesque described by François de la Brétèque: rural geography and topography, physical structures representing key social ones, familiar archetypes, and customary social practices and rituals. Moreover, the rural milieu in French Canadian folktales is similar to de la Brétèque's village universe, which functions as a kind of metonymy for the territory (both cultural and national) encoded in the *mise-en-scène* of the tales' description of the land. The image of the village universe significantly embodies the "fantasy of return" (de la Brétèque 1992, 61) to the *ancien régime* of the past and the rural-agrarian way of life, which, in the context of Québécois culture, connotes the French colonial régime and the strong time of French Canadian cultural autonomy prior to Anglo invasion and conquest.[5]

In the French Canadian regional picturesque, the main feature of the rural geography and topography is the landscape, which has two distinct types, *wilderness* and *pastoral*, each with its own iconography and enduring archetypes. The wilderness landscape, associated with the period of New World discovery and early colonial foundations and characterized by forbidding natural terrain (mountains, forests, rivers, and lakes), is not as prominent in the folktales as the pastoral one, which corresponds more closely to the postsettlement village universe of agrarian French Canada. Nonetheless, the folktales and films frequently refer to the rugged archetypical persons of the wilderness, legendary for their fortitude

The "habitant" costume of the snowshoers in *Les Raquetteurs* reaffirms the festival's celebration of collective Québécois identity.

and resourcefulness in negotiating the backcountry and instantly recognizable in the unique apparel which represents their *métier* or vocation. These include the famous *voyageurs*, or "canoe men" of the North American waterways, with their buckskin jackets and coonskin caps; the *bûcherons* (loggers), with their axes and red-and-black-plaid lumberjackets; and the *coureurs-des-bois* (outlaw trappers and poachers); and *habitants* (settlers), dressed in their *tûques* (long woolen caps), *capôts* (parkas), and *ceintûres flêchées* (embroidered cloth belts with arrow patterns). This habitant costume is an important feature in *Les Raquetteurs*: as the official apparel of the participating snowshoe clubs, the costume underscores the significance of this annual congress as a ritual reaffirmation of collective Québécois cultural heritage and identity.

The pastoral landscape is typically identified by the farmhouse and the church, two outstanding physical structures that emphasize the rural milieu's association with advancing French Canadian civilization and culture. The farmhouse, which generally is located on the outskirts of the village and set picturesquely on a hillside, in a valley, or against the background of a lake or river, takes on a quasi-mythic character in Québécois folktales, novels, and cinema in its nostalgic reference to the past. The farmhouse is a symbol of French Canadian collectivity and community, whether these values are expressed through the farm family that inhabits the house, through the rural traditions they enact under its roof, or through the rural-agrarian social class they represent (Lemieux 1984, 22).

Thus significantly, in *Les Raquetteurs,* the first structure that is visible in the snowy countryside when the film cuts to the race on the city outskirts is a farmhouse, built in the traditional Norman style of the habitant home,[6] also formalized in the paintings of nineteenth-century Québec artists such as Édouard Massicotte and Cornelius Krieghoff.[7] As well, the workers' cabins in *De Montréal à Manicouagan* recall the *chantiers* or "lumber camps" (described in numerous tales), where the loggers worked and lived throughout the winter season and which similarly emphasize the importance of basic creature comforts and companionship within the rural milieu.

The interior of the habitant farmhouse is dominated by one central room *(la grand'chambre),* described in the literature and folktales as a sacred place. It is where one is born and where one dies, and the place where all daily activities and rituals take place (Lemieux 1984, 23). This central room contains four prominent fixtures: the large table in the middle, where the family prepares its meals, dines, or does its chores; the crucifix, altar, or icon of Jesus or Mary, to which the family addresses its daily prayers; and the fireplace or wood-burning stove, used for cooking and heating and which acts as the emotional hearth of family and community life (Tétu de Labsade 1987b, 205). Finally, there is the rocking chair, strategically placed by the fire, the warmest and most comfortable spot in the house and one usually reserved either for the patriarch or matriarch of the family or such honored visitors as the *curé* or *conteur,* the traditional storyteller invited to tell his tales to gathered guests at a *veillée,* or private social gathering.

The grand'chambre is recalled in the films' depictions of communal gathering spaces. For example, in *Golden Gloves,* most of the scenes detailing boxing contender Ronald Jones's home and family life are shot at the kitchen table. In other films *(La Lutte, Un jeu si simple, Margaret Mercier, À Saint-Henri),* the domestic, private spaces of the nuclear family are supplanted by public spaces such as sports arenas, stadiums, theatres, nightclubs, restaurants, and taverns, which represent gathering spots for the new "national family" that assembles there en masse to participate collectively in celebrations or performances of Québécois cultural identity.

The church, symbol of the Catholic faith and parish community in the rural milieu, is appropriately depicted in the regional picturesque at the direct center of the village, its gleaming Gothic steeple towering

In *La Lutte*, the ethereal effect of the powerful lights shining down on the ring enhances the mythical significance of the wrestling match.

over neighboring structures and visible from afar. In the films, images of the church and religious ritual suggest that the Catholic faith is still a tangible presence. For example, in *À Saint-Henri,* a shot of a neighborhood church echoes images of country churches in traditional landscape paintings and on picture postcards. However, the rural church's typically bucolic décor of interlaced pine branches has been replaced here by overhead power lines and streetcar wires. Another striking religious reference in the film is the twilight radio broadcast of *le chapelet* (the rosary): as the camera pans over the houses of Saint-Henri, we hear the familiar litany; by means of this nightly religious ritual, the community's collective culture and identity are continually reaffirmed.

The church's resonant power is also felt in *La Lutte,* in the film's depiction of the Forum, the famous Montréal sports arena, as a modern-day shrine.[8] The overhead lights inside the arena, shining down on the ring and illuminating the canvas, cast a glow that seems almost ethereal. Nondiegetic music includes the sounds of Gregorian chants and a Bach-Vivaldi concerto: this piece, transcribed from Vivaldi, is one of many which Bach composed to the "honor of God" during his lifelong career as a church cantor and organist (Schrade 1973, 10). Though the filmmakers may be using these religious elements to make ironic statements about professional wrestling and mass popular culture, at the same time they are also alluding to the continuing symbolic currency of the church within Québécois society.

Another feature of the folktales related to geography/topography as well as customary social practices and rituals is the cycle of seasons. This cycle both determines and is in turn reflected in other cycles of rural-agrarian life (agriculture, the tides, reproduction, and religious cycles of birth/death/rebirth) that provide structure and meaning, as well as regulate the inhabitants' social customs and practices. The most enduring season in the Québec rural milieu is winter, which lasts on average sixteen to eighteen weeks, at least five weeks longer than in the urban areas (Provencher 1986, 12). The length of this season is duly reflected in the frequent depictions of winter sports and recreational activities (hockey, ice-skating, sledding, and sleigh rides) and celebrations of sacred and secular holidays which fall during the winter months (Christmas and Midnight Mass, New Year's, Lent, Carnival, and Easter). As well, the most prominently depicted form of socialization among friends, family and neighbors is the veillée or the *soirée de campagne* ("country evening" of feasting, singing, dancing, card playing, practical joking, and storytelling), which was originally institutionalized in the rural milieu to pass the long winter nights. Significantly, the soirée de campagne frequently provides both the setting for the folktale and the occasion for telling it.

True to the conventions of the regional picturesque, films use mostly winter settings for the kinds of collective cultural activities in which people participate. Some of these activities, such as snowshoeing in *Les Raquetteurs* and hockey in *Un jeu si simple*, take place specifically during the winter season. In other films, winter provides a recognizable setting, as in *La Lutte*, as indicated by the snow outside the Forum and the overcoats worn by the wrestling fans, or in *Margaret Mercier*, as the ballerina trudges through the snow every day on her way to and from the theater. Winter also provides familiar context for collective merrymaking that recalls the soirée de campagne, as in the gala party that ends the snowshoers' congress in *Les Raquetteurs*, and numerous other social gatherings that take place in taverns, dance clubs, social halls, or restaurants, as in *Golden Gloves*, *À Saint-Henri*, or *Jour après jour*. The prominence of winter in the films can be explained simply by this season's length: a great deal of film production would naturally take place during this time, and outdoor scenes would automatically contain shots of snow and ice. Yet I believe that such winter scenes (for example, the racers in

Les Raquetteurs moving across the snow-covered rural landscape) owe as much, if not more, to the conventions of representation established in the folktales.

As noted earlier, in addition to appropriating the visible markers of the regional picturesque formalized in the folktales, the films are also structured and presented like folktales. The filmic techniques and conventions through which the cinéma direct filmmakers attempted to capture and transmit the "unmediated truth" of the contemporary Québécois social reality are not dissimilar from those used in earlier, traditional forms of pictorial representation. These conventions include contextualization; the presence of a conteur, either in the form of an on-screen character or folk performer who narrates the action as well as provides eyewitness authentication of the event; and the use of certain narrative devices and structuring patterns, such as cycles, which similarly shape traditional ways of life in the rural-agrarian milieu. While these conventions, like the signposts of the regional picturesque, do not individually justify the claim that these films function as folktales, together they make a compelling argument,

Contextualization is one method that makes the folktales and films more accessible: the more they are contextualized to a local, recognizable milieu, the more seemingly authentic their representations of surrounding social reality become. Contextualization may take the form of recognizable landmarks, such as the neon sign identifying the Forum in *La Lutte*, the familiar skyline of Saint Henri, or the office towers and concourse shops of Place Ville-Marie identifying downtown Montréal in *Margaret Mercier.*

Equally important to the setting or scene of the story is its actual telling. Thus, a key component of contextualization is the presence of the *conteur* or "storyteller"; he or she is the narrator who simultaneously describes the action, acts out the roles of the characters, and imparts the tale's subtextual ideological message(s) as well as participaing in the event being retold. The conteur's participation is particularly significant: by means of his or her self-insertion into the story, the conteur establishes him or herself as an eyewitness to the event, thus corroborating the truth of its occurrence and the authenticity of the account. At the same time, the conteur identifies him or herself as one of the crowd gathered for this folk performance. In paintings of the regional picturesque, this perspective is achieved through the pictorial first person, namely an eye-level position which places the artist (and the viewer) in the center of the picture plane and thus in the midst of, or within reach of, the action.

In the films, the conteur's self-insertion is similarly achieved through the pictorial first person by means of cinéma direct techniques, such as the mobile, handheld camera and the use of panning and tilting, instead of cutting, to mimic the movements of a human spectator and thus further attest to the actual physical presence and personal testimony of the filmmaker. In *Les Raquetteurs,* the camera gets into line with the marchers in the parade or mingles with the crowd on the sidelines. In *À Saint-Henri,* the camera follows a young couple as they walk down the street, hand in hand, turning when they turn, pausing when they stop to kiss. In each of these examples, the camera-conteur inserts itself within the social context and culture of the on-screen community.

The presence of the conteur as off-screen narrator or on-screen performer also draws attention to the ritual of storytelling itself. In *À Saint-Henri* and *Golden Gloves,* narration is delivered via off-screen voice-over. In *Bacheliers de la cinquième,* however, the narration, provided by folksinger Gilles Vigneault, is more an overt performance. The film intercuts between diegetic shots of the protagonists vainly seeking employment and nondiegetic shots of Vigneault singing directly to the camera in the recording studio, thus positioning the folksinger as both part of the sequence and an integral conveyor of its meaning. Further suturing the folksinger into the action as a kind of one-man Greek chorus lamenting this tragic aspect of Québécois social reality is the combination of the song's lyrics (which describe the causes and hardships of unemployment) and its delivery (through which Vigneault acts out the respective roles of the employer and the unemployed). At the same time, we are still conscious of the conteur's performance, and thus of our own participation in this familiar folk-song ritual.

Another important facet of the conteur's storytelling performance is his or her use of language to describe or act out events in the tale and strengthen the bond with the audience. The language of the conteur is both verbal in its utilization of colloquialisms, idiomatic expressions, trade jargon, and local patois that are specific both to the conteur and the particular region (Guilbault 1991, 10), and physical (i.e., body language) in its reliance upon distinctive gestures, mannerisms, and facial expressions (Calame-Griaule 1974, 195–96) that are a hallmark of the conteur's particular style and repertoire. Language importantly impacts both the performance of the tale and the representation of the society described, conferring a creative liberty and agency upon the conteur that makes him or her both the transmitter and author of the tale.

Language is also an important contextualizing element within the films. Language has always been the chief defining element of Québec's

distinctive national identity. Whereas in previous periods of folk reviv-
alism, language was primarily an instrument for safeguarding and preserving French Canadian identity from assimilation into the dominant
Anglo culture, during the Quiet Revolution it became less of a defensive
measure and more of a specific target for reform by the newly elected
Liberal government.[9]

For the Francophones at the NFB looking to liberate Québécois film
from the constraints of Anglo-Canadian cinematic conventions, language became an important instrument for taking back the controls of
cultural representation. Making films in French enabled the filmmakers
to distinguish themselves and their work from the NFB's general output
but also importantly permitted their on-screen characters to tell their
own stories directly: in their own language, in their own words, in their
own accent and idiom. Thus, French is spoken in the films everywhere
and by everyone, unmediated by voice-over commentaries or subtitles
typical of NFB productions.

One may even argue that the cinematic techniques in the films
function as a kind of language in and of themselves. The trademark
devices of the cinéma direct movement mentioned earlier (the mobile
camera, movement within the frame and between frames to evoke the
rhythms of modern urban living, and the use of montage to replicate
the rhythms of construction and labor) function in a way similar to the
storytelling devices of the conteur—the gestures, colloquialisms, and
intonations—which place the viewer/listener at the scene, while at the
same time capturing a sense of its immediate social reality. Overall,
as in the folktales, language in the films operates simultaneously as
a hallmark of style, a means of contextualization, and, perhaps most
importantly, as a form of authorship that enables the filmmaker-con-
teur to control the means and method of representation, and thus take
possession of culture and identity.

One other folktale convention used in the films that has important
bearing on their narrative structure is the device of cycles that signal
recurring beginnings and endings, arrivals and departures. The most
prevalent cycle motif is the journey or voyage. To a considerable degree,
the journey motif has a mythic function in providing the means by
which we travel back to the time of national origins. The journey device
provides the structural basis for *De Montrèal à Manicouagan*, providing
the means by which we travel between these two geographic sites, and
simultaneously between past and present and old and new national
identities. Similar journey motifs mark the beginnings and endings of
Bachéliers de la cinquième, in the boys' boat voyage to and from the North

In *Jour après jour*, the image of smokestacks provides bookends for the journey to and from the mill, and the beginning and end of the film.

Shore, and *Jour après jour,* in the shots taken inside the car traveling to and from the paper mill.

The voyage or journey cycle may also be viewed as one version of the *mise-en-abyme,* or story-within-a-story, effect common in Québécois folktales, which is like a narrative hall of mirrors. The *mise-en-abyme* device entails not only the repetition of the story itself, from one conteur and audience to the next, but also repetition of the surrounding conditions when the story is told and when the actual event took place. Such conditions also signal that the storytelling ritual is about to take place. One such condition is the venue, which provides a space for the conteur/storyteller to address the audience, gathered around in a group. Whereas in the folktales, the performance takes place in an intimate living or workspace (a habitant home, a lumber camp, a blacksmith's shop), in the films, in keeping with the urban context, the venue is larger, more public. Yet it still provides the requisite materials for the ritualized folktale performance, including the circular seating for the gathered crowd, as seen in *Les Raquetteurs* in the stadium where the races take place and the podium set up at the gala to crown the festival queen; in

In *Un jeu si simple*, the hockey arena provides the venue for a ritualized folk performance.

the arena that encircles the wrestling ring and hockey rink in *La Lutte* and *Un jeu si simple;* and in the rows of seats facing the theater stage in *Margaret Mercier*.

Other elements establishing atmospheric conditions are the presence of liquor and smoke from the fireplace, stove, or tobacco. While the smoke provides an appropriate atmosphere for the more mysterious or mystical elements of the folktales, liquor is always passed around the room immediately preceding the telling of the tale; *p'tits coups* or shots of rum or whisky not only provide additional warmth on a cold winter's night but also loosen tongues and imaginations and enhance the already-formidable talents of the conteur. In the films, the presence of liquor and smoke seems more routine and less ritualized than in the folktales, perhaps due to the waning power of the church as an agent of social and moral control. Much of the action in the films takes place in public venues (taverns, nightclubs, arenas), where drinking and smoking are not only unrestricted but part of the natural local atmosphere. One film that does make ritualistic use of atmosphere is *La Lutte:* the combination of smoke from the spectators' cigarettes and steam from the

Bûcherons de la Manouane intercuts shots of modern technology with those of traditional logging methods.

powerful overhead lights creates an ethereal ambience that enhances the mythical significance of the wrestling match.

Taken together, all of the various iconographic and narrative elements of folktales utilized in the cinéma direct films provide important ties to the historical and cultural past and preceding conventions of pictorial representation. These elements, in turn, counterbalance the processes of modernization, suggesting the need for continuity through tradition, as underscored by the films' frequent counterpointing images of the old and new Québec. For example, *Les Raquetteurs* constantly intercuts between the downtown core and outskirts of Sherbrooke, and the party scene at the end of the film presents striking contrasts between traditional and modern modes of dress (traditional habitant costumes versus contemporary suits and evening gowns), modes of music (folk versus jazz) and styles of dancing (contemporary versus folk). Similarly, in *Bûcherons de la Manouane,* shots of loggers using motorized chain saws are intercut with ones depicting others using old-fashioned axes, while shots of men loading logs onto waiting transport trucks are juxtaposed with ones of men loading logs onto horse-drawn sleds. Continuity with the past is further strengthened by the extradiegetic sound of ringing axes that reverberates throughout all the scenes, even those that do not portray logging. The rhythmic blows of the axes suggest the beat of custom afnd tradition that continues to regulate life in the lumber camps (and by extension, Québec).

In comparable fashion, the boat trip down the St. Lawrence River in *De Montréal à Manicouagan* is a journey both toward Québec's future and back into its past because it reiterates the historical voyage of Jacques Cartier, the discoverer of Québec, who sailed up this river in 1534. Each site passed along the way is laden with both contemporary and historical significance: Donnacona, once the historic meeting place of Cartier and the Indian chief, Stadacona, is now the location of a paper mill. Laval, named for the first bishop of New France, is now the home of Laval University. These juxtapositions stress Québec's advancement to a state of modernity, as well as its ability to assume mastery of its own destiny—to say, "Look how far we've come." At the same time, this attention to key points of origin also tells us to "look back where we came from."

This chapter demonstrates the way contrasts between past and present, and tradition and modernity, in these films draw attention to important shifts taking place in Québécois society, while at the same time corroborating the continued presence and power of traditional culture in developing new modes of cultural expression and representation. The chapter offers only a very general overview, which can provide the basis for a more detailed study of the historical evolution and relevance of traditional Québécois culture, one which analyzes additional modes which could not be covered here (picture postcards, poetry, dance, traditions, and rituals).

Québécois filmmaker Gilles Carle once said that in cinéma direct, "the picturesque has yielded to the familiar" and "the myth...has yielded in the face of reality" (Clandfield 1987, 43). This statement, though ideologically consistent with the aims of this movement, is not true of the films, which portray the picturesque and familiar, and myth and reality, as two sides of the same cultural coin.

As these films clearly indicate, for Francophone filmmakers at the NFB during this period of revolution and change, Québec's folk heritage was equally as rich a resource for their nationalist agenda as its social and political history. Preservation of the past and its traditions could and did provide them with a viable means of preserving creative control over the representation of their culture and nation.

Notes

1. *Temps présent* was not produced as a series in the usual sense of the term. Rather it is the title given to this group of films that were made by the NFB and subsequently organized into a series of screenings or airings for Radio-Canada, the French arm of the CBC. For this reason, the NFB has never released or distributed these films as a series. They are only available under their individual titles.

2. I emphasize Québec to avoid any confusion with *direct cinema*, which typically refers to the American cinéma vérité and, more particularly, to the fly-on-the-wall observational style of documentary filmmaking associated with Robert Drew, Richard Leacock, the Maysles brothers, D.A. Pennebaker, and others. Cinéma direct and direct cinema tend erroneously to be used as interchangeable terms, with the former often regarded as a derivative of the latter. However, this is "historically inaccurate inasmuch as [Canadian developments in cinéma vérité] actually anticipate those in the United States upon which they supposedly draw" (Elder 1979, 87), beginning as early as the mid-1950s with the *Candid Eye* TV series produced by the NFB's English-language documentary unit (Unit B) and, a few years later, in several TV series produced by the French film unit, including *Temps présent* as well as *Panoramique* (1957) and *Coup d'oeil* (1958) (Véronneau and Euvrard 1978, 30). For more on Canadian and Québécois cinéma direct, see also Gilles Marsolais (1974), Marcel Jean (1991), and Yves Lever (1995).

3. Although *Margaret Mercier* was aired as part of *Temps présent* with the other films mentioned, it is not discussed in any of the standard historical and critical texts on the cinéma direct movement I have come across thus far. This omission may have occurred because Kaczender was not Québécois, but rather a Hungarian emigré who came to the NFB in 1952, where he made only two documentary films, *Margaret Mercier* and *City Scene* (1964), which was produced for the English series *Comparisons* (1959–64). *Margaret Mercier* is a sadly overlooked treasure, for it provides not only an excellent example of pure cinéma direct technique but also a prime demonstration of "motion as change" via the movement of the human body engaged in an athletic competition or aesthetic performance.

4. Miron was the driving force behind *L'Hexagone*, the radical poetry journal and publishing house that became a major center for nationalist poetry during the Quiet Revolution.

5. The "fantasy of return" to the golden age of French colonial times in Québec is implicit in the slogan *Je me souviens*, which is the provincial logo on Québec automobile license plates. The phrase translates as "I remember," referring to the decisive 1763 battle between French and English forces on the Plains of Abraham outside Québec City, where the French were defeated and subsequently colonized by Great Britain.

6. This style of architecture, in *l'esprit français*, or "French spirit," meant a two-story structure with a pavilion or mansard pitched roof, dormer windows, a wide porch, and clapboard or fieldstone construction (Tétu de Labsade 1987, 205).

7. Artists such as Krieghoff, Massicotte, and Raphael and later, caricaturists such as Henri Julien were well known for their "picturesque and anecdotal"

depictions of "happy, frolicking *habitants* engaged in perpetual revelry" and
the performance of local customs and traditions (Harper 1969, 82).

8. The sports media in Montréal often described hockey as a "religion" and
the Forum as its "shrine" (Goyens 1996, 71). This image was reinforced by
the religious services that frequently took place there, including Christmas
Midnight Mass and prayer meetings held by various religious groups and
leaders, such as Billy Graham, Aimée Semple McPherson, and the Jeho-
vah's Witnesses, as well as funeral and memorial services for important
public figures and celebrities like hockey star Howie Morenz

9. Several language laws legislated throughout the 1960s and 1970s effectively sought to "francisize" Québec to safeguard French culture and promote a greater sense of national cohesion among Québécois at all levels
of society. This process of francisization was effected in several ways:
first, by guaranteeing the preeminence of French over English in schools
and places of businesses; second, by ensuring that new immigrants to the
province were required to learn French; and third, by making French the
national language of Québec (Tétu de Labsade 1987, 104, Dickinson and
Young 1993, viii–xii).

Filmography

Les Bachéliers de la cinquième (1962). 28 min. Clément Perron
Bûcherons de la Manouâne (1962). 28 min. Arthur Lamothe
City Scene (1964). 28 min. Gordon Burwash and George Kaczender
Coup d'oeil (1958). 10 min. Michel Brault and Grant Crabtree
Golden Gloves (1961). 28 min. Gilles Groulx
Un jeu si simple (1964). 28 min. Gilles Groulx
Jour après jour (1962). 28 min. Clément Perron
La Lutte (1961). 28 min. Michel Brault, Claude Fournier, Claude Jutra, and
    Marcel Carrière
Margaret Mercier, ballerine (1963). 28 min. George Kaczender
De Montréal à Manicouagan (1962). 28 min. Arthur Lamothe
Les Raquetteurs (1958). 15 min. Michel Brault, Gilles Groulx, and Marcel
    Carrière
À Saint-Henri le cinq septembre (1962). 42 min. Hubert Aquin

Works Cited

Brunet, Michel. 1964. La présence Anglaise et les Canadiens. Études sur l'histoire
    et la pensée des deux Canadas. Montréal: Beauchemin.
Calame-Griaule, Geneviève. 1974. Project de questionnaire pour l'enquête sur le
    style oral des conteurs traditionnels. In *Les langues sans tradition écrite: Meth-
    ods d'enquête et de description,* ed G. Manessy and J. M. C. Thomas, 195–96.
    Special no. 3. Actes du colloque international du CNRS ténu à Nice, 28 juin
    au 2 juillet, 1971. Paris: SÉLAF, La société détudes linguistiques et antho-
    pologiques de France.

Carpenter, Carole Henderson. 1979. Chapter 5: " Je me souviens ": Folklore and French Canada. In *Many voices: A study of folklore activities in Canada and their role in Canadian culture,* ed. Carole Carpenter and Diamond Jenness, 205–63. Canadian Centre for Folk Culture Studies. National Museum of Man Mercury Series 26. Ottawa: National Museums of Canada.

Clandfield, David. 1978. From the picturesque to the familiar: Films of the French unit at the N.F.B. (1958–1964). *Cinétracts* 1 (4) :50–62.

———. 1987. *Canadian film.* Toronto: Oxford University Press.

Coulombe, Michel, and Marcel Jean. 1991. *Le dictionnaire du cinéma Québécois.* Rev. ed. Montréal: Éditions du Boréal.

de la Brétèque, François. 1992. Images of Provence: Ethnotypes and stereotypes of the south in French cinema. In *Popular European cinema,* ed. Richard Dyer and Ginette Vincendeau, 58–71. London/New York: Routledge.

Dickinson, John A., and Brian Young. 1993. A short history of Québec. 2nd ed. Toronto: Copp Clark Pitman.

Elder, Bruce. 1979. On the candid-eye movement. In *Canadian film reader,* ed. Seth Feldman and Joyce Nelson, 86–94. Toronto: Peter Martin and Associates.

Goyens, Chrystian. 1996. *The Montreal forum: Forever proud.* Montréal: Les éditions Effix.

Guilbault, Nicole. 1991. *Contes et sortilèges des quatres coins du Québec.* Québec: Bibliothèque nationale du Québec.

Hall, Stuart, and Paddy Whannel. 1964. *The popular arts.* London: Hutchinson Educational.

Harper, J.R. 1969. *Painting in Canada: A history.* Toronto: University of Toronto Press.

Jean, Marcel. 1991. *Le cinéma Québécois.* Montréal: Boréal Express.

Lemieux, Denise. 1984. *Une culture de nostalgie.* Montreal: Boréal Express.

Lemieux, Germain, ed. 1981. *Les vieux m'ont conté 17.* Annotated and transcribed for the Centre Franco-Ontarien de Folklore. Montréal/Paris: Éditions Bellarmin/Maisonneuve et Larose.

Lever, Yves. 1991. *Le cinéma de la révolution tranquille de panoramique à Valérie.* Rev. ed. Montréal: Bibliothèque nationale du Québec.

———. 1995. *Histoire générale du cinéma au Québec.* 2nd ed. Montréal: Éditions du Boréal.

Marsolais, Gilles. 1974. *L'aventure du cinema direct.* Paris: Seghers.

Miron, Gaston. 1996. *L'homme rapaillé: Poèmes 1953–1975.* Montréal: Typo.

Morris, Peter. 1984. Temps présent. In *The film companion,* 291. Toronto: Irwin Publishing.

Parti pris. 1964. 7.

Provencher, Jean. 1986. *C'était l'hiver: La vie rurale traditionelle dans la vallée du Saint-Laurent.* Montréal: Éditions du Boréal Express.

Rodnitzky, Jerome.1976. *Minstrels of the dawn: The folk protest singer as cultural hero.* Chicago: Nelson Hall.

Schrade, Leo. 1973. *Bach: The conflict between the sacred and the secular.* New York: Da Capo Press.

Shek, Ben-Z. 1991. *French Canadian and Québécois novels.* Toronto: Oxford University Press.

Tétu de Labsade, Françoise. 1987a. Le mouvement des idées. In *Le Québec: Un pays, une culture*, 133–57. Montréal/Paris: Éditions de l'Hexagone.
———. 1987b. La maison. In *Le Québec: Un pays, une culture*, 203–8.
Véronneau, Pierre. 1987. Résistance et affirmation: La production Francophone à l'ONF 1939–1964. In *Les dossiers de la cinémathèque*, no. 17, 37–41. Montréal: Cinémathèque Québécoise/Musée du cinéma.
Véronneau, Pierre, and Michel Euvrard. 1978. *Les cinémas Canadiens*. Montréal/Paris: Cinémathèque Québécoise.

2

Elvis Gratton

Québec's Contemporary Folk Hero?

JULIE M-A LeBLANC

How can a fictional film character potentially be considered a Québécois folk hero in a contemporary narrative setting? The attempt to suggest or discuss the heroic nature of Robert (Bob) "Elvis" Gratton (affectionately known as Elvis Gratton), the Québécois film character and social political parody, is a daunting task because of the sheer oxymoron it represents. Though the very notion of Elvis Gratton as a folk hero in Québec seems unlikely to viewers of the film series, the character's phenomenal status in popular Québécois culture makes it feasible to consider him that way. When I discussed my interpretation with potential participants in this research, many reacted in the same predictable manner: "You're trying to discuss Elvis Gratton as a folk hero in Québec?" In response to their quizzical expressions, I outlined my hypotheses: proposing the rather unpromising character as a hero and perhaps antihero. These discussions provided me with a detailed approach to the topic during formal interviews online and in person. This essay recounts the points highlighted during the interviews and suggests viewing this popular film character as an invented satirical hero.

This character's creation and life have become as important in contemporary media narratives as the romanticized legendary heroes of traditional lore. One may also characterize Elvis Gratton as what Richard Dorson calls a mass-culture hero. Dorson distinguishes between the folk hero, a character known and talked about locally or in an occupation, and the legendary hero, whose "fame spreads into subliterary channels, like county histories or chapbooks or dime novels, which enlarge the circle of his admirers through printed means but on levels close to folk groups and influential on local tradition" (1959, 199). He reserves a third category for the mass-culture hero, one whose existence and deeds are created by resort promoters, movie producers, or other forms of popular culture (199–200), as is the case with the character of Elvis Gratton. As

Dorson points out, few folk heroes exist in oral tradition. With Gratton, the categorical definitions of mass-culture and folk "hero" are blurred in cross-cultural perceptions and popular culture.

Over the past twenty years, the Elvis Gratton creators—film director Pierre Falardeau and actor Julien Poulin—have developed three "epic" films centered around the character's parodic sociopolitical rants and slapstick humor. These films have been enormously popular with audiences since the first short film appeared in 1981. The film character charmed groups ranging from film critics to Falardeau and Poulin fans to parody lovers. Most Québécois know about the character Elvis Gratton and his impressive, albeit burlesque, life adventures.

Although some Elvis Gratton films have won praise from general crowds, various film festivals in other Canadian provinces such as Ontario, and English-speaking communities, they are chiefly geared toward French-speaking communities and the Québécois public in the hopes of jolting a political reaction, and perhaps inciting a social revolution. As a result, I decided to continue my research on heroes and antiheroes in narratives by showing how this unique character in Québécois cinema can ultimately be considered a contemporary folk hero/antihero.

Comparatively speaking, this film character may share a place within Québécois folklore similar to other legendary heroes in Québec's narrative tradition such as Joseph "Jos" Montferrand or Ti-Jean. Elvis Gratton, a character who is known, talked about, and serves as an embodiment of social concerns shared by particular groups is presented as a stereotypical embodiment of popular (mis)conceptions.

In this chapter, I examine Elvis Gratton as the popular representation of class and nationalist expressions through published interviews with the films' controversial director as well as personal interviews and one focus group. I also discuss the way an entertainment medium uses the image of the character implicitly and explicitly to promote socioeconomic and political reform and cultural changes for Québec.

Terms such as hero and antihero are defined from the perceptions of both the participants and authors who have used regional characters from the past as examples of national heroes. Works on the hero pattern and tradition by Lord Raglan ([1936] 2003) and Vladimir Propp ([1968] 2001) are supplemented with those by Horace P. Beck (1971) and Alan Dundes (1978) to support the discussion of heroic displays and their interpretations. I include Dundes's criticism of Raglan's and Propp's theories to illustrate how comparative functionalist and structuralist studies can be applied to film narratives. While I do not base my entire study on Raglan's and Propp's early twentieth-century work, I do use their studies as a potential frame to extract similar elements about what makes up a hero, and, conversely, an antihero from Elvis Gratton. This research examines the atypical ways a hero may be conceived and created in contemporary narratives and illustrates how cinema as a folk transmitter is a visual stimulus in Québec's contemporary narrative tradition.

Elvis Gratton: Who Is He?

Elvis Gratton is not a particularly handsome man, nor does he look like Elvis Presley, though he desperately tries to when impersonating him. This discrepancy explains why some of my participants felt using the term hero and Elvis Gratton in the same context was bizarre. As an unpromising hero, however, Elvis Gratton illustrates the effects of irrational political thought by becoming the satirical stereotype of a Canadian Federalist in Québec. In all three features, Gratton is challenged by Falardeau and Poulin's personal conceptions of the stereotype and overcomes various obstacles but ultimately pays the consequences for an uninformed political opinion.

Falardeau introduced the character of Elvis Gratton to viewers across Québec in 1981 in a thirty-minute short film. The character instantly became popular, making it possible to create two more short films and combine them into a feature in 1985. The Elvis Gratton films circulated as bootleg copies, traveling from household to household. Those who knew the film character, either by word of mouth or viewing the early films, were initiated through family members or friends who asked them if they knew about the Elvis Gratton films. For some, the experience of watching the combined film, *Elvis Gratton: le king des kings* (1985), was like viewing any other cult film. Audience participation reaches an "event" form akin to watching *The Rocky Horror Picture Show* (1975), where the viewer also experiences the performance of others who know the upcoming jokes either starting to laugh before them, or even saying the lines as the actors pronounce them on the screen. Watching the Elvis Gratton films creates a setting for mimicry. How many times have I heard the line, "Pasta Dental...Linda! C'est d'la pâte-à-dent!" (Pasta Dental...Linda! It's toothpaste!), referring to a scene where Elvis Gratton's wife, Linda (Denise Mercier), rubs toothpaste on his back thinking it is sunscreen. This scene, reenacted among Elvis Gratton fans, is as entertaining as the one that follows, where both actors are lobster red from sunburns. That fans react to the line without the visual stimulus reveals an insider's knowledge of the scene and reflects the shared experience and familiarity with the character.

The phenomenon surrounding the way the lines are repeated and how they affect viewers makes Elvis Gratton a popular legendary character in Québec. Insiders repeat these film lines when they refer to or acknowledge something or someone resembling Elvis Gratton. Some of my interviewees even stated that it was his stereotyped accent, one from Brossard, a south-shore suburb of Montréal, that made him more comical. Some of my interviewees described the accent as a "colon" or "habitant" accent, a derogatory term referring to either a member of a farming class of early colonial Québec, one with little or no education, or even a lower-class or social-welfare-type person. Although the character is quite successful in his hometown, the owner of a *gros* garage ("large automotive" garage), he is portrayed as a kitschy, blue-collar suburbanite impersonating Elvis Presley on weekends to entertain himself and the fans in his community. The character, also seen as a "redneck Québécois" (Claude Leblanc 2004), is almost too real to be fictitious, and the first films created a plausible image of a person someone might actually know. Both director and actor wished to transmit precisely this impression to viewers. The character was meant to convey the idea that he could very well be living in your neighborhood, could be one of your family members, a friend, or even you.

The problem with discussing this character as a hero is that although those who know him see him as a phenomenon , they do not necessarily regard him as a contemporary folk hero for the Québécois. As a result, I also tried to examine antihero as well as hero definitions to see whether a character that represents a form of social embarrassment and political criticism may function as both hero and antihero.

The Making of a Potential Hero

Over the course of six months, I interviewed, formally and informally, French and English Canadians on the subject of the Elvis Gratton films and how they perceived the works of Falardeau. I asked interviewees if they could define, in their own terms, hero and antihero with examples. In general, and in accordance with the data collected, they perceived a hero as a person who is admired and imitated; who has no moral, intellectual, or physical faults; who is capable of extraordinary accomplishments; who wins and makes significant contributions to the well-being of others even in dangerous situations; and who is honorable. Some of these qualities are in keeping with dictionary definitions, for example,

Special edition and restored version of *Elvis Gratton, The King of Kings.*

that a hero is brave and capable of great acts. According to Lord Raglan's *The Hero: A Study in Tradition, Myth and Drama*, a hero can belong
to a mythical as well as a historical period. His story is "altered to make
[it] conform to a ritual pattern," or he is someone in "whose [life] ritual
played a predominant part" (2003, 186). Horace P. Beck comments that
"Raglan, like most of the other writers, is talking about mythological,
epic, or culture heroes" (1971, 122). Similar to Beck's interest in what
defines the "popular, national legendary heroes" (1971, 122), I approach
Elvis Gratton as a popular, national, legendary hero with traits similar
to those found in the structuralist works of Lord Raglan and Vladimir

Propp. I do acknowledge that some of Raglan's and Propp's characteristics should be applied tentatively, but they remain nonetheless valuable in developing a hero or antihero analysis in a contemporary narrative medium such as film.

While Raglan's work enumerates twenty-two "features and incidents" that may reveal a hero ([1936] 2003, 174–75), Propp's *Morphology of the Folktale* identifies thirty-one "functions of the dramatis personae" ([1968] 2001, 25–65) that illustrate how a folktale is developed. The absence of the hero's death in Propp's final functions was criticized by Alan Dundes in "The Hero Pattern and the Life of Jesus" (1978, 231) and is partially compensated for by Raglan's final pattern element in the life of a hero. Although Dundes argued that Raglan and Propp's functions apply to legends and folktales respectively, I have incorporated both structural approaches to examine briefly how it may be possible to analyze Elvis Gratton as a potential hero according to these patterns.

Raglan's first to the eighth incidents, dealing with the hero's origins and rearing, do not apply to Elvis Gratton because we receive limited genealogical information about the character other than what seems to be his native and current hometown, Brossard, Québec, Canada. Viewers are introduced to Elvis Gratton's wife, Linda, and his brother-in-law, Méo (Yves Trudel),[1] but are not given information on his birth and rearing. This factor is therefore part of the pattern element stated in Raglan's ninth and tenth features, where "we are told nothing of his childhood, but on reaching manhood he returns or goes to his future kingdom" ([1936] 2003, 174). Elvis Gratton's kingdom in the film can be loosely designated as both Brossard and the province of Québec.

In the first conglomerate film, Elvis Gratton impersonates Elvis Presley, wins first prize in a look-alike contest, and travels to a fictitious South American island named Santa Banana, ruled by a megalomaniac dwarf dictator named Général Augusto Ricochet (Reynald Fortin). A series of embarrassing events ensue, such as mistaking toothpaste for sunscreen, being sold a dead rat decorated as a beautiful native bird, listening to preregistered baseball games on the beach, and being completely ignorant that soldiers patrol the grounds to prevent contact between locals and visitors. Using Elvis Gratton's vacation, the director and actor decided to play on the extreme stereotypes about the Québécois vacationer who travels to destinations such as Old Orchard Beach in Maine or even Cuba. One of my interviewees stated that Québec once had its own specific airline carrier specializing in such southern destinations and filled with "Elvis Grattons" (O'Leary 2004). Eventually, the carrier went bankrupt, but its vacation packages were similar to all-inclusive ones sold by travel centers and airlines today. The image in the film portrays a relatively plump Québécois male in his Canadian-flag swimming trunks, wearing socks and sandals, and talking loudly in his native accent. These stereotypes have also been described to me by friends and acquaintances from Québec and the United States, who have seen these "Elvis Grattons" come to life in front of their eyes.

My interviewees had particular opinions about the image of the loud Elvis Gratton vacationer, stating that he lacked sophistication even though he thought he had some and that he reflected a particular social class that is often a basis for humor in Québec. For one interviewee, Elvis Gratton reflected the image of Canadian "snowbirds" who "envahissent 'la Florida' durant les mois d'hiver" (invade Florida during the winter months) (Charles 2004). This particular image was also projected in another comedy film, *La Florida* (1993), where one Québécois character sarcastically commented that his fellow native vacationers in Florida were "des coureurs-de-bois en Cadillac" (lumberjacks in Cadillacs). One male student from Québec City even told me that he thought Elvis Gratton was the archetype of the Québécois vacationer, although he did not personally know anyone who reminded him of the character (O'Connor 2004).

It is precisely for these stereotypical images that Falardeau and Poulin created the character of Elvis Gratton; Berger mentions that it is a common trait for screenwriters to draw on stereotypes which can ultimately "give readers and viewers of films and television shows distorted images of certain kinds of people" (1995, 160). Although the image of Elvis Gratton is not characteristic of a traditional hero, he plays that role in Québec's popular culture and, according to Falardeau and Poulin, surfaces in the Québécois subconscious to awaken the dormant revolutionary that may live in them.

For one female student in Montréal, Elvis Gratton is the embodiment of the universal idiot (Cormier 2004). The general impression is that Elvis Gratton is grotesque, extreme, raw, and antiseparatist. Ultimately, Elvis Gratton does not embody the Québécois people as a whole; he represents all that is hated by separatists, one of many subpolitical groups in Québec. How then can Elvis Gratton qualify as a hero? Perhaps the character's essence is not heroic according to the director's views, but his popularity has made him legendary.

Looking further at Raglan's heroic incidents, we can see the metaphors associated with heroic traits thirteen and fourteen when Elvis Gratton "becomes king....For a time he reigns uneventfully" ([1936] 2003, 175) in the *King of Kings* film. If we transfer these traits to a contemporary

setting and alter the long voyage taken by the traditional hero in Propp's ninth function ([1968] 2001, 36–38), Elvis Gratton's trip to Santa Banana changes his character significantly. As though being tested on his trip, and relevant to Propp's eleventh and twelfth functions ([1968] 2001, 39–42), Elvis Gratton amusingly overcomes tourist traps as well as technological and physical obstacles, returns to his homeland and his garage in Montréal, and tries to remedy the political turmoil of Québec to fit a federalist agenda. Upon his return, Elvis Gratton's political deeds are less than noble; he makes financial arrangements akin to bribery with the mayor of Montréal.[2]

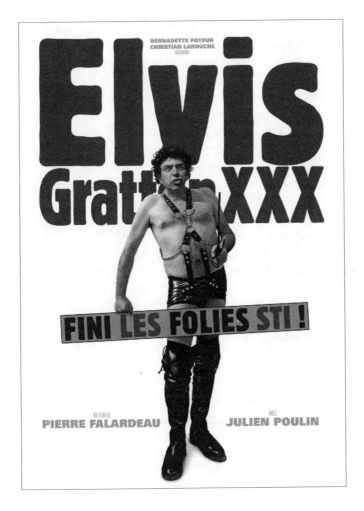

In the first feature film, Elvis Gratton explicitly offers offensive opinions on socialism and critiques welfare, students, and the health-care system in Québec. His monologue also describes separatism and the downfall of the independence movement in Québec. This behavior obviously reflects the satirical image Falardeau wishes to portray. Coincidentally, Elvis Gratton's opinions and political influence may also be compared to Raglan's fifteenth trait, that of the hero who "prescribes laws" ([1936] 2003, 175). Raglan's sixteenth and eighteenth traits, where the hero "later…loses favour with the gods and / or his subjects, and…he meets a mysterious death" ([1936] 2003, 175) may be reflected in the way

Elvis Gratton creators Falardeau and Poulin took the roles of the gods in question and killed the hero in the first feature film.

Ironically, the less-than-perfect image of traditional heroes can make them even more likable, just as they may lose favor with gods or subjects in legends and tales. This is reinforced by Beck's brief illustrative point that dishonesty in American heroes such as Davy Crockett and Ethan Allen was excusable because they both "cheated the cheatable" (1971, 128). Robin Hood is another example of a hero who performed a not-so-noble gesture such as stealing, but because he took from the rich and gave to the poor, it was excused as a necessary deed. The vigilante and rebellious nature of Robin Hood as an important antioppressive hero is what makes him virtuous (see Holt 1960; Keen 1961; and Raglan [1936] 2003, 45–53). The charismatic examples found in Davy Crockett, Ethan Allen, and Robin Hood may be compared to Elvis Gratton because they appear the same to those who admire noble heroes, for it is the notoriety of a character that often makes him larger than life. Elvis Gratton's political role in the films would not die with the character in the first feature film. While Falardeau prepared other politicized films, Elvis Gratton merely slumbered.

The Politics Surrounding Elvis Gratton

Falardeau, as an independence-movement activist, created many political documentaries on the nature of Québécois politics and used this first fiction film as a social criticism about the need to reexamine independence causes leading to separation from Canada. The desired effect was to stimulate a cultural shock and possible revolution within the social, political, and cultural realms in Québec. Falardeau and Poulin's Elvis Gratton was molded out of their frustration about the failed Québécois separation referendum of 1980 (LaFrance 1999, 74; Lussier 2004, 3; Bégin 2004, 120). In Pierre-Luc Bégin's interviews with Falardeau, the film director clearly states his intentions about Elvis Gratton. In fact, the second film was specifically released in theaters on Canada Day (July 1), a planned event much in the essence of Falardeau's philosophy, as he stated, "Faire mes films comme on pose des bombes" (making my films is just like placing bombs) (Bégin 2004, 85).

After reading Mireille LaFrance's interviews in her book *Pierre Falardeau persiste et filme!* and viewing Falardeau and Poulin's projects from the 1970s on, I learned just how political both artists were in their early stages as film director and soundman who constructed collages of media footage and metaphorical images to convey their political beliefs.

Looking at Falardeau's filmography is like witnessing an evolution of social angst, artistic rebellion, and political reactivism toward a system that does not favor egalitarian hegemony, but rather a dominant, central, capitalist institution governing the entire nation. As a master's student in anthropology, Falardeau was fascinated by works from Claude Lévi-Strauss and Roland Barthes (LaFrance 1999, 17–22; Bégin 2004, 62–67, 204). Being a product of Québec's Quiet Revolution and using what he had learned in anthropology, Falardeau envisioned his films as a way to express himself politically. As noted by Sherry B. Ortner in her 1984 compiled historical outlook, "Theory in Anthropology since the Sixties," the seventies saw a particular interest in symbolism in "class or group identity, in the context of political/economic struggles of one sort or another" (142). This resonated in Falardeau's approach to cinema and his narrative development. With the help of Poulin, Falardeau was able to use what he had learned in anthropology and create a character that embodied social criticism.

Falardeau and Poulin's personal political opinions have also often been discussed in the media. It was their strong opinions in their works together prior to the Elvis Gratton films that branded them as political activists within an artistic medium. Falardeau became a controversial film director with separatist, sociodemocratic ideals that bordered on cultural manifestos and were in keeping with left-wing nationalist movements. This ties in with the Elvis Gratton as hero or antihero debate since it was after the first screening of Elvis Gratton in 1981 that Falardeau and Poulin realized to what extent they had created a "monster." Such a monster was specifically manifested in the second feature film, *Elvis Gratton II: Miracle à Memphis* (Elvis Gratton II: Miracle in Memphis) (1999). After the first Elvis Gratton film won the award for best short fiction film at the Festival de Lille in 1982, and then a 1982 Genie Award in Toronto, Falardeau and Poulin sought to continue the adventures of the "héros national du bourrelet" (fat national hero).

Holy Gratton!

Elvis Gratton, a duly politicized character, also becomes a supernatural figure through this second film. He miraculously resurrects at the end of the first feature to continue spreading his notions of life and entertainment in the sequel. Elvis Gratton suffers a severe heart attack while performing in an Elvis sequined suit clearly too tight for him. The resurrection takes place during his funeral march; he bursts out of his coffin before the planned burial. In a way, the end of the first feature illustrates

Raglan's twenty-first heroic pattern of the "body not buried" ([1936] 2003, 175). That Elvis Gratton resurrects three days after his death "like Jesus" (as noted in the film synopsis) is particularly significant.[3] Though *Elvis Gratton II* appeared in theaters fourteen years after the release of the first feature in 1985, the sequel states that Elvis Gratton resurrected three days after his death and aged surprisingly quickly. However, the current events portrayed at the beginning of the sequel date from 1998, making the chronological explanation moot.

It can be argued that Elvis Gratton plays a similar supernatural role to that of Jesus, or even King Arthur, as a slumbering king or sleeping messiah/warrior (Raglan [1936] 2003, 41). The resurrection has parallels to the sleeping warrior motif, where "the story of the Sleeping Warriors is connected with a coronation ritual, a ritual intended to qualify the new king to impersonate the old king" (Raglan [1936] 2003, 42) and echoes Elvis Gratton's return from death and reexamination of social issues in Québec. Viewers learn in this second film that Elvis Gratton will use his miraculous return to life as a commercial ploy to sell his own image in the entertainment and business worlds. Elvis Gratton resurrects like an allegorical hero and profits from this miracle to become the commercial "king des kings." With the help of a wealthy corporate Texan mogul (Barry Blake) called Donald Bill Clinton or preferably D. Bill, Elvis Gratton creates items out of his image to sell to the masses. As an interesting play on words, D. Bill in French sounds like *débile*, meaning "stupid" or "idiotic," which is yet another personal opinion Falardeau shares with his audience on wealthy tycoons and excessive commercialism.

From a sociolinguistic perspective, the use of specific terms in French, to deride the English character in this case, illustrates the deeper level where Falardeau is encoding his opinions and the way viewers should decode them. Linguist Edward Sapir notes that a specific group decodes what they "experience" and its reference to their identity (1921, 12–13). In Alan Cruse's *Meaning in Language*, this intention also shapes the way a sender's message is conveyed, especially since in language "signs are the property of the speech community and have stable semantic properties" (2004, 6). Unless you are part of the French-speaking community and understand the thick *joual* accent (Québécois slang) pouring out of Elvis Gratton's mouth, you may not understand most of the linguistic derision in the script. The identifying markers and associative speech also confirm the specific audience Falardeau expects to view the films. The community of viewers must at least be initiated into the film's language and meanings to understand the message.

Pierrette Thibault's 1993 definition of sociolinguistics in the *Dictionnaire critique de la communication* describes the Labovian approach to linguistics, that is, acknowledging a community as having its own communication system subject to variations according to constructed identities (1993, 286). The variation of French represented by jouale is an example of the way language works in the Elvis Gratton films to draw in particular listeners and identify a specific group in Québec. Falardeau's use of the Texan mogul to mock the excesses of commercialization is clear not only through his name D. Bill (débile) and what it conveys to French speakers but also through the way he capitalizes by marketing Elvis Gratton as a product.

Through the overblown marketing strategies implemented by D. Bill and his committee, as well as the ridiculous activities that mark Elvis Gratton's own involvement in the campaign, Gratton experiences worldwide popularity, performs his own shows around the world, and sells personal products while advertising others at his shows. Even his Presley-like purple latex jumpsuit is plastered with product and company logos. This concern with commercialism becomes the main theme in the second feature film, one viewers also see expressed by other Canadians like Naomi Klein in her critiques of the corporate world and its name-branding phenomenon (Klein 2000).

Elvis Gratton, the Puppet: Falardeau's Voice and Criticism

Falardeau always tries to convey social criticism in his films, and it is fitting that between the first conglomerate Elvis Gratton film and the second feature he kept his voice heard in Québécois popular politics by creating a series of serious films and documentaries. In his 1994 tragic drama, *Octobre*, he presented a version of Québec's Quiet Revolution and the early 1970s assassination of Minister of Labor Pierre Laporte by members of the Front de libération du Québec (FLQ) that provoked as strong a reaction as his previous films. The film and director received much attention from the media as well as politicians in Québec and other provinces in Canada, who felt this interpretation might have romanticized the image of a radical rebel group and their drastic measures for independence. Falardeau started the project research for the film *Octobre* in 1981 when Poulin was still very involved in its creation, but the film was only released to the public in 1994. Even though Falardeau's timing seemed to be by chance, it perfectly aligned with the second referendum for separation in Québec, which took place one year after the release of *Octobre* on October 31, 1995. The day after the referendum echoed the same sense of defeat and confusion that Falardeau remembered from 1980 (LaFrance 1999, 74).

After creating a short advertising commercial for the Yes campaign, Falardeau did what he knew best: create another film in response to the referendum failure. The public then witnessed the rebirth of Elvis Gratton in 1999 through *Elvis Gratton II: Miracle à Memphis*. This rebirth, in keeping with the metaphorical awakening of the slumbering king, served as a political reminder for Québec. It represented Falardeau's own serious attempt to stimulate historical events leading to a possible new order in Québec.

Since 1990, Falardeau had wanted to direct a project on the final letters of the Chevalier de Lorimier, a Patriote who was executed in 1839 for rebelling against the British crown's neglect to govern those inhabiting Lower Canada (the province of Québec today) responsibly. The Patriotes were also present in Upper Canada (parts of the present provinces of Ontario and Québec), but what interested Falardeau was representing a common Québécois political movement. It was during LaFrance's interviews with Falardeau that he shared his views of national heroes in Québec, and the irony that de Lorimier, the hero of his film *15 février 1839* (2001), was a martyr, hanged for his political beliefs, became apparent. The actor who portrayed de Lorimier, Luc Picard, was the same person who played Francis Simard, the FLQ member involved in the assassination of Pierre Laporte in the film *Octobre*. As though recycling these serious images, Falardeau chose Luc Picard as the hero for his political tragedy and Julien Poulin as the one in his political satire.

Is Elvis Gratton a Hero or an Antihero?

Compared with other heroes in Québec's legend tradition, such as the southwestern Québécois strongman Joseph "Jos" Montferrand, or even the cunning and shrewd Ti-Jean (Little John) who outwits the colonial British, Elvis Gratton may not seem as directly heroic. When I interviewed people and asked them whom they considered to be a hero, some named religious figures like Jesus Christ, the Virgin Mary, or one of the saints; some suggested mythological heroes such as Hercules and Ulysses; others offered comic characters such as Superman, Lucky Luke, Tintin, and Astérix; sports fans even mentioned hockey player Maurice Richard and basketball star Michael Jordan. One interviewee named Québec's popular past prime minister, René Lévesque (from the Parti Québécois).

I was intrigued to learn my interviewees' definitions of antihero and the examples they gave to counterbalance certain qualities of Elvis

Gratton. Julie said that an antihero "atteint, par le hazard des choses, un but meilleur que le sort qui lui était destiné. La population le supporte parce qu'il démontre des caractéristiques humaines qu'on ne veut mettre en évidence" (obtains, by chance, his goal, which is greater than what is truly destined to him. The population supports him because he demonstrates human traits that they do not wish to place in evidence) (Hamel 2004). Derry felt that the antihero shows his "faiblesses, c'est la personne que l'on ne veut pas être mais, à un certain moment, on prend tout de même sa part puisqu'il est ce qu'il est. L'anti-héro est le 'born-loser' mais on l'encourage pareil" (weaknesses, is someone whom we do not wish to be, but at times, we support him because he is what he is. The antihero is a born loser, but we still encourage him) (O'Connor 2004). Other interviewees commented that the antihero does things out of his own interests and may put other people's lives in danger, which is neither idolized nor idealized.

Examples offered as antiheroes were as various as the ones for heroes and some were even exact opposites when the interviewees thought that an antihero is contrary to a hero. In the political realm, Hitler, Stalin, and George W. Bush were mentioned; for comic characters, Captain Hadock in Tintin, Obélix in Astérix, Gaston Lagaffe, Charlie Brown, Andy Capp, and Wile E. Coyote were proposed. Julie thought that Elvis Gratton is an antihero much like the characters from the Québécois garage-hockey-league film series *Les Boys I, II, III* (1997, 1998, 2001), as well as those from a similar older film, *Slap Shot* (1977). Julie continued by stating that Elvis Gratton is an antihero because "le destin est plutôt un résultat de chance et Elvis se présente avec son personnage quotidien et cru" (his destiny is more of a chance result, and Elvis is a raw and everyday man) (Hamel 2004). Derry also considered Elvis Gratton to be an antihero because he is "tout ce qu'on ne veut pas être, mais, en meme temps, on se reconnaît en lui et ça nous fait rire" (everything we do not wish to be, but at the same time, we find ourselves in him and that makes us laugh) (O'Connor 2004). This, in fact, represents satirical admiration for the character, making Elvis Gratton a potential antihero but a hero as well, though an unpromising one in terms of political revolutions. Derry continued,

> Falardeau a probablement eu l'idée de montrer c'est quoi un
> hosti de raciste, cheesy, réactionnaire, fédéraliste, pro-Américain
> fétéchiste…, mais ça a rebondi un peu aussi parce qu'Elvis n'a
> pas motivé les gens de changer, il a servi un peu comme une
> célébration de tout ce qui était, et est, un peu backwards au Québec
> (et partout dans l'occident peut-être) [Falardeau probably had the

idea to show what is a "host" (expletive colloquial term similar to damn) racist, cheesy, reactionary, federalist, pro-American fetish-ist…, but it bounced back a bit because Elvis did not motivate peo-ple to change; he served…as a celebration of all that was and is a bit backwards in Québec (and probably everywhere in the Western world too)]. (O'Connor 2004)

This politicized answer showed that people understood what Falardeau wished to convey through the character, but at the same time, he created a popular cult phenomenon beyond his own political messages.

Some interviewees saw Elvis Gratton as neither hero nor antihero (Giroux 2004; Charles 2004). One of them mentioned that Elvis Gratton is simply a caricatured image like Homer Simpson and Falardeau is him-self an antihero because he "se sert de ses films pour inciter les Québé-cois à supporter la cause séparatiste en essayant de créer une perception de ceux qui ne la supporte pas comme étant des colons stupides ou des impérialistes brutal" (uses his films to incite the Québécois to support the separatist cause trying to create a perception of those who do not support the cause as stupid colonials or brutish imperialists) (Charles 2004). This is precisely the reaction Falardeau wishes to provoke when portraying the amusing, but ill-informed, Elvis Gratton.

Falardeau, quoted in a special film booklet featured in the daily Mon-treal newspaper *Journal de Montréal*, observed that the slapstick humor was not easy to create, but that "tout est dans la manière. Parce qu'Elvis, c'est de la caricature. C'est grotesque. C'est gros comme personage" (all is in the way [it is made]. Because Elvis is a caricature. It is grotesque. It is big for a character) (Rezzonico 2004, 44). In another issue of the *Journal de Montréal*, a journalist stated that "on rit de lui parce qu'il est une cari-cature ambulante, une espèce de concentré de tout ce qu'on peut trouver de pire dans l'*homo Québecus*" (we laugh at him [Elvis Gratton] because he is a walking caricature, a concentrated species of all that we can pos-sibly find worse in the *homo Québecus*) (Langlois 2004, 67).

This particular caricature and provocation continued in the sequels. On June 23, 2004, one day before Québec's provincial celebration of St-Jean-Baptiste, the third film, *Elvis Gratton XXX: La vengeance d'Elvis Wong* (Elvis Gratton XXX: The Revenge of Elvis Wong) was released. On June 30, one day before the Canada Day celebrations, I headed to Starcité (a large Famous Players multiplex cinema) in Hull, Québec, to view the film with family members and interview them for comments, reactions, and interpretations. I also watched the audience's reactions. The theater seated approximately 250 viewers, and I roughly counted 85 in the room. Fewer than 10 viewers were teenagers, and approximately

20 were between the ages of twenty and thirty-five. The target audience for this film was largely those who had seen the previous Elvis Gratton films, that is, those who were between twenty and forty in the early 1980s. That particular group was predominant in the theater. Once the film started rolling, the physical and recurring jokes from previous Elvis Gratton films made people howl with laughter. However, Falardeau's explicit attack on the media, featuring images of mass-media influence, its manipulation of the public, and its lack of factual information, and his treatment of censorship issues were not as appreciated by viewers. They responded to the slapstick humor, but the highly political messages Falardeau sent through Elvis Gratton and the character's appropriation of a national broadcasting corporation were not as popular. During my family's focus-group interview following the film, they all said they thought the political messages were overdone, and they were disappointed the film took such a propagandist approach (Claude Leblanc 2004; Marc-André LeBlanc 2004; Nadeau 2004; Westphalen 2004).

During an interview, Falardeau mentioned that he was aware of the disappointment some felt because of the evolution of Gratton's character since the second feature (Légaré 2004, 26–29 *passim*). Falardeau recently shared his reflections on the various audience members who view his films and their reactions. When interviewed by Montréal's daily newspaper *La Presse,* he stated, "C'est pas grave. Il y a des comedies que j'ai vues très jeune, qui m'ont fait rire, et dont j'ai compris la signification beaucoup plus tard" (It's not important. There are comedies that I have seen at a very young age that made me laugh and that I understood the meaning much later [in life]) (Lussier 2004, 3). This is perhaps the reaction he was hoping to get from those who saw the third Elvis Gratton film. There are some interpretations that may still be left to our imaginations.

The message in the Elvis Gratton films is simple: if you know someone like Elvis Gratton, don't be like him, but rather learn from his behavior. Falardeau's political message serves as a lesson and wake-up call about the troubles of cultural assimilation in Québec since the colonial period. Elvis Gratton, perhaps not the best hero example, is a character who fulfills a similar role as a hero, but through negative reinforcement.

Elvis Gratton: The Phenomenon

As for his popularity, can it be that Elvis Gratton's success is due to the consumers who buy into the Gratton image and see a piece of him in themselves? Falardeau and Poulin show this common man, the little bourgeois from a metropolitan suburb, suddenly seeking and finding international fame. Slews of people who have seen the films in various stages of their lives can retell events, scenes, or even sayings from the main character that relate to the stereotypes and parodies.

This reaction to the popular character brings up identity issues that surround a particular group. Alan Dundes discusses various definitions of identity that are tied to sameness and continuity in groups (1983, 237–39), and Thomas Meyer describes a phenomenon of identity that may be related to Elvis Gratton. Meyer's definition of identity as "an open process of negotiation between the self-image that the individual conjures up of himself and the image that his partners in social interaction form of him in changing contexts" (2001, 15) applies to Elvis Gratton's image as a Federalist who questions the very motives of separatism and cultural distinction in Québec. Falardeau's opinions of Federalists are reflected through Elvis Gratton. By using a Federalist satirical character, Falardeau differentiates between those who question the imposed political system versus those who follow it blindly in Québec.

The third film takes a different political approach by directly attacking the media. The political concerns are stretched to address freedom of speech and the mediated, controlled national broadcast system. The film's distributor, Christal Films, refused prescreenings to the media; in consequence, film posters, chronicles, interviews, Web site advertisements, and television rebroadcastings of the other two Elvis Gratton features took place in the weeks prior to the release of the third film. Elvis Gratton had never seen such publicity or intriguing attention from the masses and the media. Ironically, the third film ridicules this very same media that promoted its release. At the end of the film, after Elvis Gratton's second superdeath, we see a scene of his "selected" wife bearing his cloned child. This obviously opens the door for a fourth Elvis Gratton film, but how will this character evolve from the original? Will there be a difference, or has the initial character finished his transformation into his supernatural perpetuity?

This very politically incorrect film did not appeal to every viewer, but its success is not based entirely on viewers' critiques; rather it exposes the immortality of the character. Some viewers complained about the explicit messages about exploitation by the media and felt that the Elvis Gratton films had degenerated into a less subtle form of satire. The director's direct and raw personal frustrations left little to the imagination. Overall, Falardeau's concerns always remain explicit through his character, Elvis Gratton, even if the content of the films may seem excessive.

Conclusion

In retrospect, trying to explore Elvis Gratton as a contemporary folk hero made me reconsider the definitions of hero and antihero as well as the populist perception of Falardeau and Poulin's creation. After continuously watching the films, I rediscovered more clues that had led to my preliminary hypotheses about Gratton and hero cultures. What was striking about the first Elvis Gratton feature was the mayor's condolence speech at Gratton's Christmas wake. While the stiff, dead Elvis poses with a "hang-loose" finger gesture, his weeping wife, Linda, is consoled by the mayor's eulogy:

> La mort de votre mari, c'est une perte immense pour notre ville. C'est un homme irremplaçable, il s'est dévoué pendant des années pour les pauvres, les riches, les malades, il a toujours donné le meilleur de lui-même. Il laisse derrière lui de nombreux accomplissements et pour nous qui cherchons des exemples héroiques dans une société en bouleversement, Robert Gratton restera à jamais un monument pour les generations à venir. Mme Gratton, mes sincères condoléances. [The death of your husband is a great loss for our city. He is an irreplaceable man. He devoted himself for many years to the poor, the rich, as well as the sick and always gave the best of himself. He leaves behind him numerous accomplishments and for those of us who are searching for heroic examples in a changing society, Robert Gratton will forever remain a monument for generations to come. Mrs. Gratton, my sincere condolences.]

Ironically, Elvis Gratton did nothing for the poor, or the sick, but rather idolized the rich and famous as well as all that was glamorous, as one interviewee told me. Elvis Gratton did, however, become a popular icon because his cult films attracted the same public they had in the past plus a few additional viewers who had heard of the legendary character. Through laughter, Elvis Gratton managed to communicate the message intended by Falardeau and Poulin: to reexamine ourselves continuously and change what we can. His films may create the reaction needed to jolt a Québécois toward political reform. They may also remind viewers of the apathetic response some have toward cultural assimilation or may simply act like any other political satire and offer comic relief.

If any conclusion should be drawn on the subject of Elvis Gratton as a contemporary folk hero in Québec, it is that the question mark following this speculation reflects the people's own views of the character as unpromising hero, as antihero, as caricature, and as none of these. Elvis Gratton is the everyman, the underdog, but the one who manages to

reappear every so often after political debates about separation in Québec. Elvis Gratton is a man who occasionally appears at political conventions and universities in full Elvis Presley garb, and who survives his
own legend. Falardeau and Poulin created Elvis Gratton, the character
who would not die, the figure of cultural irony who "thinks big"!

What would Québec do without Elvis Gratton? Perhaps this will
be the question raised in the potential fourth Elvis Gratton film? Who
knows if Elvis Gratton's clone will continue the pseudohero tradition?
Although some may not consider Elvis Gratton to be a folk hero like
Jos Montferrand or Ti-Jean in Québécois legends, he does share their
supernatural hero traits. Comparatively speaking, these characters share
the fundamental role of folk hero, that is, a character who is known by
groups, is talked about, and is an embodiment of concerns and social
focus shared by these groups.

Elvis Gratton may not embody the desired and aspired values of
a community according to his creators, but he does reflect the fears
and shallow imperfections that may obsess the contemporary Québécois. Through this character, Québec may laugh at itself and reflect on
these stereotypes that are shared and believed to be true by Québécois
and Canadians. Examples of other films using satirical and stereotyped
images in derision to criticize or create a sense of familiarity that compare to the Elvis Gratton genre are Michael Moore's *Canadian Bacon*
(1995) and Mike Clattenberg's *Trailer Park Boys: The Movie* (2006). While
Moore's Bud Boomer (John Candy) resembles Elvis Gratton behavior-
ally, the *Trailer Park Boys: The Movie* is English Canada's equivalent to the
Elvis Gratton popular phenomenon. The characters are so vividly portrayed that they inevitably become popular with viewers. They achieve
an epitome of notoriety, a quality associated with heroes.

If the interpretations provided by those I interviewed, as well as the
ones from the published interviews with Falardeau, offer anything, it is
that the character of Elvis Gratton has a place next to other heroes in having a potential influence and playing a role in contemporary Québécois
folklore due to his surpassing popularity among a cross-generational
group of viewers. Those who share stories from the films with some
who have yet to see them perpetuate the cult among a greater body of
potential viewers. From Québec to other provinces in Canada, and even
to international places, Elvis Gratton travels farther than his film box. He
is alive and well and may even reside next to someone you know. As one
reporter from Montréal observed, "Elvis Gratton est au cinéma du Québec ce que la poutine est à sa gastronomie" (Elvis Gratton is to Québec's
cinema as poutine is to its gastronomy) (Rezzonico 2004, 44).[4]

Notes

This paper was initially presented at the twenty-second Perspectives on Contemporary Legend conference in Aberystwyth, Wales, on July 21, 2004.

1. Méo has become increasingly important in the second and third Elvis Gratton films, and during the June 30, 2004, focus-group interview, Marc-André LeBlanc noted that Méo may possibly represent the voice of the Québécois people slowly and assertively being heard and understood in the films as a counterbalance to Elvis Gratton's excessively Federalist comments.

2. This type of political and cultural endorsement has long since been an issue of great concern in Canada. In light of current affairs in Canada and as an interesting comparative example, the Liberal Party experienced serious allegations and consequent trials from the sponsorship scandals, whereby contractual work with companies created a budgetary double-dipping advantage for the party.

3. I am using the concept of Jesus as folk hero in a similar way as folklorists such as Alan Dundes (1978, 223–70) in comparing him to Elvis Gratton based on the allegorical and metaphorical portrayal implied by film director Pierre Falardeau.

4. Poutine, a mixture of fries, cheese curds, and gravy, is a conventional and subcultural dish as worth a try as viewing the Elvis Gratton epics.

Filmography

Les Boys (1997). 107 min. Louis Saïa
Les Boys II (1998). 120 min. Louis Saïa
Les Boys III (2001). 124 min. Louis Saïa
Canadian Bacon (1995). 91 min. Michael Moore
Elvis Gratton (1981). 30 min. Pierre Falardeau
Elvis Gratton: le king des kings (1985). 89 min. Pierre Falardeau
Elvis Gratton II: Miracle à Memphis (1999). 105 min. Pierre Falardeau
Elvis Gratton XXX: La vengeance d'Elvis Wong (2004). 105 min. Pierre
    Falardeau
15 février 1839 (2001). 120 min. Pierre Falardeau
La Florida (1993). 114 min. Georges Mihalka
Octobre (1994). 97 min. Pierre Falardeau
Pas encore Elvis Gratton (1985). 30 min. Pierre Falardeau
The Rocky Horror Picture Show (1975). 100 min. Jim Sharman
Slap Shot (1977). 123 min. George Roy Hill
Trailer Park Boys: The Movie (2006). 95 min. Mike Clattenberg
Les Vacances d'Elvis Gratton (1983). 30 min. Pierre Falardeau

Works Cited

Beck, Horace P. 1971. The making of the popular legendary hero. In *American folk legend: A symposium,* ed. Wayland D. Hand, 121–32. Berkeley: University of California Press.

Bégin, Pierre-Luc. 2004. *Québec libre! Entretiens politiques avec Pierre Falardeau.* Québec: Éditions du Québécois.

Berger, Arthur Asa. 1995. *Cultural criticism: A primer of key concepts.* Thousand Oaks, CA: Sage.

Cormier, Elisabeth. 2004. Interview with author. Online. May 10.

Charles [pseud.]. 2004. Interview with author. Online. May 2.

Cruse, Alan. 2004. *Meaning in language: An introduction to semantics and pragmatics.* 2nd ed. Oxford / New York: Oxford University Press.

Dorson, Richard M. 1959. *American folklore.* Chicago: University of Chicago Press.

Dundes, Alan. 1978. The hero pattern and the life of Jesus. In *Essays in folkloristics,* ed. Alan Dundes, 223–70. Meerut: Folklore Institute.

———. 1983. Defining identity through folklore. In *Identity: Personal and sociocultural, a symposium,* ed. Anita Jacobsen-Widding, 235–61. Atlantic Highlands, NJ: Humanities Press.

Giroux, Micheline. 2004. Interview with author. Online. April 26.

Hamel, Julie. 2004. Interview with author. Online. May 2.

Holt, J. C. 1960. The origins and audience of the ballads of Robin Hood. *Past & Present* 18: 89–110.

Keen, Maurice. 1961. Robin Hood—Peasant or gentleman? *Past & Present* 19: 7–15.

Klein, Naomi. 2000. *No logo: Taking aim at the brand bullies.* Toronto: Vintage.

LaFrance, Mireille. 1999. *Pierre Falardeau persiste et filme!* Montréal: L'Hexagone.

Langlois, Claude. 2004. Comment est né Elvis Gratton. *Journal de Montréal,* June 17, 67.

Leblanc, Claude. 2004. Focus group interview with author. Audio recording 2005–124. June 30. Memorial University of Newfoundland Folklore and Language Archive (MUNFLA), St. John's.

LeBlanc, Marc-André. 2004. Focus group interview with author. Audio recording 2005–124. June 30. MUNFLA.

Légaré, Jean-François. 2004. Empire et contre tous. *Famous Québec* 3 (5, June): 26–29.

Lussier, Marc-André. 2004. Vengeance, *stie! La Presse,* June 19, 3.

Meyer, Thomas. 2001. *Identity mania: fundamentalism and the politicization of cultural differences.* London / New York: Zed Books.

Nadeau, Jean-François. 2004. Focus group interview with author. Audio recording 2005–124. June 30. MUNFLA.

O'Connor, Derry. 2004. Personal online interview with author. Online. May 4.

O'Leary, Alain. 2004. Interview with author. Audio recording 2005–124. March 11. MUNFLA.

Ortner, Sherry B. 1984. Theory in anthropology since the sixties. *Comparative Studies in Society and History* 26 (1): 126–66.

Propp, Vladimir. [1968] 2001. *Morphology of the folktale.* Repr. and rev, Austin: University of Texas Press.

Raglan, Lord. [1936] 2003. *The hero: A study in tradition, myth and drama.* Repr., Mineola, NY: Dover.

Rezzonico, Philippe. 2004. Elvis Gratton est au cinéma du Québec ce que la poutine est à sa gastronomie. *Journal de Montréal,* Cinéma Weekend sec.: Elvis Gratton: Toujours vivant, June 19, 44.

Sapir, Edward. 1921. *Language: An introduction to the study of speech.* New York: Harcourt, Brace.

Thibault, Pierrette. 1993. Sociolinguistique. In vol. 1 of *Dictionnaire critique de la communication,* ed. Lucien Sfez, 286–89. Paris: PUF.

Westphalen, Tammy. 2004. Focus group interview with author. Audio recording 2005–124. June 30. MUNFLA.

3

A Strange and Foreign World

Documentary, Ethnography, and the Mountain Films of Arnold Fanck and Leni Riefenstahl

Rebecca Prime

With its celebration of mountains and masculinity, of pure white land-scapes and strong white men, the popular genre of Weimar cinema known as the mountain film (Bergfilm) lends itself readily to interpretations that emphasize its relation to Nazi ideology. A number of factors have encouraged the perception of the mountain film as Aryan-myth wish fulfillment. The growth of the genre closely mirrors the rise of National Socialism, with production petering out once the Third Reich was established in 1933. Additionally, the content of the films conforms to popular conceptions of Nazism: the white, athletic characters can be seen to represent the ideal Aryan "super race," while the narrative emphasis on heroism, self-sacrifice, and submission to force (nature, in this instance) seems tailor-made to educate ideal fascist subjects. Finally, film history has been instrumental in casting the mountain film in the role of Nazi collaborator. In his study of Weimar cinema, Siegfried Kracauer set the tone for much subsequent scholarship in characterizing the mountain film as "an exclusively German genre...rooted in a mentality kindred to the Nazi spirit" (1947, 110, 112).[1]

Whereas Kracauer's interpretation bears the mark of his historical circumstances as a German exile trying to understand the horrors of the Third Reich, a number of recent, revisionist studies have brought a more nuanced eye and contextual approach to the mountain film. Eric Rentschler has called attention to the connections between the mountain film and two other popular genres of Weimar cinema: the fantastic and the street film (1990). In separate analyses, Nancy Nenno discusses the mountain film in relation to the rise of mass tourism during the Weimar period and the cultural significance of the Alpine landscape (2003, 1996). What both Rentschler and Nenno bring to the fore is the highly complex relationship between modern and antimodern impulses characteristic of Weimar Germany and expressed in the mountain film's distinctive mix of technology and tradition. Compared to that of Britain and France, Germany's experience of industrialization was late and sudden, and the arrival of modernity consequently had a greater impact. What resulted was a form of "reactionary modernism"that harnessed new technology to the rhetoric and ideals of the past (Herf 1984, 2). By relating the mountain film to the paradoxes of Germany's embrace of modernity, Rentschler and Nenno open up the interpretive playing field dramatically.

In this chapter, I contribute to this process of unearthing the layers of signification buried in the mountain film by taking as my focus two important, but as yet little studied, dimensions of the genre: the documentary and the ethnographic. During a period when film production was almost exclusively studio based, mountain films were exceptional for their commitment to location shooting in the Alps. While concessions to narrative wormed their way into the genre as it developed during the course of the 1920s, they were never at the expense of the documentary component; the spectacular Alpine landscape remained a significant character in these films, lying at the heart of the genre's appeal. Related to the genre's documentary aspects is its engagement with the ethnographic, by which I mean the depiction of traditional culture and people in these films. A peripheral presence in films such as Arnold Fanck's *The Holy Mountain* (1926) and Fanck and Georg Pabst's *The White Hell of Pitz-Palü* (1929),the Alpine villagers play a much more significant role in one of the later mountain films, Leni Riefenstahl's *The Blue Light* (1932). In view of the central political role that folklore and the idealized notion of the *Volk* came to play in the construction of the Third Reich, emphasizing the ethnographic may prove a revealing intervention into the debates surrounding the relationship between mountain films and Nazism.

" A Strange and Foreign World"

In her account of her early career, Leni Riefenstahl describes her reaction to seeing her first mountain film, Fanck's *Mountain of Destiny* (1924):

> Beginning with the first shots, I was strangely affected by what I saw: mountains and clouds, alpine slopes and naked rock cliffs moved past me. I was looking at a strange and foreign world. Who would have thought that the mountains were so beautiful? I knew them only from postcards; they seemed lifeless and rigid, but yet they intoxicated me with their undreamt of splendor....The beauty and strength of the film attracted me so much that, even before the film was over, I had decided to visit the mountains and see them for myself. (Hinton 1978, 4–5)

Riefenstahl spent four weeks touring the Alps, at the end of which she met Luis Trenker, the star of *Mountain of Destiny*. Despite her lack of acting (not to mention mountain-climbing) experience, Riefenstahl persuaded Trenker to pass along a becoming photo of herself to the director, Dr. Arnold Fanck. In doing so, she set in motion the transformation of the genre Fanck had pioneered. A geologist by training, Fanck was drawn to motion pictures not by his cinephilia (his directorial debut, *The Miracle of Skiing*, made in 1919, was only the second film he had seen!) but by his desire to capture the beauty of the mountains (Hinton 1978, 1).

Fanck's initial forays into film were documentary depictions of the alpine landscape, where the primordial battle waged between man and nature suggested by titles such as *The Struggle with the Mountain* (1921) fulfilled any need for narrative. Despite the box-office success of these early films, Fanck felt that to keep the public's interest, the mountains needed human costars. For his first dramatic film, *Mountain of Destiny*, he selected a narrative—the true story of a son conquering the mountain that had killed his father—rich in Oedipal overtones, a choice that connects the mountain film to the broader cinematic milieu of Weimar Germany.[2] As had Fanck's earlier films, *Mountain of Destiny* depicts the Alps as a masculine domain, a realm of male camaraderie and bonding.[3] Making her debut in Fanck's *The Holy Mountain* (1926) just two years later, Leni Riefenstahl carved a permanent niche for herself in this exclusively male preserve, becoming the star in the majority of Fanck's mountain films.

With the addition of Riefenstahl, the mountain film took a turn toward melodrama, with plots revolving around love triangles in which Riefenstahl provided an alluring center.[4] These changes were not always well received, with critics quick to heap scorn on Fanck's formulaic narratives and lofty sentiments. Kracauer and Lotte Eisner echo the views of many contemporary critics in calling attention to what they see as a fundamental opposition between the documentary value of the images and the cliché demotions of the narrative (Kracauer 1947, 110; Eisner 1952, 312).[5] Reviewing *S.O.S. Iceberg*(1933), the *Berliner Tageblatt* laments that in "virulent contrast to this divine work of nature, the film's tacked-on plot becomes here, quite frankly, a prime example of the human intellect's capacity for presumptuousness" (Rentschler 1990, 148). The reviewer singles out Leni Riefenstahl for criticism, arguing that by her very presence, she undermines the power of the film's documentary qualities. "In the midst of a horizontal setting larger than life, this romantic silliness struck one as unbearable kitsch"(Rentschler 1990, 152).

How would the mountain film have evolved if Leni Riefenstahl had not seen *Mountain of Destiny* and tracked down Luis Trenker, if Trenker had not passed along her photo to Fanck, and if Fanck had not become enraptured by her image? With *Mountain of Destiny*, Fanck was already moving away from documentary and toward melodrama, a trajectory in line with the direction of cinematic development during the period. Indeed, Johannes von Moltke sees Fanck's career as "exemplary in that it leads directly from the early 'view' aesthetic" [the static framings characteristic of travel and landscape films]"through its gradual dynamisation by way of technical innovations and heroic stunts, to its more or less successful (in)fusion with fictional narrative in *The Holy Mountain, Battle for the Matterhorn* (1928), and *Avalanche* (1930)" (2002, 21). Considering these broader trends, the mountain film likely would have met melodrama with or without Riefenstahl. However, the complex conjunction between gender and aesthetics she introduces bears fuller exploration and provides the focus for my next section in which I situate the mountain film vis à vis other developments in the documentary genre during the 1920s.

"We Really Froze"

Since its inception, cinema has shown a fascination for the real. Some of the earliest films, the documentary actualités of the Lumière brothers, were simple depictions of scenes from everyday life. The appeal of natural landscapes contributed to the extreme popularity of early nonfiction travel films and expedition films (Gunning 1997). While these types of films may more or less correspond to our contemporary conception of the documentary—based upon the presumed authenticity of the indexical relationship between the image and external reality, or the objective presentation of verifiable "facts"—during the 1920s documentary was a rather more fluid and undefined concept. As Kevin Brownlow puts it, "In the silent days, film-makers never realized they were making documentaries. They set out to make pictures about actual events, and they failed or succeeded, according to their individual talents. There was no formula" (1979, 403). Perhaps the most involved attempts to define the documentary occurred in France, where a number of influential early film critics had succeeded in legitimizing the cinema as an art, and therefore worthy of serious consideration (Abel 1988; Williams 1992). In 1923, the critic Riccioto Canudo wrote that the mission of the documentary was to "integrate the lives of men with that of their surroundings" (Ghali 1995, 292; my translation), an elegant formula that emphasizes documentary cinema's ties to social realism.

For others, the essence of the documentary lay in its ability to reveal reality's secret poetry, to capture the expressive potential of the material world. Documentaries could be realistic or poetic, "pure" (where "lived realities filmed on the spot" are related in "a relatively dry fashion") or fictional ("in which the facts are more often selected, interpreted, and idealized by the artist for a better cinematic rendering") (Dréville [1930] 1988: 42–43). Yet another early attempt to define the documentary came from Paul Rotha, whose 1935 survey of the genre delineates the following divisions: the naturalist (romantic) tradition (Flaherty, Cooper and Schoedsack); the realist (continental) tradition (Cavalcanti, Ruttmann, and Ivens); the newsreel tradition (Vertov); and the propagandist tradition (Grierson, Riefenstahl, Dovzhenko).

Where does Fanck fit into this constellation of documentary directions? It is worth recalling that Fanck's obsession lay not with cinema but with the mountains. Even in his later films, with their hackneyed, melodramatic plots, Fanck's depiction of the dramatic beauty of the Alps remains fresh and engaging. In the opinion of Kracauer, the "fictional element, rampant as it was, did not interfere with an abundance of documentary shots of the silent world of high altitudes. As documents these films were incomparable achievements" (1947,110–11). This enduring fascination with landscape suggests connections both with travelogues and educational films and, more specifically, with the French landscape (and seascape) films of André Antoine, Jean Grémillon, and Jean Epstein, all of whom grasped the narrative power immanent in the physical world.[6] Fanck's mountain films conform most closely to the naturalist (romantic) tradition—to adopt Rotha's terminology—characteristic of the films of Robert Flaherty, Merian Cooper, and Ernest Schoedsack.

Flaherty, Cooper, and Schoedsack all saw themselves first and foremost as explorers, not filmmakers (Rony 1996, 99). As "camera explorers," they embodied the nonsynchronicity characteristic of Weimar Germany and modernity more generally in their attempts to capture the timeless struggle of Man against Nature through the use of modern technology (the cinematic apparatus). Although Fanck's explorations were limited to his own backyard, comparatively speaking, his was nonetheless a similarly romantic quest for a lost, ahistorical past to be recovered in the Alps. During the nineteenth and early twentieth centuries, the Alps were culturally constructed as an antiurban, antimodern space, fulfilling the "quintessentially modern desire for the ahistorical" (Nenno 1996, 310).

Another defining feature of films of exploration is the cultural fascination with the heroic that they reflect. Throughout the 1920s and into the 1930s, the explorer was a prominent public figure, appealing to a desk-bound society's dreams of freedom and adventure. And although more efficient means of transport put explorers in danger of becoming a thing of the past as undiscovered territories became an increasingly rare commodity, modern media made it possible for their endeavors to impress a broader public than ever before, magnifying their glory.[7] The exploration filmmaker trafficked in this rhetoric of courage and daring, making the film's production a spectacle equal to the finished product. Merian Cooper's filmmaking motto—Distant, Difficult, Dangerous—could equally apply to Fanck, who routinely placed himself and his actors in danger, most perilously during the filming of *S.O.S. Iceberg* in Greenland, when the iceberg on which Fanck and his crew were standing began to crumble (Infield 1976). Eric Rentschler observes that contemporary reviews emphasized the "onscreen heroism" and "behind-the-scenes feats of strength" undertaken by a community of "athletic actors" and "daring assistants" (1990, 152). Marc Sorki, assistant director on *The White Hell of Pitz-Palü*, describes his work on the production in terms suggestive of the heroic mindset Fanck demanded:

> That was a wonderful picture. The original was shot on location in Switzerland, and it was terribly cold in the mountains in winter. Most of the cast and crew came down with pneumonia. Pabst and Fanck both had a sadistic drive. We really froze. All night long we drank hot wine and punch just to keep breathing (Infield 1976, 28).

How "wonderful!" "We really froze!" The conjunction is telling. The ideal of self-sacrifice central to the plots of many mountain films was a lived reality during their production.

Considering Fanck's mountain films in the light of other films of exploration helps to illuminate why Leni Riefenstahl's presence was considered so disruptive. Explorers traded on their masculine authority, using their cameras as tools of conquest and control. They also reaffirmed traditional notions of masculinity, satisfying the public's need for "an antidote to anxieties about the depletion of agency and virility in consumer and machine culture" (Shapiro 1999, 59). With a few rare exceptions, expeditions were male endeavors.[8]

The Alps themselves were another factor in the mountain film's discourse on masculinity. Reflecting its historical construction as the repository of German national identity, the Alpine landscape provided an effective setting for the reassertion and recuperation of German masculinity in the aftermath of World War I (Nenno 1996, 312). By welcoming Leni Riefenstahl to the mountains, Fanck committed an act of generic transgression. But transgressive acts are compelling, and the conflict between Riefenstahl's gender and the dangerous world of the mountain film helped propel her to stardom, and, in addition, earned her the admiration of her colleagues.[9]

Having situated Fanck's films in relation to other documentaries of the period, I now move into a more detailed discussion of the mountain film's specifically documentary qualities. David Hinton, one of the few scholars who have paid much attention to Fanck's conception of cinematic realism, credits the director with initiating "one ofthe earliest realist film movements in cinema history" (1978, 2). The claim is jarring in its breadth but is not without merit in that Fanck's innovations were contemporaneous with advances in realist aesthetics in French cinema, to note just one example.

What made Fanck's a realist cinema? First and foremost was his commitment to location shooting. As Kracauer concedes, "These films were extraordinary in that they captured the most grandiose aspects of nature at a time when the German screen in general offered nothing more but studio-made scenery" (1947, 110). Perhaps because of his limited exposure to film, Fanck had not internalized cinematic conventions and consequently found them easy to reject. He was opposed to the stylized, expressionistic acting that dominated German cinema in the years following World War I. His directorial style was minimal; he gave his actors few instructions but insisted they be natural in both their movements and appearance. Particularly in his nonnarrative early films, physical ability counted for more than acting expertise in any case. Accordingly, he hired athletic amateur actors and unknowns such as Luis Trenker with the ironic result of transforming them into stars. With regard to film structure, Fanck disliked the linear narratives and quick tempo of Hollywood films, aiming instead for a cinema of "contemplation and meditation" (Rentschler 1990, 142). Echoing both the Russian avant-garde filmmaker Dziga Vertov's notion of the kinoeye and the French concept of *photogénie*, which referred to the transformative power of the camera, Fanck believed that in its capacity for revelation, the camera surpassed the human eye, claiming "nature remains mute and unexpressive unless captured by a camera" (Rentschler 1990, 146).

Because of the crucial narrative role played by the natural landscape in the mountain film, maintaining the illusion of documentary verisimilitude remained important even after Fanck had made the transition to narrative. The opening titles of *The Holy Mountain* broadcast Fanck's anxiety about authenticity: "The well-known sportsmen who participated in the making of *The Holy Mountain* ask the audience not to mistake their performances for trick photography. All shots taken outdoors were actually made in the mountains, in the most beautiful parts of the

The awesome mountain slopes of *The White Hell of Pitz-Palü* (1929).
(Photo from the collection of Kevin Brownlow.)

Alps, over the course of one and a half years." Assertions aside, the literature on mountain films includes much debate regarding whether or not Fanck used studio reconstructions for certain scenes, particularly the dramatic climax on the ledge in *The White Hell of Pitz-Palü* (Hinton 1978, 12; Eisner 1952, 312). Eisner's claims that these scenes were recreated in the studio using salt and white powder to simulate the frozen landscape are countered by Riefenstahl's insistence that what distinguished Fanck from other mountain filmmakers was his refusal to compromise his commitment to cinematic realism (1952, 312). "The difference between our mountain films and those made by other directors," Riefenstahl explains, "is that Dr. Fanck never wanted to use a double, didn't use tricks. He wanted everything to be real, like the time I was buried by an avalanche" (Infield 1976, 28). However, I believe that Fanck's (and Riefenstahl's) overarching commitment was to their notion of heroism; realism was merely the prerequisite to maintain the illusion since the power of Fanck's films as spectacles would be severely diminished if the audience did not perceive the dangers faced by his characters as real.

With their clumsy, conventional narratives, Fanck's mountain films would today never be mistaken for documentaries, although they do bear similarities to other documentary approaches of the period. Like the

Leni Riefenstahl and co-star Gustov Diessl keep each other warm in
The White Hell of Pitz-Palü (1929).
(Photo from the collection of Kevin Brownlow.)

French realist film, they reveal an elective affinity between the cinematic
medium and natural landscapes. Like the expedition film, they revel in
the images of heroism they evoke. Modernity provides the connective tis-
sue among these documentary styles; it is the context they are respond-
ing to and reacting against. In Fanck's case, it is a reaction infused with
German romanticism and its celebration of the self. His conception of the
camera's potential for revelation updates "Schelling's belief that man's
awareness of himself and the world around him brings 'the unconscious
life in nature to conscious expression'" (Rentschler 1990, 146).The films'
intra- and extratextual celebration of a juvenile and self-sacrificing heroism recalls romanticism's elevation of passion and irrationalism (Kracauer 1947; Herf 1984). Where Fanck departs from his own purported
aesthetic ideals is his casting of Leni Riefenstahl: her status as a woman
disrupts the mountain film's generic ties to the expedition film, her
renown as a dancer shatters any illusions of documentary authenticity.

"A Wild, Innocent Mountain Girl"

As noted earlier, Fanck's claims to realist cinema were undermined by
his attachment to melodrama, at least in the opinion of contemporary
reviewers, for whom Fanck's narratives departed too dramatically from
the conventions of other documentary styles, such as the expedition film.

Leni Riefenstahl likewise considered this disjuncture between form and content problematic; as she told director Ray Müller in his 1993 documentary about her life, "Dr. Fanck's films, although realistic, were set in fairy tale landscapes. I found that a conflict."

Riefenstahl's directorial debut, *The Blue Light*, represents her attempt to address the stylistic contradictions of Fanck's films by recasting the mountain film in the narrative mode of a fairy tale, complete with a "crystal mountain," magical stones, and an outcast heroine. However, *The Blue Light* contains plenty of intriguing aesthetic disjunctions of its own, experimenting with techniques associated with realist modes of production to achieve effects that pay tribute to romanticism. Eric Rentschler has characterized these discordances in terms of Weimar Germany's particular brand of reactionary modernism:"Riefenstahl's debut, a film that mines the romantic legacy with the tools of modernity, provides a curious merging of anti-modernism and instrumental will, a blend of romanticism and enlightenment, a pronounced double talk at once conscious of the appeal of the past and equally wise to the ways of the present" (1989, 50).

Another lens through which to read the curious disjunctions of *The Blue Light* is an ethnographic one. Perhaps to an even greater degree than the documentary, the ethnographic film was an ill-defined genre in the 1920s and 1930s. For example, Robert Flaherty's *Nanook of the North* (1922), usually considered the first ethnographic film in standard texts in the discipline, was hailed for its contribution to the development of *documentary* film in contemporary reviews. Nor was Cooper and Schoedsack's depiction of the epic migration of the Persian Bakhtiari tribe in *Grass* (1925) praised for its ethnographic qualities, although it was lauded for its "startling novelty" and the power of its "simple emotional and esthetic honesty" (*Literary Digest* 1925, 27).

As a discipline, ethnography was still in its salad days, with a number of foundational texts such as Bronislaw Malinowski's *Argonauts of the Western Pacific* (1922) and Franz Boas's *Anthropology and Modern Life* (1928) published in the 1920s. More generally, the interwar period presented an "ethnographic moment" during which the rise of modernism fueled a corresponding fascination with the primitive. While ethnographic film may not yet have been articulated as a genre, films such as *Nanook of the North* nonetheless incorporated—intentionally or not—ethnographic principles such as Malinowski's concept of participant observation.[10]

Historical context aside, what makes a film ethnographic? Ethnographic filmmaker and theorist David MacDougall foregrounds the intercultural aspects of ethnography: "An ethnographic film may be regarded as any film which seeks to reveal one society to another. It may be concerned with the physical life of a people or with the nature of social experience...the aim of interpreting one society to another is what underlies its kinship with anthropology. Without this aim, a film like Leni Riefenstahl's *Triumph des Willens*, so revealing of Nazi psychology and values, could properly be called an ethnographic film" (1969–1970:16). Yet offering *Triumph of the Will* as a counter example to the ethnographic film's intercultural emphasis may not be entirely apt if we consider the film in light of the cultural climate of 1930s Germany and the political mission of the Reich. In its concern to construct a unified German identity, the Reich mobilized the concept of the Volk, the true German people or race. The traditional peasant was thought to embody this desired racial and cultural purity, a symbolic transformation of the internal Other to the national ideal.[11] By the early twentieth century, the majority of Germans lived in towns and cities, and the creation of the peasant cult so central to National Socialist ideology can be considered an intercultural act, between urban and rural, if not national cultures (Peukert 1993, 10; Kamenetsky 1972).

With this notion of the intercultural in mind, to what degree can *The Blue Light* be considered an ethnographic film? Based on "a mountain legend from the Dolomites," a phrase overheard by Riefenstahl while on a hiking tour and used in the film's opening credits, *The Blue Light* draws its source from folklore, a discipline allied to ethnography in its emphasis on traditional culture. While both concerned with customs and rituals, the folkloric film and the ethnographic film differ in the latter's traditional focus on *non-Western* societies and the collaborative role frequently played by anthropologists (Sherman 1998, 57–63).[12]

Rather than recreate the traditional culture of the Italian Alps using actors or constructed sets, Riefenstahl wanted to film the real thing and spent four weeks location scouting in the Dolomites until she found a village that matched the picturesque ideal she had imagined. However, her plan to persuade the villagers to participate in her project proved challenging as David Hinton's account of Riefenstahl's experience in the village of Sarentino suggests:

> It was no easy task to get them to perform before her cameras, since none of them had an idea what a film was, and few of them had ever ventured beyond the secluded valley in which they were born. Riefenstahl's first attempts even to converse with them were silently rebuffed, so she rented a room in the village's small boarding house and spent days slowly making acquaintances in the village. She was determined to win their confidence, since their rugged, individualistic faces, which seemed to her to be right out

of a Dürer etching, mirrored the right amount of suspicion and distrust for the villagers of Santa Maria. Slowly but surely the villagers came to trust her, and finally agreed to do what she was asking.
(1978, 20–21)

In establishing herself in the village and gaining the people's trust over
time, Riefenstahl adopted a modified version of the time-intensive
approach advocated by other early ethnographic filmmakers such as
Flaherty, Cooper, and Schoedsack, who spent at least a year (significantly more in the case of Flaherty) in the field with their subjects. What
this description also makes clear is the extent to which Riefenstahl was
dealing with a foreign culture; not only did the villagers speak a different language, but they lived in a different era, their geographic isolation
having sheltered them thus far from the onslaught of modernity.

Riefenstahl's visual treatment of the peasants also recalls that of
indigenous peoples in other ethnographic films. In a manner reminiscent of Flaherty's famous portrait of Nanook, she lets the camera linger
closely on the villagers, their wizened faces a synecdoche for their traditional way of life. Riefenstahl's "ethnographic gaze" did not go unnoticed; Hinton mentions that the *"Berliner Morgenpost* was particularly
excited about the performance of the villagers, noting that, 'appearing
as if carved out of hardwood, they give the film background and color'"
(1978, 21), while the Nazi film historian Oskar Kalbus "praised the
racial hardiness of their physiognomies, the features of people who had
descended from the Visigoths" (Rentschler 1989, 61). *The Blue Light* was
also the film that brought Riefenstahl to Hitler's attention. Considering
his perception of the peasant as the "cornerstone of the whole nation,"
his approbation further suggests the alignment between Riefenstahl's
romantic representation of the villagers and the function of the peasant
in Nazi ideology (Kamenetsky 1972, 228).

But with visual representation comes the risk of exploitation, for, to
varying degrees, reality is almost always manipulated to serve the filmmaker's purposes. This risk is particularly acute in ethnographic film
because of the cultural differences and imbalance of power that divide
the filmmaker from the subject. The disjunctions of *The Blue Light* surface
in relation to this issue of exploitation. Set amidst dramatic Alpine scenery, the film tells the story of Junta (Riefenstahl), a mysterious young
woman who is treated as a pariah as a result of her unique ability to
access a remote mountain grotto whose crystals emit an entrancing blue
light. An admirer of Junta's succeeds in following her to the grotto and
shows a map of the route to the villagers, thus putting an end to her
mountain sanctuary and indirectly leading to her death.

On the one hand, *The Blue Light* can be read as a critique of the pillaging of nature at the hands of modernity. Not only is Junta's cave destroyed by rapacious villagers eager to sell its crystals for a profit, but the legend that surrounds Junta after her death contributes to the village's transformation into a tourist site. On the other hand, outside of the text, Riefenstahl takes full advantage of the setting and the innocence of the villagers to realize her romantic vision of purity and beauty. Similarly, although she repeatedly describes her character, Junta, as an innocent mountain girl, this designation "contrasts with the less than innocent strategies of Riefenstahl's camera, its presentation of the mountain girl as an erotic presence and a seductive force" (Rentschler1989, 65). Belying its veneer of simplicity, *The Blue Light* is technically sophisticated—Riefenstahl developed a new method of shooting day for night—and assured work in which the fledgling director expertly packaged both herself and the national past.

Like most fairy tales, *The Blue Light* is an ambiguous text, open to a number of interpretations. In the film's simultaneous critique and practice of exploitation, Rentschler sees "a striking self-legitimating brand of instrumental rationality" that foreshadows the actions and ideology of the Third Reich (1989, 62). Taking an opposite position, Hinton argues that the film should be read as "a warning against Hitler, not a preparation for him" because of its negative depiction of the Volk as avaricious and closed minded (1978, 23). If we believe Riefenstahl, the film was just a chance to give free rein to her "juvenile sense of romanticism and the beautiful image" (Infield 1976,29). That the film won the approval of no less an audience than Hitler suggests the success of Riefenstahl's ethnographic endeavor; by deeming traditional culture an appealing background for her film, Riefenstahl both reflects and reinforces the concept of the Volk cultivated by National Socialism.

Fantasies of *Fernweh*

In her memoirs, Riefenstahl ascribes the impetus for *The Blue Light* to her subconscious. "I began to dream," she writes, "and my dreams turned into images of a young girl who lived in the mountains, a creature of nature. I saw her climbing, saw her in the moonlight" (Rentschler 1996, 30). What this description suggests and the film confirms is that *The Blue Light* is the dream of a romantic tomboy. Junta succeeds where men fail, affirming her superiority by ascending the mountain that has caused the death of many men. Yet she is also the film's object of sexual desire, always attractively disheveled and winning the heart of the handsome young

Leni Riefenstahl as Junta in *The Blue Light* (1932).
(Photo from the collection of Kevin Brownlow.)

man from Vienna. By foregrounding the exceptional physical abilities of its female heroine, *The Blue Light* challenges the mountain film's conflation of masculinity and heroism. However, the film's fairy-tale structure contains this challenge within acceptable social norms, transforming the independent outcast into a more conventional damsel in distress. The folkloric framework provides the ideal setting for Riefenstahl's "dream"; the semiethnographic depiction of peasant life lends the film the air of authenticity and legitimacy Riefenstahl craved, while the generic familiarity of the fairy-tale narrative works to neutralize the more transgressive aspects of the film's treatment of gender. In its marriage of the ethnographic and the fantastic, folklore likewise provides a way for Riefenstahl to reconcile the formal incongruities of Fanck's earlier mountain films with their documentary realism and melodramatic plot lines.

Riefenstahl was not the only filmmaker demonstrating an interest in traditional culture during the 1930s. Departing from the non-Western focus of his earlier films, Robert Flaherty returned to the land of his forebears to film *Man of Aran* (1934) on the Aran Islands, off Ireland's western coast. Flaherty's desire to depict Irish traditional culture was so strong that he encouraged the islanders to revive activities—such as the use of harpoons in the shark hunt depicted in the film—they no longer practiced. Yet, as in his other ethnographic films, Flaherty went abroad in his romantic quest for an ahistorical past unpolluted by modernity.

What distinguishes *The Blue Light* and the mountain films of Arnold Fanck from other expedition and ethnographic films of the period is that, while these genres are portraits of "elsewhere," of foreign people in foreign lands, in the mountain film, elsewhere is right here in Germany. The German concept of *Fernweh*, the impossible dream of the faraway place where wholeness awaits, may suggest an explanation. By definition, *Fernweh* is a state of unfulfillment, of longing, of becoming, a dream of elsewhere that must remain unrealized. Instead of another country, in the mountain film, elsewhere is the idealized landscape of beauty and purity articulated by German romanticism and made all the more attractive through contrast with modernity. Unlike the propaganda films produced for the Nazi's "Blood and Soil" program, the mountain films of Fanck and Riefenstahl remain shrouded in a romantic, egocentric quest for self-fulfillment that to some degree sequesters them from the realm of the political. And in choosing to adopt an ethnographic approach in her version of the mountain film, Riefenstahl underscores the extent to which traditional culture was considered distinct from that of modern, urban Germany, an observation that distances her work from the Third Reich's attempt to naturalize the peasant as a symbol of German national identity.

Notes

1.   In her essay "Fascinating Fascism," Susan Sontag recapitulates Kracauer's position in suggesting that the mountain films present "an anthology of proto-Nazi sentiments," although she does acknowledge that such political interpretations are anachronistic considering the genre's apolitical contemporary status (1980, 76). Other popular studies follow Kracauer's lead in promulgating the erroneous view of the mountain film as "an exclusively German" genre (1947, 110); see also David A. Cook, *A History of Narrative Film* (second ed, 1990, 129–30n, cited in Rentschler (1990, 138). Such interpretations ignore the fact that Switzerland, Austria, and France also produced films set in the Alps during the 1920s as well as the influence of

earlier Swedish landscape films, such as Victor Sjostrom's *The Outlaw and His Wife* (1918) and Mauritz Stiller's *Snows of Destiny* (1919). See Richard Abel, *French Cinema: The First Wave, 1915–1929* (1984, 102).

2. Kracauer popularized this perception of Weimar cinema in *From Caligari to Hitler* (1947), in which he suggests the "master narrative" of both Weimar cinema and culture to be that of Oedipus. According to Kracauer's analysis, the Oedipal logic of the dramas depicted on screen served to reflect the crisis of male subjectivity that ensued from Germany's defeat in World War I and the political and economic instability of the 1920s. For a critique of this perspective, see Patrice Petro, *Joyless Streets: Women and Melodramatic Representation in Weimar Germany* (1989, 9–17) and Thomas Elsaesser, *Weimar Cinema and After: Germany's Historical Imaginary* (2000).

3. The relationship between the mountain film and the crisis in masculinity is discussed in Rentschler (1990) and Nenno (1996). Rentschler notes the emphasis on "masculine authenticity" in contemporary reviews of mountain films, while Nenno persuasively suggests that in the mountain film, the Alpine setting—through its cultural construction as the German national landscape—provides a site of recuperation for German masculine identity damaged as a result of defeat in World War I.

4. The structure, while most clearly observable in *The Holy Mountain*, also exists in variation in *The White Hell of Pitz Palü* (1929), *Avalanche* (1930), and *S.O.S. Iceberg* (1933).

5. Kracuaer writes disparagingly of Fanck's fondness for "combining precipices and passions, inaccessible steppes and insoluble human conflicts" (1947, 110), while Eisner notes "the discordances inherent in the conjunction of natural images and melodramatic plots, which is what we get in most mountain films" (1952, 312).

6. See Antoine's *Les Travailleurs de la mer* (1919), Jean Grémillon's *Gardiens de phare* (1929), and Jean Epstein's *Finis Terrae* (1929), all filmed on location using non-actors, at least in part (Abel 1984, 500–513).

7. Documentary accounts of the Antarctic voyages made by Scott (*The Undying Story of Captain Scott*, 1913) and Byrd (*With Byrd at the South Pole, 1930*), and of Mallory's ascent of Mt. Everest (*Epic of Everest*, 1924) were among the popular expedition films of the period (Brownlow 1979). In *S.O.S.Iceberg* (1933), the story of a search party sent to rescue a missing expedition in Greenland, Fanck references the expedition genre directly.

8. Francis Flaherty accompanied her husband to the Canadian arctic for the filming of much of *Nanook of the North*; and the husband and wife team of Osa and Martin Johnson made numerous films of their travels in Africa and the South Seas (Brownlow 1979). Marguerite Harrison, a journalist and spy, accompanied Cooper and Schoedsack on their arduous Persian trek, but her presence in the film is minimal.

9. Marc Sorki's praise for Riefenstahl is predicated upon her gender: "Riefenstahl was wonderful...in this picture (*The White Hell of Pitz-Palü*) she was driving herself as hard as anybody and more. She worked day and night...She would work extremely hard, harder than anybody. Even Pabst had to admire her. He said: 'It's terrible. What a woman!'" (cited in Infield 1976, 28).

10. Some critics and scholars consider *Nanook* a collaborative work because Flaherty showed rushes to his Inuit crew and encouraged their participation in all aspects of the production. See Rony, 1996, 118.
11. Marianna Torgovnick notes in her study of modernist primitivism, "fascism had both positive and negative versions of the primitive...the Aryan folk were the 'vital' primitive" (1990, 253–54).
12. Since the 1970s, a paradigm shift has occurred within ethnographic filmmaking practice as filmmakers have increasingly trained their cameras on themselves and their own societies. Another important recent development within ethnographic film is the advent of indigenous media production. For further discussion of these changes in relation to folkloric film, see Sherman (1998:63).

Filmography

Avalanche [Stürme über dem Mont Blanc] (1930). 73 min. Arnold Fanck
Battle for the Matterhorn [Der kampf ums Matterhorn] (1928). 82 min. Mario Bonnard and Nunzio Malasomma
The Blue Light [Das blaue licht] (1932). 70 min. Leni Riefenstahl
Epic of Everest (1924). J.B.L. Noel
Finis terrae (1929). 80 min. Jean Epstein
Gardiens de phare (1929). 80 min. Jean Grémillon
Grass: A Nation's Battle for Life (1925). 70 min. Merian C. Cooper and Ernest B. Schoedsack
The Holy Mountain [Der heilige berg] (1926). 106 min. Arnold Fanck
Man of Aran (1934). 76 min. Robert Flaherty
The Miracle of Skiing [Das wunder des schneeschuhs] (1920). Arnold Fanck
Mountain of Destiny [Der berg des schicksals] (1924). 60 min. Arnold Fanck.
Nanook of the North (1922). 79 min. Robert Flaherty
The Outlaw and his Wife [Berg-Ejvind och hans hustru] (1918), 102 min. Victor Sjöström
Snows of Destiny [Herr Arnes pengar] (1919). 122 min. Mauritz Stiller
S.O.S. Iceberg [S.O.S. Eisberg] (1933). 90 min. Arnold Fanck
The Struggle with the Mountain [Im kampf mit dem berge] (1921). 54 min. Arnold Fanck
Les Travailleurs de la mer (1919). André Antoine
Triumph of the Will [Triumph des willens] (1935). 110 min. Leni Riefenstahl
The Undying Story of Captain Scott (1913). 90 min.
The White Hell of Pitz-Palü [Die weiße hölle vom Piz Palü] (1929). 150 min. Arnold Fanck and Georg Wilhelm Pabst
With Byrd at the South Pole (1930). 82 min. Joseph T. Rucker and Willard van der Veer
The Wonderful, Horrible Life of Leni Riefenstahl [Die macht der bilder: Leni Riefenstahl] (1993). 181 min. Ray Müller

Works Cited

Abel, Richard, ed. 1988. *French theory and criticism: A history/anthology 1907–1939.* 2 vols. Princeton, NJ: Princeton University Press.

Boas, Franz. 1928. *Anthropology and modern life.* New York: Norton.

Brownlow, Kevin. 1979. *The war, the West, and the wilderness.* New York: Alfred A. Knopf.

Dréville, Jean. [1930] 1988. Le Documentaire, âme du cinema. In *French theory and criticism: A history/anthology 1907–1939,* 2:42–43.

Eisner, Lotte. 1952. *The haunted screen.* Paris: L'Ecran Démoniaque.

Elsaesser, Thomas. 2000. *Weimar Cinema and after: Germany's historical imaginary.* New York: Routledge.

Ghali, Noureddine. 1995. *L'Avant-garde cinématographique en France dans les annéesvingt: Idées, conceptions, theories.* Paris: Editions Paris Expérimental.

Gunning, Tom. 1997. Before documentary: Early nonfiction film and the "view"aesthetic. In *Uncharted territory: Essays on early nonfiction film,* ed. Daan Hertogs and Nico de Klerk, 9–24. Amsterdam: Nederlands Film Museum.

Herf, Jeffrey. 1984. *Reactionary modernism: Technology, culture, and politics in Weimar and the Third Reich.* Cambridge: Cambridge University Press.

Hinton, David B. 1978. *The films of Leni Riefenstahl.* Metuchen, NJ: The Scarecrow Press, Inc.

Infield, Glenn. 1976. *Leni Riefenstahl: The fallen film goddess.* New York: Thomas Y. Crowell Company.

Kamenetsky, Christa. 1972. Folklore as a political tool in Nazi Germany. *Journal of American Folklore* 85: 221–35.

Kracauer, Siegfried. 1947. *From Caligari to Hitler: A psychological history of German film.* Princeton, NJ: Princeton University Press.

The Literary Digest. 1925. An epic movie of man's fight with nature. April 25, 27.

MacDougall, David. 1970. Prospects of the ethnographic film. *Film Quarterly* 23: 16–30.

Malinowski, Bronislaw. 1922. *Argonauts of the western Pacific: An account of native enterprise and adventure in the archipelagoes of Melanesian New Guinea.* London: Routledge and Sons.

Nenno, Nancy. 1996. Projections on blank space: Landscape, nationality, and identity in Thomas Mann's *Der Zauberberg.* *The German Quarterly* 69: 305–21.

———. 2003. "Postcards from the edge": Education to tourism in the German mountain film. In *Light motives: German popular film in perspective,* ed. Randall Halle and Margaret McCarthy, 61–83. Detroit: Wayne State University Press.

Petro, Patrice. 1989. Joyless streets: Women and melodramatic representation in Weimar Germany. Princeton: Princeton University Press.

Peukert, Detlev. 1993. *The Weimar Republic.* New York: Hill and Wang.

Rentschler, Eric. 1989. Fatal attractions: Leni Riefenstahl's *The blue light. October* 48: 46–68.

———. 1990. Mountains and modernity: Relocating the *Bergfilm. New German Critique* 51: 137–61.

———. 1996. *The ministry of illusion: Nazi cinema and its afterlife.* Cambridge, MA: Harvard University Press.

Rony, Fatimah Tobing. 1996. *The third eye: Race, cinema, and ethnographic spectacle.* Durham, NC: Duke University Press.

Rotha, Paul. 1935. *Documentary film*. New York: W.W. Norton & Company.

Shapiro, Michael. 1999. *Cinematic political thought: Race, nation, and gender*. New York: New York University Press.

Sherman, Sharon R. 1998. *Documenting ourselves: Film, video, and culture*. Lexington: University of Kentucky Press.

Sontag, Susan. 1980. Fascinating fascism. In *Under the sign of Saturn*, 73–105. New York: Farrar, Straus, and Giroux.

Torgovnick, Marianna. 1990. *Gone primitive: Savage intellects, modern lives*. Chicago: The University of Chicago Press.

Von Moltke, Johannes. 2002. Evergreens: The *Heimat* genre. In *The German cinema book*, ed. Tim Bergfelder, Erica Carter, and Deniz Göktürk, 18–28. London: BFI Publishing.

Williams, Alan. 1992. *Republic of images: A history of French cinema*. Cambridge, MA: Harvard University Press.

II.

TRANSFORMATION

4

PC Pinocchios

Parents, Children, and the Metamorphosis Tradition in Science Fiction

HOLLY BLACKFORD

WHAT VIEWER OF *2001: A Space Odyssey* (1968) can forget the moment when the computer HAL 9000 faces his death and sings "A Bicycle Built for Two"? The melody winds down as HAL loses consciousness. It is a poignant moment in which the technological creation, a conscious being whose increasing power we are supposed to fear, regresses to the point of his seemingly innocent creation. The melody reminds us that he was created like a child and sung to by a creator who must have deployed the song as, on the one hand, a recording test and, on the other, a nurturing lullaby. It is a moment that asks us to consider our parental responsibilities and changing relationships to the beings we create, whether organic or machine. In fact, the film asks us to consider the fine line between machine and organic creations through lyrical scenes in which the human characters wear and depend upon various technologies to eat, breathe, and move. The technological child is one that human beings create again and again, only to regard it with horror as it seizes the tools of the father and rises to power in a classic Promethean or Frankenstein plot.

Suspicion of the technologies we spawn has become a folklore plotline in itself. A recent spoof of *2001* in the children's cartoon *Recess* (ABC/UPN, 1999–present) reveals that both parents and children are expected to identify with aspects of this story ("Schoolworld" episode). This plot has become a parable that seeks to teach parents and children to consider the mysteries of creationism and child development. But it also regards these mysteries with suspicion, asking us to consider the relationship between children and technology. Are our technological creations offspring that we shun because they threaten our authority and bring about our obsolescence?

These questions are overtly addressed at the end of the introduction to *AI: Artificial Intelligence* (2001), adapted from Brian Aldiss's

1969 story "Super-Toys Last All Summer Long." In *AI,* David (Haley Joel Osment) is a cyberchild, programmed to love its parents but then rejected by them. The film posits the idea that, while we can create a simulated child with emotions and consciousness, it is much more difficult to find parents who can return a child's love and raise him or her with a proper sense of ethics, responsibility, and morality. The technological child evokes our sibling rivalry; once we recognize its independence as a created being, we seek to disconnect it. *AI* depicts the sibling rivalry between two children, one cyborg and created to love unconditionally, the other an organic child who looks partially cyborg due to assistive devices for walking. Who is the monster in this film? The father/programmer, the computer, or the human sibling, a symbol of the peer community that fears it?

Frankenstein's creature, HAL, and Spielberg's artificial child are Adams of our genesis impulse. They are born in innocence and tragically engineered by environment to act in particularly monstrous ways. What does it mean to develop as a human being, these films ask? How have technological creations come to stand for our sentiments about universal patterns of child development, today's computer-aged children, and our own flaws as a parenting culture?

It is perhaps not surprising that the dawn of the computer age features science-fiction films with the Frankenstein theme of a child surpassing the powers of the creator, who, like the divine being of Genesis, built it from clay, simulated flesh, or wires and electricity. The theme of development from tabula rasa to monster or outcast explains the genre's popularity with family audiences, particularly teenagers. In many films, machines simultaneously replace or threaten youth *and* mirror the concerns of both young people and their parents regarding human development. For example, in Disney's *The Computer Wore Tennis Shoes* (1969), a student, Dexter (Kurt Russell), merges with a computer and becomes intellectually gifted but forgets basic human values such as friendship. In *Tron* (1982), another Disney film, we encounter the cosmic battle between a corporate father figure and his progeny, both a computer that displaces its creator and a hacker whom the father has dispossessed because of the hacker's gaming skill. In *WarGames* (1983), a teen hacker is asked to develop a relationship with and reform a computer system that was created as a child substitute but has become monstrous and needs to recall the innocent play of early childhood.

The restoration of a proper childhood is echoed in *Terminator 2* (1991) and Warner Brothers' animated feature *The Iron Giant* (1999), both of which represent the computerized machine as a reprogrammable child that only needs the touch of a real child to learn how to play, feel, and respect life.[1] Perhaps the most childlike cyborg of all is Data (Brent Spiner) of *Star Trek's The Next Generation* (syndication, 1987–1994). In *Star Trek: Insurrection* (1998), Data obtains lessons from a real child in how to play, something that these films feel is necessary to aid wholesome growth and human understanding. *AI* is only the logical culmination of the genre's testing ground for what makes a child-creature human and how we can resolve our conflicted feelings toward child development in the computer age, which seems to have robbed children of innocence and allowed them to surpass adults in skill, power, and authority.

The theme of childlike machines and machinelike children is pervasive enough to justify what Mikel J. Koven calls a "motif spotting" methodology (2003, 183), the enumeration of traditional folklore motifs in what I see as the dynamic, modern storytelling of popular film. While the relation of film to traditional folk storytelling is a question for folklorists, as a children's literature critic, I feel that an analysis of pervasive motifs across cinematic and literary texts can illuminate ambiguities (particularly toward children) localized in our collective, cultural unconscious. In my view, the films that I discuss are coming-of-age tales that endlessly replay the power of the transformation folktale to capture our Western view of child development. Computer characters grow from a state of puppetry, given genesis but not freedom, to adulthood, which means determining their own destiny and understanding the meanings and responsibilities of being human—but not without growing pains that are experienced as monstrous. These science fiction films appropriate the traditional folkloric motifs of magical transformation (D0–D499), magic objects (D800–D1699), and creation of man (A1200–A1299) through the motif of inanimate objects coming to life.

These narrative elements are common to folk-based stories of child development that have become staples of children's literature in such stories as Carlo Collodi's *The Adventures of Pinocchio* ([1881] 1996) and Margery Williams's *The Velveteen Rabbit* ([1922] 1958). As animals and folk heroes have traditionally functioned, toys are simultaneously child characters and more than children. They stand for children when they embark on journeys to understand their relationship to their creators and develop their own sense of consciousness and agency; characters undergo metamorphosis when they have explored and mastered what it means to be human.[2] A tough adolescence typically intervenes in this quest for mastery. Science-fiction films have adopted the toy-folklore combination to express similar themes with computer progeny. While computer "children" function as folk heroes, exploring human development in the universal sense described by Donna Rosenberg (1997) in her collection of folktales for children, they also express our wonder at and fear of today's computer-age children, who threaten adults with obsolescence.

The Toy Story

AI's intertext of Pinocchio reveals the analogy between the computer character and the toy, animal, or human protagonists in traditional folk narratives that, in the eighteenth and nineteenth centuries, were increasingly adapted to children's literature. Unlike much of today's literature written expressly for children, folktales and classic children's literature influenced by them were dual audienced to explore adult and child points of view on human development simultaneously. A brief glance at the history of adapting folktales for children teaches us that both oral and literary stories for children embed pedagogical relationships between adults and children. As tales were collected and used to educate children, they became structurally more literary and thematically more didactic.

Always a part of the folktale, the fable came to the foreground when adapted for children. Ruth Bottigheimer comments, "By the eighteenth century, then, the only folk-tale genre to have survived for children's reading was the fable" (1996, 163). Thus "Little Red Riding Hood" transformed from "a ribald story" to "a solemn cautionary tale warning children about the perils of disobeying mother's instructions" (Tatar 1992, 3). However, tales do not impart a simple message; listeners creatively interpret them, and tales contain contradictory meanings. Listeners can enjoy Little Red's disobedience and consequent adventure as much as they may appreciate its parable message. If we take the anthropological point of view, we can presume that folk and fairy tales adapted for children have lasted because they ritualistically meet the complex needs of both tellers (adults) and listeners (children).

Even while transforming their audience, tales, such as the Jack tales, maintained their hopefulness for the ingenuity of the underdog and, if Jack Zipes is correct, shaped a subversive sense by which everyday folk could undertake a journey and triumph against all odds, often altering the power structure (1988). In the fairy tale, essentially defined not by fairies but by its structure of journey and metamorphosis (Warner 1995, xix–xx), the protagonist undergoes significant transformation as a reward for perseverance. The related genre of myth explores connections to the divine. However, children never found the distinction between relations to the gods and those with elders very meaningful. Both types of tales spoke to their sense of powerlessness and need to persevere in the face of larger, quasi-divine beings (parents, elders) with power over them and greater access to societal tools (such as fire), tools that children need to become equal to their creators. It is not hard to see why children identify with the protagonists of folk, fairy, and myth tales. Little Red, Jack, Cinderella, Prometheus, and Pinocchio are "small" or insignificant when thrown into a world they do not control. But through the narrative, they journey, rise, work, or steal to challenge those in power.

The role of the protagonist in the folktale became culturally linked to child development in Western culture when these stories became the province of children's literature. But their universal appeal to adults, particularly parents, incorporated them into tale telling in the family setting. Folktales are also linked to the progress of Western children from an oral to a literate culture, teaching them the foundations of literary structure and formal patterns, such as those defined by Vladimir Propp. This is probably because they represent an oral tradition that became increasingly important in the schoolchild's transition to literacy. The adoption of *Aesop's Fables* as a textbook is a case in point (Bottigheimer 1996, 162).

The tale of the puppet Pinocchio loosely and episodically adopts many different folktales, including biblical ones with common folk motifs: creating a child from wood (A1252) or similar materials such as clay (A1614.2.1.2); the stolen child expressed in captivity motifs (R0–R99); the trickster (cat and fox) animals common to deception motifs (K0–K99); the descent and journey through the belly of the whale that mirrors otherworld journeys (F0–F199); the transformation in fables into a donkey and drum skin to concretize laziness (D132.1 and others in D100–D199); the prodigal son (P233.8); and various motifs of metamorphosis, resurrection, and rebirth (which range from resuscitation motifs, E0–E199, to reincarnation ones, E500–E699). It represents an overall fairy tale with (unlike many) a real fairy, an odyssey that is actually a picaresque literary form. It is this picaresque literary form that Spielberg adopts in *AI*, which gives the film its loosely connected structure as his cyborg child David continually quests to find the Blue Fairy and meets unlikely adventures and, finally, his creator. The difference is that Pinocchio cannot do anything right, while David cannot do anything wrong, but both are not "real" and must prove their worth to be considered that way.

Both are toys of adults, created to meet their makers' need to overcome loneliness. It is not an accident that Spielberg pairs his cyberchild with a sex toy, Gigolo Joe (Jude Law), who cares for him more deeply than any human can. Both are born of men without women, and both seek the redemption of a mother figure's love, to be reborn into a real being and thus recognized as human. Qualities associated with the feminine are precisely what machines lack. Both are on a journey that is supposed to teach them something, which the reader/viewer can learn but the characters cannot because they are wooden and embody the child archetype of culture, changeable like the oral tradition rather than permanent like print. The Flesh Fair of Spielberg's film mirrors Pleasure Island in *Pinocchio*; the humans are the real monsters because they encourage or program children to be one way and then cannot deal with the consequences, so they become violent and hostile to these children. Both leave or are abducted from their creators, whom they cannot honor once given the breath of life, and both return to their creators after undergoing significant journeys in the world. Pinocchio, however, redeems his incorrigible nature at the last minute when he saves Gepetto from the whale, even after repeatedly failing morally in relation to both Gepetto and the fairy. Spielberg's David, on the other hand, is good throughout his journey and finally turns violent when he finds his creator's laboratory and discovers he is mass produced. Like a Cain and Abel parable, the two "unique" robots in *AI* cannot coexist, so one kills the other and then tries to kill himself, but is, like Pinocchio, resurrected to achieve wholeness with his mother, however briefly.

Spielberg's cyberchild story features the question of individual identity in the same way as Disney/Pixar's children's film *Toy Story* (1995), in which characters who think they are unique discover that they are mass produced. The film also highlights sibling rivalry by deploying competition between a wooden and a plastic toy (children in developmental stages) for attention from their owner. In *Toy Story*, Buzz Lightyear believes he is *the* Buzz, rather like Tigger being "the one and only Tigger" in A.A. Milne's stories and must come to terms with his identity as a mass commodity. *Toy Story 2* (1999) continues the identity theme by having Woody discover that he is not only unique but a collector's item, not meant for children at all, instead designed for a pedestal rather than relationships and family.

Like folktales that explore what it means to be a unique human being yet a member of a community, these toy stories bridge developmental issues of both parents and children. In her analysis of toy stories, Lois Kuznets delineates the characteristics of toy narratives that explore developmental and existential concerns. As toys develop into animate beings, they "embody human anxiety about what it means to be 'real'" (1994, 2) or independent of powers greater than they. However, they are also toys and thus vulnerable to the manipulations of others, either "known or unseen forces": "And when toys come alive by being created by humans (usually male), they replicate 'divine' creation and imply vital possibilities for human creativity while arousing concomitant anxiety about human competition with the divine. These creations also threaten human hegemony" (Kuznets 1994, 2). She also comments on the increasing "competition between adults and children for the control of toys" (1994, 2). Who has the right to ascribe value to toys, and whose sense of value is more valuable?

This increasing competition seems to signify the dual function of the folk protagonist-turned-toy as a symbol of *both* child and parental concerns. Is human development a sign of progress or destruction, something to be welcomed or feared? The cybertoy, or computer created by a parental programmer, is both welcomed and feared; pitted against a real child, it splits our alliances into being partially "for" developing children and partially "against" these inclinations. The toy arouses feelings of powerlessness in adults, who engineer conditions of maturation yet wish to maintain control and stay in charge. Toy characters evoke parental anxiety because parents face questions about their relationship with children and their own obsolescence. The abandoned toy Jesse, in *Toy Story 2*, is a case in point. Parents have to accept their similarity to discarded technologies; in other words, the older generation is destined to relinquish its power and social role to the next one. This developmental inevitability is only compounded by a technologically changing world where parents may well feel that they are continually out of date. *AI*'s desire to immortalize a nine-year-old boy and halt development is the crux of the true monstrosity in the film. David cannot undergo metamorphosis like Pinocchio because he is not in a fairy tale, and his reward for perseverance is really the curse of immortality, engendered by a community of parents who fear technology and computer-age children, leary of their identification with the once-loved and now-discarded toy. Everyone has abandonment issues, along with an insatiable need for love.

The story of *The Velveteen Rabbit* exemplifies the dual nature of the rabbit as child and parent. The rabbit quests to be real but does not understand what it means to be real. As a stuffed toy that lacks the buzzes and whistles of other toys in the nursery, he feels inadequate to the task of development. He asks the skin horse what it means to be real and how he will know if he has achieved real status. The skin horse explains that you become real through the love of a child; this necessitates a long relational process through which you get worn and shabby (life takes its toll and demands sacrifices) but you *become.*. The rabbit indeed becomes the transitional object of a child, as defined by D.W. Winnicott (1971), who argues that objects chosen by the child stand for the mother when the child learns about separateness; such objects are intermediaries between the developing self and the outside world, joining the child in a shared reality, yet symbolizing the mother and the child's inner world (1971, 46). Worn and shabby as the rabbit is, it is clear that in the story he stands for both child and parent developmental concerns. He is an object of competition between child and parents when the child becomes sick and the parents throw out the cherished toy for fear that he carries germs. The rabbit is also a teen when he is ridiculed by real rabbits (peers), which notice he cannot run and jump because he has no hind legs.

After his descent into the trash, mirroring Pinocchio's descent into the belly of the whale and David's heroic descent into various other worlds such as the forest, the Flesh Fair, and the sea, a female spirit of nursery magic steps in to change him into a real rabbit of flesh and blood. This deus ex machina resolution undercuts the first definition of relational reality with a child into a second definition with a community of equals (Kuznets 1994, 60–62). The rabbit's quest to understand what makes him real, like an adopted child's quest to know who his or her real mother is, is a question about what makes a person of any age develop into a valuable human being and how relationships aid and hinder the quest. The deus ex machina answer, common to folk narratives, is only as false as the aliens that Spielberg offers David in lieu of the Blue Fairy.

The Brainchild of Science Fiction

One mixed sentiment about today's children is that they are technologically sophisticated beyond their years and parents, but they have lost some respect for basic human values. This theme manifests itself throughout science-fiction films about computers that take the place of toys and stand for child development and coming of age which represent a cultural paradox. On the one hand, middle-class parents and educators have become proponents of early learning through toys and strategies that enhance neurological development in children. On the other hand, the propensity of children for tech toys such as video and computer games, for using the Internet to circumvent adult supervision, and for using a mouse before they can even tie shoes frightens adults and reinforces the idea that youth is simply out of control.[3]

Disney explores the theme of the precocious youth, whose learning is computer assisted, in *The Computer Wore Tennis Shoes*, produced in 1969 and remade in 1995. In the 1969 film, Dexter Riley, a student at a mediocre state university and a member of a juvenile crowd that likes to defy the administration's rules, finds a benefactor to donate a computer to his school. He needs a benefactor because the administration does not believe in allocating resources to technology; they are the antiquated past. During a storm, Dexter falls into the new computer, subsequently becoming the smartest student in the nation and thus coveted by Ivy League deans, who fight with the dean of his school for this now-brilliant youth. The long, outrageous scene of the youth being sucked into the computer symbolizes that time period's sense that young people were being sucked into the information-processing revolution. Yet the computer is offered as the smart tool of future leaders. In fact, the tone of the film mourns the fact that "today's kids" are not as perfect as the computer.

With the aid of the computer, this youth now has societal value. However, Dexter grows conceited and neglects his friends. It turns out that this computer given to his school, and now a resident of his brain, was actually designed to store data from gambling sites run by the donor. This "creator" turns out to be an "evil" designer, revealed when the system starts breaking down and recklessly listing the gambling dens that he owns. Thematically, then, the student himself is innocent of deserting his friends and values because an evil machine has infiltrated him. "Bad files" are never the fault of the young but of an evil (adult) programmer behind the scenes. The child as a machine has no agency, and his actions are entirely the result of an environment orchestrated by good or evil educators. This conclusion indicates a rather pervasive cultural pattern by which we refuse to blame the young for having gone awry.

Partly, this film helps historically to locate the emergent definition of the brain as an information-processing unit, coinciding with the information-processing revolution occurring in the cognitive sciences during the 1950s and '60s (Hall 2004, 1). The parallels between the learning brain of a young person and the computer became apparent in everyday language, such as "memory," "artificial intelligence," and "motherboard," an organic metaphor commonly applied to technology. The idea of learning from environment became central to the definition of childhood. It was not uncommon for psychologists to discuss cognitive codes, storing and recovering processes, and auditory processing. Once the child and the brain have been defined as processing units, the designer of information content and flow becomes of paramount importance. Science-fiction films became obsessed with the possibility of technologically manipulating a person's memory "files" and consciousness, but culture seems to believe this quite natural when it comes to parenting and educating children.

In a fascinating return to romantic visions of childhood, tinged with Locke's educational philosophy of the tabula rasa, the young person affected by technology becomes an innocent product of good or bad design. *The Computer Wore Tennis Shoes* is on the cusp of a culture entering the computer age and questioning its future impact. When youth and computers combine, we find a force with which to reckon. The creator or benefactor in the film has to chase down the child to stop him from revealing his own secret evils; youth is only a symptom of cultural evil unleashed into the world. In the end, the youth and computer have to be detached because the evil must be removed from the young. As Dorothy realizes in Oz, the youth has to learn that there's no place like home with your friends and your mediocre state school. Because it is growing too smart—a word we equate with being disrespectful—youth is put back in its place. The youthful character has tried in various ways to be mature and recognized as valuable by adult society, but he has to accept that rising to power and valuing community are incompatible. Dexter ostensibly matures by shedding technological power, a feat that actually keeps adults on top.

The culture's mixed feelings about children growing up in the computer age crystallized in depictions of gaming. As children entered the world of gaming, soon to be dominated by "the culture of Nintendo," David Sheff notes, "Some [parents, teachers, and sociologists] saw video games as insidious hypnotizers and mind destroyers; others viewed them as training tools for the cybernetic world of the future. One proponent claimed that children who excelled at one game, 'Tetris,' scored higher on intelligence tests" (Sheff 1993, 9). In 1982, *Tron*, the first computer-animated film that I can recall, portrayed a similar paradox, whereby youth's gaming culture is out of control yet also a formative path toward the world's future and our safety. In the film, a gamer has to retake control of a computer creation with his hacker skills. Clearly we want to have our cake and eat it, too; we want to conceptualize the nature of the child brain as plastic and permeable enough to be programmed and supported with smart tools, and yet we simulate child development in machines of fiction to express regret that children cannot be children. In *Tron*, the creator/father figure is Mr. Dillinger (David Warner), the adult with full access to the world of corporate power, which by the 1980s was a major player in the commodification of children and teens. Dillinger has written and helped to create the Central Computer Manager (CCM), which quickly shows up his "father" by surpassing him and taking over the gaming company. In an early scene between Dillinger and a cocreator of the CCM, the latter a grandparent figure who mourns the loss of the early days of technological innovation in a garage rather than corporate setting, Dillinger dismisses his cofounders and asserts sole (corporate) possession over his technological creation. However, this consolidation of power only undoes the father in the end because it spawns a monstrous technological progeny. His computer, the CCM, asserts its own independence and maintains that it now knows much more than its programmer.

The CCM needs to be contained and disconnected by a real child of Dillinger's. The youthful Flynn (Jeff Bridges), shown playing with teenagers in his arcade, is a former employee of Dillinger's who has been fired. He embarks on a journey to challenge the father and subdue the CCM sibling, which he does by being young and an expert gamer. While hacking into the CCM, he is physically sucked into the computer, much the same way Dexter is in *Tennis Shoes*. The CCM makes Flynn play games to survive. In the end, Flynn with the help of Tron, a freedom-fighter program authored by a colleague, liberates the system.

By the 1980s, the concept of virtual reality had been shaped. Each of the young hackers in the film has a counterpart in the video game itself. Their virtual counterparts worship their users with a kind of reverence that displays the film's hopeful sense that our technological children live to serve us. The virtual selves try to communicate with the users and find salvation and faith when they see one in the virtual world. *Tron* establishes the spiritual significance of our ability to achieve immortality by building virtual worlds. In *Tron*, however, we witness not just one parable between a creator and his child but several cycles of development by which youthful hackers and creations repeatedly displace their fathers. The obsolescence of the parental figures is both inevitable and terrifying. It is the elder's own thirst for immortality and power through creation that undoes his place on the throne. This age-old paradox is quite recognizable; the moment Adam is created, the moment Pinocchio is crafted, the father realizes he has given life in his own image and fashioned a rival.

The teen-associated or teenaged hack became a stock figure, one both revered and feared as an example of the way in which computer-age youth develop into Promethean figures that steal fire from the gods for greater social change. *WarGames* can be seen as a response to the coupling of youth and computer. In this film, David (Matthew Broderick) hacks into the nuclear-defense system, and the computer Joshua, named after the designer's dead child, starts calling him to play chess. David maintains his innocence: "Joshua called *me!*" As in *Tron*, there is a thin line between gaming and reality, a congruity between play and intergenerational struggles for power. The child-replacing computer begins to play war games and initiate nuclear war, having had so much fun learning and playing with his new friend. David (as organic child) has to stop him by making him regress and play a game that will teach him fundamental lessons about life. In a telling scene, in which David takes the "bad child" Joshua in hand and reprograms him, David tells the machine to play tic-tac-toe against itself to determine that there are games no one wins. The message of the film is that any three-year-old knows that war games are bad for everyone and that, if we had all had a proper childhood, full of traditional play, we would have learned our proper moral center.

The way in which the computer Joshua thieves youth, replacing a real child and perverting play, mirrors *Tennis Shoes* and *AI*, but it also advances the irony that we wish to see childhood and the computer age as incompatible, even while we want to explore developmental issues with computer toys.[4] When computers supplant real children, they emblem common sentiments about today's youth along with the ironies of our belief in the reprogrammable child machine and our faith that technology makes kids smarter. Culturally, we live with this irony. We demand technology in the schools but get angry when children have uncensored access to the Internet; we quiver with pride at our children's ability to push us aside and recover our files but quake in our boots when they glue themselves to the television set rather than play outside, stare endlessly at our car's DVD player rather than peer at the open road, and endlessly e-mail and play video games rather than interact with us.[5] The machine child hyperbolizes our belief in the ability of young people to reform and asks us to measure our responsibility in manipulating their behavior, particularly in restoring a proper childhood to them.

Terminator 2 in 1991 and *The Iron Giant* in 1999, the latter explicitly made for children, both put forth the message that a proper child can reform the computer age. In *T2*, the terminator from the first film (Arnold Schwarzenegger) is reprogrammed by freedom fighters to be a protector of the future resistance fighter John Connor (Edward Furlong). The two, machine and child, engage in a Huckleberry Finn-like quest wherein the adult is both protector of and subservient to the all-powerful child. The child instructs the machine not to kill because human life should be respected; the child explains why people cry when the machine asks him, as if he were the velveteen rabbit imploring the wise skin horse for a definition of being real; and the child teaches the machine playfulness by having him "give five" and then move his hand as a joke. John is rewarded when the machine sacrifices itself. The machine recognizes its responsibility and proves its humanity by killing itself and thus destroying the last artificially conscious computer chip, which will alter the future. The sacrifice parallels the tragic sacrifice of Data at the end of the *Next Generation* series.

In *T2*, John Connor is all powerful because he is an expert on human values and, in particular, emotions. It is assumed that children are inherently good and playful (or that play makes them good) and that they have the ability to reform evil, technology, and bad programming. However, like other toys, the machine in *T2* is both an adult and a child. Like Data, the machine questions and endeavors to understand the world as a child would. We are asked to sympathize with machines because they are purely logical and learning entities, without the ability to feel. We are asked to pity machines that contain our knowledge but do not know how to use it.

However, the machine is also a reformed father. The mother in the story regards the machine as "the sanest choice" of a father in an insane world, where fierce passions and intemperate emotions prohibit real concern for others. And the film is part of a tradition where fathers have to learn the value of family and children to prove their humanity. By being both parent and child, the machine suggests that "the child is father to the man" and that, given the computer age, it is no longer clear whether parents or children have greater adaptive skills.

Similarly, *The Iron Giant*, adapted from the novel by Ted Hughes (1999), reclaims the computer's innocent, tabula rasa nature as if it were the American Adam figure analyzed by R.W.B. Lewis, combined with the paradoxes analyzed by Leo Marx in *The Machine in the Garden: Technology and the Pastoral Ideal in America* (1999). The paradox involves simultaneously valuing the innocent past of childhood and admiring progress, which undoes the pastoral ideal. In this film, a child gets to know an iron giant, which unfortunately happens to contain a nuclear-defense program, activated when the giant is threatened. The child develops a relationship with the iron giant before understanding its reactive programming. The child shows the giant the world, the junkyard, art, and play. The child teaches the giant basic things about the human world, leading to a metamorphosis by the machine. When adults who fear the giant "other" threaten it with tanks and guns, their actions activate the giant's defense program to kill. However, in a scene imitating Joshua's reprogramming based on tic-tac-toe, the child tells the giant that it does not have to kill. This rhetoric of choice—to desert programming and decide for yourself a course of action—is the novelist's vision of maturation; as in the other films, the choice is to reify human values. The giant proves to be the child's friend, while the adults are more militant and machinelike in their natures.

Like Terminator and Data, the machine demonstrates its successful learning of humanity by sacrificing its life for humans, symbolizing our desire to separate proper childhood from the computer age. The machine essentially becomes what American literary critics call "the noble savage," based on Hoxie Neale Fairchild's (1928) definition of the term. Because of racial paradigms in American culture, writers such as James Fenimore Cooper, Edgar Allen Poe, Herman Melville, and Mark Twain tended to pair a white protagonist and ethnic subordinate to represent democratic fraternity, only to close democratic possibility by having the noble savage gracefully exit the scene after proving his civilized values. This paradigm is apparent in Cooper's Mohican (1826) who fades into the wilderness; Lydia Maria Child's Hobomok (1824) who graciously gives up his white wife when she no longer wishes him; Harriet Beecher Stowe's Uncle Tom (1852) whose nobility kills him; Melville's Queequeq (1851) whose coffin buoys up the protagonist; and Twain's Jim (1885) who sacrifices his freedom for the rascal Tom and, of course, Huck. But this paradigm is hardly a lone artifact of the nineteenth century. In American films such as *Field of Dreams* (1989) and *The Legend of Bagger Vance* (2000, based on Steven Pressfield's 1995 novel), African-American characters inspire and enable the full human potential of the white protagonists, after which they conveniently walk off into the sunset. In the tradition of science fiction that I trace here, machines take the role of the subordinate racial Other. They allow an exercise in the acquisition of Western civilization and then reveal their civilized and humane characters by acquiescing to their own demise, thereby bowing to the society bred by white fathers. After all, aliens and cyborgs are part of science fiction film's efforts to give us a final frontier, and how would Americans know themselves without frontier folklore?

In the character of Data in *The Next Generation*, we find the perfect metaphor for our culture's conflicted feelings about the nature of childhood and development in the technological age. By the time we get to the film *Star Trek: Insurrection*, we can see that Data is a metaphor for a child who seeks to understand what being human means and then, like the velveteen rabbit, wishes to become. From confronting his father and evil brother to finding his mother, Data also represents the potential within all of us to quest for a fuller humanity. *Insurrection* embeds the story of Data's relationship to a child within its main plot of betrayal within the Federation and the quest for eternal youth. The Enterprise travels to the planet of the Ba'ku, a small group of people who, though once technologically sophisticated, have retreated to a simpler way of life. Yet they have done so by abandoning their children who, of course, become monstrous. Like a group of Thoreaus on Walden Pond, the Ba'ku have purposely tried to avoid the contemporary universe and, in doing so, have found a source to prolong youth, denying their obsolescence. Everyone wants to possess and control this source—everyone except Data, who is, for all practical purposes, immortal. Only Data quests for a real childhood.

But Data is a digital-age product and thus a threat to real childhood; he is at once a childlike being and a symbolic threat to the pastoral idea of childhood. In fact, in the beginning of the film, we are duped into thinking that Data has undergone a dramatic change and become a violent teen rebel; however, in his sojourn on the planet, he meets a real child (Zachary Williams) who is frightened by his seemingly "adolescent" behavior, and he courts the friendship of this child to explore and compare their differences. Data wants to know what it is like to feel growth, to have legs, and to play, the quality that the child claims most defines childhood. In the twentieth century, ironically, the very beings (computers) that have replaced other methods of playing do not seem to understand it. The child, on the other hand, actually feels that the android is lucky to be beyond the restrictions of childhood.

Parallel scenes introduce the quest of each to be more like the other. In the opening scenes, the child's head pops out of a haystack, where he has been playing, and Data's pops out of the air, where he has been invisible. By the end of the film, we see Data's and the child's heads simultaneously pop out of a haystack and look at each other in complete equality. Called by his "mother" ship, Data says to the child, "I have to go now," like any ten-year-old boy. Data has successfully become a child, which a machine must do to metamorphose into a human adult. Even earlier in the film, Captain Picard (Patrick Stewart) sings to Data to recall him to a sense of human relationship, just like HAL's death chant reminds us that his creation mimicked a human birth.

The film communicates a double message. It suggests that organic life, apart from technology and simulation, must be preserved and allowed to flourish. Youth here symbolizes what it often does—a more primitive state of culture, or the childhood of Western civilization. Yet the one who most effectively heeds this lesson is a machine, whose very simulation of childhood embodies the irony that childhood is most appreciated by those who are not children ("youth is wasted on the young"), that it is adult viewers who gain something in seeing the world as simulated children again, and that children themselves see mastery of the machine, and identification with the fictional machine, as a welcome sign of maturation and freedom from childhood. Data consistently breaks barriers (shattering force fields, walking into water) that a real child cannot. Thus, we are left with a question: for whom is this vision of restoring a proper childhood as an antidote to the technological age intended?

Conclusion: Conflicting Data on the Next Generation

The folkloric pattern of the transformed computer toy reveals conflicts in our conceptualizations of child development that are only compounded by our digital age. What are these films saying to adults, when they absolve the child/teen of guilt for problems created by the Faustian impulses of adults? What are they saying to adults, when children are the reforming agents of the computer world? What are they saying to teens, who are betwixt and between our culture's sense of what youth means and what real power is? What are they saying to children, who see themselves "gone bad" as much as they see themselves save the day in the end?

The machine, computer, or toy is not inherently good or bad, much like the child in post-Lockean educational theory is neither our spiritual savior nor our original sin. However, the machine is inherently in conflict with our persistent romantic ideas about organic childhood, which include the child's playful and imaginative soul, its connection to nature, and its regenerative powers for us all. This model of childhood is simply in conflict with our image of children as learning machines, whose environment we engineer. Deep down, what adults are really facing in these fables is what their children may already know: computer-age children, with their flexibility and adaptability, will grow into a world we cannot know, one for which we cannot really prepare them. We have little confidence in our teaching abilities, yet we have constructed child entities that are little information processors from birth. In these films, we pit the organic child with pedagogical and technological skills against the childlike machine of our own creation to see who wins. The game that they play indicates *our* ambivalence about whether to love or hate the very idea of the next generation.

In the machine, adults see themselves being led by the next generation, and we feel sorry for our confusion. Films like *AI*—and characters like Data— ask us to sympathize with technology and feel badly not about its imperfections but our own. They ask us to cope more effectively with intergenerational challenges and become better parents and teachers. They ask us to be noble savages and embrace our own obsolescence, for we are in an age and culture that value youth more than ever before. One of the roles of folk narratives is to stand between youth and elders and thereby resolve developmental dilemmas. This image of the computer receiving the breath of life, seeking guidance, and surpassing creators continues a very old tradition in representing and attempting to resolve the paradoxes with which we regard Jack-the-giant-killers.

As in all stories passed down to children, the meaning of this story differs widely depending on the developmental status of the listener, viewer, or reader. The lesson of Margery Williams's stuffed rabbit and Collodi's Pinocchio is that somehow the next generation holds the key to a real understanding of life. The real child is an antidote to environments that are unsympathetic to youth and human values. But we do not know what this real understanding of life is, so we describe the search for it again and again. Ironically, we prefer to romanticize the real child and symbolize the struggles of child development in the machine. In the meanwhile, we all play a great game of pretend. For even as we experience insatiable hunger for the ever-wondrous technologies of film, we pretend that it is the machine's fault we do not have children anymore.

Notes

1. To explore poignant connections among youth, child development, and technology, I could have also chosen to analyze *The Lawnmower Man* (1992); *Johnny Mnemonic* (1995); *Minority Report* (2002), based on the 1956 story by Philip K. Dick; and *The Matrix* (1999), where Neo's journey is parallel to Lewis Carroll's *Alice's Adventures in Wonderland* ([1865] 2000) and L. Frank Baum's *The Wonderful Wizard of Oz* ([1900] 1984). Neo's awakening into the matrix is the descendent of Jack's discovery of the giants, rendered again and again in coming-of-age folktales.
2. For an exploration of the way Pinocchio achieves humanity, see Willard Gaylin (1990).
3. This theme manifests itself in quite another manner in horror films from the 1960s on. *The Exorcist* (1973), *Carrie* (1976), *Rosemary's Baby* (1968), *It* (1990), *Pet Sematary* (1989), *Village of the Damned* (1960 and 1995), and related films echo the growth of science fiction films about evil forces "possessing" children and separating them from a real or authentic childhood.
4. This contradiction mirrors the irony that we enjoy science-fiction films partly for their technological innovations, even while they seek to teach us that our zest for technology undoes us and threatens our future—our children. For example, *Johnny Mnemonic, Minority Report,* and *Dark City* all contain the theme that machines have displaced children and childhood.
5. One can similarly see the retarded Jobe Smith (Jeff Fahey) in *The Lawnmower Man* (1992) as an abused child who becomes an accelerated learner through gaming and technology.

Filmography

AI: Artificial Intelligence (2001). 145 min. Steven Spielberg
Carrie (1976). 98 min. Brian De Palma
The Computer Wore Tennis Shoes (1969). 91 min. Robert Butler
The Computer Wore Tennis Shoes (1995). 87 min. Peyton Reed
Dark City (1998). 100 min. Alex Proyas
The Exorcist (1973). 132 min. William Friedkin
Field of Dreams (1989). 105 min. Phil Alden Robinson
The Iron Giant (1999). 86 min. Brad Bird
It (1990). 193 min. Tommy Lee Wallace
Johnny Mnemonic (1995). 98 min. Robert Longo
The Lawnmower Man (1992). 107 min. Brett Leonard
The Legend of Bagger Vance (2000). 127 min. Robert Redford
The Matrix (1999). 136 min. Andy Wachowski and Larry Wachowski
Minority Report (2002). 146 min. Steven Spielberg
Pet Sematary (1989). 102 min. Mary Lambert
Recess (1997–2001). ABC/UPN
Rosemary's Baby (1968). 136 min. Roman Polanski
Star Trek: Insurrection (1998). 103 min. Jonathan Frakes
Star Trek: The Next Generation (1987–1994). Syndication
Terminator 2: Judgment Day (1991). 139 min. James Cameron
Toy Story (1995). 81 min. John Lasseter
Toy Story 2 (1999). 92 min. John Lasseter
Tron (1982). 96 min. Steven Lisberger
2001: A Space Odyssey (1968). 141 min. Stanley Kubrick
Village of the Damned (1960). 166 min. Wolf Rilla and Anton Leader
WarGames (1983). 114 min. John Badham

Works Cited

Aldiss, Brian. 1997. Super-toys last all summer long. *Wired,* January. http://www.wired.com/wired/archive/5.01/ffsupertoys.htm
Abrams, M. H. 1999. *A glossary of literary terms.* Boston: Heinle & Heinle.
Baum, L. Frank. [1900] 1984. *The wonderful wizard of Oz.* Repr., New York: New American Library.
Bottigheimer, Ruth B. 1996. Fairy tales and folk-tales. In *The international companion encyclopedia of children's literature,* ed. Peter Hunt, 152–65. New York: Routledge.
Carroll, Lewis. [1865] 2000. *The adventures of Alice in wonderland.* Repr., New York: Signet.
Child, Lydia Maria. [1824] 1986. *Hobomok and other writings on Indians.* Repr., New Brunswick: Rutgers University Press.
Collodi, Carlo. [1881] 1996. *The adventures of Pinocchio.* Trans. Ann Lawson Lucas. Repr., New York: Oxford University Press.
Cooper, James Fenimore. [1826] 2006. *The last of the Mohicans.* Repr., Ann Arbor: Ann Arbor Media.
Dick, Philip K. 1991. *The minority report.* New York: Citadel Press.

Fairchild, Hoxie Neale. 1928. *The noble savage: A study in romantic naturalism.* New York: Russell & Russell.

Gaylin, Willard. 1990. *Adam and Eve and Pinocchio: On being and becoming human.* New York: Viking Press.

Hall, Richard H. 2001. Information processing theory. http://medialab.umr. edu/rhall/educational_psychology/2001/vlza/info_new.htm

Hughes, Ted. 1999. *The Iron Giant.* New York: Yearling Books.

Koven, Mikel J. 2003. Folklore studies and popular film and television: A necessary critical survey. *Journal of American Folklore* 116: 176–95.

Kuznets, Lois Rostow. 1994. *When toys come alive: Narratives of animation, metamorphosis, and development.* New Haven, CT: Yale University Press.

Lewis, R. W. B. 1959. *The American Adam: Innocence, tragedy, and tradition in the nineteenth century.* Chicago: University of Chicago Press.

Marx, Leo. 1999. *The machine in the garden: Technology and the pastoral ideal in America.* New York: Oxford University Press.

Milne, A. A. [1926] 1992. *Winnie-the-Pooh.* Repr., New York: Puffin Books.

Pressfield, Steven. 1996. *The legend of Bagger Vance: A novel of golf and the game of life.* New York: Avon Books.

Propp, Vladimir. 1968. *Morphology of the folktale.* 2nd and rev. ed. Trans. Laurence Scott. Publications of the American Folklore Society, bibliographical and special series 9. Austin: University of Texas Press.

Rosenberg, Donna. 1997. *Folklore, myths, and legends: A world perspective.* Lincolnwood, IL: NTC Publishing Group.

Sheff, David. 1993. *Game over: How Nintendo zapped an American industry, captured your dollars, and enslaved your children.* New York: Random House.

Shelley, Mary. 2000. *Frankenstein.* Ed. Johanna M. Smith. Boston: Bedford/St. Martin's.

Stowe, Harriet Beecher. [1852] 1994. *Uncle Tom's cabin; or, life among the lowly.* Repr., New York: W. W. Norton and Company.

Tatar, Maria. 1992. *Off with their heads! Fairy tales and the culture of childhood.* Princeton, NJ: Princeton University Press.

Thompson, Stith. 1955–58. *Motif-index of folk-literature: A classification of narrative elements in folk-tales, ballads, myths, fables, medieval romances, exempla, fabliaux, jest-books, and local legends.* Rev. ed. Bloomington: Indiana University Press.

Twain, Mark. [1885] 1985. *Adventures of Huckleberry Finn.* Repr., Berkeley: University of California Press.

Warner, Marina. 1995. *From beast to blonde: On fairy tales and their tellers.* New York: Farrer, Strauss and Giroux.

Williams, Margery. [1922] 1958. *The velveteen rabbit.* New York: Doubleday.

Winnicott, D. W. 1971. *Playing and reality.* London: Tavistock.

Zipes, Jack. 1988. *Fairy tales and the art of subversion: The classical genre for children and the process of civilization.* New York: Methuen.

5

From Jinn to Genies

Intertextuality, Media, and the Making of Global Folklore

MARK ALLEN PETERSON

There is scarcely a tale in the whole of the *Nights* which does not have its precursors, derivatives or analogous versions. Tales evolve into other tales and they replicate, elaborate, invert, abridge, link and comment on their own structure in an endless play of trans-formation—but was there ever the first version of any story? It is almost always impossible to tell when a story was first told and when it was first written down, or how it was transmitted, and impossible too to say what the last telling and final version of a story will be. Good stories pay little attention to cultural or linguis-tic frontiers. (Irwin 1994, 64–65)

Introduction: Global Folklore

THE TRANSNATIONAL CIRCULATION of people and media that helps define both contemporary and colonial globalization makes it possible for us to speak of global folklore. This chapter explores the emergence of global folklore by focusing on the transformation of the figure of the *jinn* as it moves intertextually from Arab folklore through the transcultural *Arabian Nights* collections into Euro-American film and television, and back into Middle Eastern media and oral performance in transmogrified forms. *Genie* in this essay refers to the Orientalist construct of powerful, wish-granting beings trapped in objects, while *jinn* alludes to the free-willed, invisible beings of Middle Eastern and Islamic lore. My argument is that in the process of traversing time and space through repeated entextual-izations, the free-willed, potentially dangerous jinn of Arab folklore have become the enslaved gift-giving genies of global folklore. Like the vam-pire and the cyborg (Latham 2002), the genie is a mythic figure whose relevance is tied to the emergence and spread of consumer society. As a magical figure that can circumvent hard work, inheritance, successful investment, and other traditional modes of attaining the wealth neces-sary to fulfill the limitless desires associated with capitalism, the genie is an important character in modern fantasy. With the increasing (but never completed) replacement of local economic systems of production and reciprocity with common global economic structures—wage labor, income taxation, international trade—the genie came to the Middle East and moved in, coexisting with the jinn, and frequently emerging in hybrid forms—forms which reflect local ambivalences about globalization and consumption.

For several decades, the "performative" approach in folklore has turned away from the classic study of the motifs and structures of folktales to emphasize the situations in which tellers produce folk narratives. Oral performance emphasizes the ways narrative structures and performance conventions are modified to meet the specific exigencies of situated tale-telling. The fixed and commodified nature of films should not cause us to lose sight of the emergent characteristics of tale-telling. As with any oral folktale, a film expresses the social relations, broadly conceived, of the time it was constructed. Like the tale-teller in the Egyptian coffeehouse, the writers, producers, and directors of a film create their story with a particular audience in mind. At the same time, the elements that are rewoven into text after text take on a certain life of their own; the collective body of representations of a particular figure—such as genies— become an intertextual web whose uses change over time but always in patterned ways. The rise of global folklore is thus made possible by the capacity of the global-culture industries to appropriate local images, transform them, and circulate them across ever-wider routes of distribution. But it also depends on the capacity of local culture industries to imitate and transform media to suit local audiences (Peterson 2003). Finally, it also relies on the capacity of people to appropriate materials from the media and integrate them into their oral performances (Peterson 2005b).

The People of Fire and Air

In Islamic cosmology, the universe is structurally divided into a seen and an unseen world. In the unseen world, angels, devils, and other beings respond to God according to their moral nature. In the seen world, human beings do the same, being divided (individually) into those who accept God and his messengers and those who do not. Jinn occupy a special, liminal status; they are of the earth, yet unseen on it.[1] They can see and hear the unseen angels, but they can also see the human world. Unlike angels, but like humans, their choice to follow or not follow God is partly a matter of will, not inherent in their nature (Martin 1982; Izutsu 1987).

The comedy *Sirr Taqiyyat al-'Ikhfa'* (Mystery of the Vanishing Cap, Niyazi Mustafa, 1959) features a Hollywood-style genie whose antics cause problems for a young reporter and a little boy. (Photo from the collection of Muhammed Bakr.)

Although belief in jinn predates Islam, their inclusion in revelation makes them an article of faith for most Muslims. The Qur'an tells us that while angels were made of light, and humans of clay, jinn were made of "the fire of hot wind" (15:27) or "smokeless fire" (55:15). Actually, the Qur'an notes that Jann, who most commentators take to be the father of the jinn as Adam is the father of humans, is made from smokeless fire. This opens the possibility that jinn may not necessarily be made of fire, just as Adam's descendants are not made of clay but clots of blood. Although humans cannot see jinn, the jinn can see them (7:27). Jinn who possess great powers are called *'afārīt* (singular, *'afrīt*). Unlike angels, who "do not rebel in what God has commanded them and do whatever they are commanded" (66:6), the jinn have free will, and among them are both those who have submitted to God and those who are evil (72:11–15). Like humans, jinn are mortal, and righteous jinn will enjoy paradise, while evil ones will suffer hell (41:24, 72:15). An evil jinn who seeks to tempt mortals into unrighteousness is called a *shaytān* (plural, *shayāṭīn*); and, of course, a shaytan has links with the Western tradition of Satan.

Middle Eastern folk cosmologies offer more complex versions of the interactions between the seen and unseen forces that coexist within the material world (El-Aswad 2002). Many supernatural creatures in folktales do not appear in the Qur'an. Padwick (1924) points out that the *ghūl* and the *mārid*, as well as shayāṭīn, jinn, and *'afārīt*, are often used interchangeably in folktales and everyday discourse. *'Afrīt* also frequently refers to a ghost—the Egyptian comic films *'Afrīt Samārah* (Samarah's Ghost, 1959), and *'Afrīt am 'Abdu* (The Ghost of Abdu, 1953), are both about ghosts who return to complicate the lives of families.

In accordance with their liminal status, jinn dwell in ruined houses, abandoned or isolated wells, graveyards, crossroads, caves, and other places on the borderlands of everyday human social life.[2] When they haunt houses, they are especially associated with the bathroom; some people say a short prayer each time they cross its threshold (Ghannam 2002). Jinn can take many shapes, especially a serpent, scorpion, lion, wolf, or jackal, but they may also assume the guise of a particularly lovely or especially ugly man or woman. In folktales and films, animal characteristics often reveal a person's identity as a jinn. In the 2001 comedy *Ga 'ana al-Bayan at-Tali* (We Have Just Received the Following Report), reporters investigating a phony miracle worker flee when he shows them his (false) goat legs because they think he is a jinn; when they tell their tale to the first man they meet, he reveals his own goat's legs. Whatever form they take, jinn are most active at dusk, betwixt and between day and night.

The dangers of jinn are the subject of countless folktales and have made their way into local films at least since the 1930s. Although stories are told of good jinn rewarding virtuous humans who are suffering unfairly, most jinn lore concerns evil examples. Several health disorders are attributed to jinn, especially mental disorders (Hammad et al. 1999; Younis 2000). Because jinn are dangerous, various rituals and musical performances are employed to ward off or exorcise them (Doubleday 1999, 126), and amulets are sold to protect people from their evil intentions (McGregor 1997, 267). Sorcerers are also often said to employ jinn. The widespread *zār* cults of North Africa and the Sudan use music and dance to both invoke and exorcise jinn. Midwives are commonly associated with jinn and may be asked to help negotiate with them. But anyone may leave a gift at a place known to be haunted by a jinn and petition for the punishment of an enemy, good luck for an enterprise, or help winning someone's love (Gingrich 1995).

In the 1988 Egyptian film *Ta'wīzah* (Talisman), for example, a real estate developer hires a sorcerer to command a jinn to drive family members from the home they refuse to sell him. In accordance with lore, the jinn is usually invisible, and much of his haunting centers around the bathroom, where blood rains from the shower and the floor ripples under people's feet. The film reflects the ambiguity of jinn in the battle between good and evil. Although he is a terrifying creature with red skin, goat's legs, and bull's horns, the jinn's evil actions are in fact compelled by a spell. The filmmakers dwell in detail on the drawing of magic circles, the knotting and tearing of cloth, and the uttering of spells which coerce the jinn. The prayers that save the family from the jinn's attacks do not seem to harm him so much as free him from his bonds. When the jinn is finally driven off by prayer, he turns on the sorcerer and real estate developer, tearing the skin from one and impaling the other on his horns. Middle Eastern films like *Ta'wīzah* reflect regional understanding of jinn as free willed and dangerous occult beings.

The Thousand-and-One Incarnations of One Thousand Nights and a Night

The transmogrification of such fearsome jinn into the gift-giving genies of Hollywood films begins in the colonial period with the appropriation by Western print capitalism of the most widely circulated collection of jinn tales, *'Alf Layla wa Layla* (One Thousand Nights and a Night). *'Alf Layla wa Layla* is an intertextual opus. Scholars have identified sources or parallels between stories in *'Alf Layla wa Layla* and Arab and Asian folktales, as well as ancient Near Eastern mythology, Indian folklore, traditions of the prophet Mohammed, and Ottoman literature.

In spite of its polyglot nature, the work has a number of themes that weave through all or most of the tales. Primary among these is the inability of men to control women (Malti-Douglas 1997; Najmabadi 2000a, 2000b) and, more generally, the inability of men to control their own lives and futures. Stylistically, *'Alf Layla wa Layla* is notable for its capacity suddenly to juxtapose diverse elements: the visible and the invisible, the small and the great, the mundane and the fantastic, life and death. Indeed, as Beaumont notes (1998, 127), all these juxtapositions are present in the very first lines of Shahrazad's first tale.

Jinn loom large in *'Alf Layla wa Layla* as agents for these themes. A jinn appears in the framing story—an encounter with a jinn and his human slave/wife convinces Shahriyar of the uncontrollability of women and hence drives his transformation into mass murderer. Shahrazad's first tale concerns a merchant whose life is ransomed from a jinn by three fantastic stories. Padwick (1924) points out that the jinn in *'Alf Layla wa Laya* represent a more urbanized class than those in North African and Arab folktales. There is a greater emphasis in *'Alf Layla wa Layla* on the magical powers of the jinn, who can build palaces overnight, produce

The film *Ta'wīzah* (Talisman, Muhammad Shebl, 1988), while borrowing many elements from the American horror genre, offers a more traditional and terrifying jinn.
(Photo from the collection of Muhammed Bakr.)

jewels the like of which no one has ever seen, and transport people in the wink of an eye. These mighty jinn serve many functions. They are guardians of treasure; vengeful spirits; agents of justice or punishment; instruments of sorcery, wives, and kin; and, of course, slaves of rings and lamps. Above all, they are powerful narrative devices for explaining the sudden changes in fortune for which the text is famous. It is these urbane and almost cosmopolitan jinn, articulate and magically powerful, who move into the European imagination.

From *'Alf Layla wa Layla* to *The Arabian Nights*

European translators have continued to emulate the anonymous Arab authors and redactors, revising and interpolating stories as they write. The most influential, Galland's *Mille et une nuits* and Burton's *Thousand and One Nights*, are less translations than reconstructions. Galland inserted into the text both the Sindbad cycle, taken from another Arabic manuscript, and several stories taken from a Syrian Christian living in Paris—including the most influential story of jinn in European literature, the tale of Aladdin and his marvelous lamp. Two of the tales that have become iconic of *The Arabian Nights* as a whole are thus not in fact part of any known medieval manuscript of *'Alf Layla wa Layla*. They reflect a good deal of Galland's own imagination (Larzul 2004) and have strong parallels with some European folktales (Coote 1880). They were subsequently translated into Arabic and incorporated from the nineteenth century on into the most popular versions of *'Alf Layla wa Layla*.[3]

In creating *The Arabian Nights*, the changing media industry has, over more than two centuries, expanded *'Alf Layla wa Layla* into a vast trove of tales and versions of tales expressed in every medium devised by human technology. From books to motion pictures to comics to tape cassettes, *The Arabian Nights* has become a centerpiece of global folklore. I have argued elsewhere that media industries are systems that appropriate cultural forms, reproduce them in transformed ways according to particular modes of production, and return them to public circulation in retextualized and remediated shapes (Peterson 2003). These systems are selective. Of all the jinn in *The Arabian Nights*, there are only two tales, representing key aspects of jinn, that have been routinely appropriated and transformed by Western media. The first is the dangerous jinn released from the bottle from the "Tale of the Fisherman and the Jinn," and the second is the slave of the lamp from the "Tale of Aladdin and the Marvelous Lamp." Of all the possible ideas about jinn, then, Western media culture came to focus on two: jinn are potentially powerful for either good or ill, and jinn are tied to objects.

The first theme is central to *'Alf Layla wa Layla*. In Western literature, though, the more general idea of the phenomenal world coexisting with an invisible world whose inhabitants can bring our best efforts to naught is subordinated to a particular focus on the choices made by the fisherman. In the tale, the fisherman releases a jinn who, furious that no one has freed him before now, threatens to kill his benefactor. The fisherman tricks the jinn back into the bottle so he can negotiate more favorable terms. The tale of the jinn in the bottle has gained its greatest popularity as a metaphor circulating in headlines and news stories. The metaphor of the dangerous jinn who, once let out of the bottle, may reward but may also destroy us, seems to be most commonly used today to describe the "nuclear genie" but can refer to all manner of other things as well, from the emerging hydrogen fuel industry (Pinkerton and Wicke 2004) to steel tariffs (*Wall Street Journal* 2003), gene therapy (McLean 2001), the

Internet (Walker 2003), political regimes (Negus 2002), and even technology itself (Lightman, Sarewitz, and Desser 2003).

This version of the jinn—free willed, powerful, and therefore potentially dangerous—has not passed readily into the movies. In my review of some eighty *Arabian Nights*–inspired movies, I have found the fisherman and the jinn sequence only once, in the 1940 classic *The Thief of Bagdad*—although it certainly has appeared in some animated shows for children. However, at least one fearsome jinn has made its way into Hollywood horror films via Wes Craven's *Wishmaster* series *(Wishmaster* [1997], *Wishmaster 2: Evil Never Dies* [1999], *Wishmaster 3: Beyond the Gates of Hell* [2001], and *Wishmaster 4: The Prophecy Fulfilled* [2002]). Although the filmmakers claim to have based their scripts on "ancient Persian mythology," theirs is no Arabian jinn like the one in *Ta'wīzah* but a Hollywood genie bound to grant wishes. Like a shayṭān, though, he twists people's wishes around to destroy them.

Genies from the Dream Factory

Arabian Nights tales were being filmed as early as the turn of the twentieth century. In Hollywood—and in Western popular culture generally—master narratives quickly emerged in popular *Arabian Nights* representations of jinn. In the first, which I call the "brass bottle" narrative, some member of a modern society finds a jinn, plunging himself or herself into a multitude of problems. The second master narrative consists of the many versions of Aladdin, in which the eponymous hero defeats an evil wizard and wins the caliph's daughter with the aid of a jinn bound to a magic lamp. In each of these narratives, the Arabian jinn is transformed into the genie through bringing not just the powers but the agency of the jinn under control.

There are dozens of film versions of Aladdin with its enslaved jinn, beginning with a French silent in 1900. In the Galland, Burton, and other early versions, the story of Aladdin and the marvelous lamp is long and complex. It features three villains (the sorcerer, his brother, and the jealous *wazir*), and two jinn, the slave of the lamp and the slave of the ring. Filmmakers have streamlined and condensed these multiplicities. In the original tale, and its most faithful film versions, possession of the lamp allows Aladdin to accomplish virtually anything; the only limits are his imagination and his morality. The danger is that the lamp can be stolen, and the powerful jinn will then have to obey the new owner. Filmmakers were faced with the dilemma of producing dramatic tension in a situation where the jinn can solve any problem. In addition to the theft of the lamp, then, filmmakers began to limit the jinn's powers—primarily by reducing the unlimited benefits of the lamp to a mere three wishes. This choice has the added advantage of introducing an additional narrative tension: the possibility that wishes will be squandered or misused.

The brass bottle narrative takes its name from a novel by F. Anstey, originally published in 1900. It was made into a successful play (1911) and filmed at least three times (1914, 1923, 1964). In the story, unsuccessful architect Horace Ventmire buys an ancient brass bottle at an auction in hopes of impressing the Orientalist father of his fiancée, who disapproves of their engagement. Breaking the seal of Solomon which is stoppering the bottle, Ventmire releases the jinn Fakrash al-Amash, who has been imprisoned for three thousand years.

Fakrash's eagerness to reward his benefactor seriously complicates the young man's life. The essence of the gag is the incapacity of a jinn to do anything for someone living in a "surveillance society" (Foucault [1977] 1995), where the origins of gold bars, suitcases of money, palaces (or housing developments), and so forth must be documented so the wealth can be taxed. Indeed, Ventmire's resistance to accepting assistance from the jinn because of the penalties he *may* suffer if his wealth is discovered by authorities is a very model of "the nexus between power relations and practices of the care of the self" at the heart of Foucault's arguments about surveillance and self-discipline (Vaz and Bruno 2003, 272). It contrasts dramatically with Aladdin, whose self-aggrandizement is part of his strategy to marry the caliph's daughter. This irony is compounded by the social and cultural incompetence of a jinn whose knowledge of the history of the world has a three-thousand-year gap in it.

The story offers a hybrid narrative of elements from the "Tale of the Fisherman and the Jinn" and "The Tale of Aladdin and the Marvelous Lamp." The crucial difference between the Aladdin stories and brass bottle ones lies in the power and agency of the jinn. In the Aladdin tales, the jinn is the slave of the lamp and must obey its owner and, especially in post-World War II versions, offers only three wishes. In the brass bottle narrative, the jinn is initially free willed and powerful but limited in its understanding or competence. The brass bottle theme is employed in a number of films and television shows, including *Where Do We Go From Here?* (1945), the Three Stooges' vehicle *Three Arabian Nuts* (1951), *The Wizard of Baghdad* (1960), *Wildest Dreams* (1990), *Bernard and the Genie* (1991), *The Genie from Down Under* (1996), *Kazaam* (1996), *The Incredible Genie* (1997), and *The Genie from Down Under 2* (1998). But its most influential transformation was almost certainly the Sidney Sheldon television series *I Dream of Jeannie,* which ran from 1965 to 1970 and successfully merged the brass bottle and Aladdin themes.[4]

In *I Dream of Jeannie,* astronaut Tony Nelson (Larry Hagman) is stranded on a desert island after his spacecraft malfunctions. He discovers and opens a decorative bottle, releasing a two-thousand-year-old blonde female genie in a harem costume (Barbara Eden), who was trapped in the bottle long ago by the evil Blue Djinn. The genie, whom Nelson calls Jeannie, keeps the astronaut alive and healthy until rescue arrives. Nelson warns Jeannie that she can have no place in his world, but she stows away in his bag when he is rescued. Over the next five years, Jeannie greatly complicates Nelson's life in at least four ways. First, she is in love with him, so she jealously ruins all his relationships (they marry during the show's fourth season). Second, she was socialized into the world of *the Arabian Nights,* so she uses her powers inappropriately in the twentieth-century United States. Third, Nelson's work is highly secret, so he is under even greater surveillance than most people, including routine psychological evaluations. Finally, Jeannie's own world keeps impinging on Nelson's in the form of relatives, invisible dogs, and genies in training.

This last aspect of the program required the producers and writers gradually to evolve a cosmology. Initially Jeannie serves her master out of gratitude, but over time she becomes a "slave of the lamp" in the Aladdin style, such that she must serve whoever possesses the bottle—a useful plot device. Over the five years of the series' run, and in its 1985 and 1991 sequels, viewers learned that genies live in a separate plane centered in a transcendental Baghdad and that they can only dwell in the mortal world so long as they have a master. A crucial element in this cosmology is that it removes the last vestiges of Islam from the genie mythos. In *'Alf Layla wa Layla,* jinn routinely call on God, declare themselves believers, and look to divine revelation as the ground for moral action. Early *Arabian Nights* films often replicated this discourse as part of their characterizations of genies, but by the early 1970s, the genie had become entirely secularized. These transformations influenced almost every subsequent entry in the brass bottle genre, not only the movies already mentioned but also imitative television series such as the British *Pardon My Genie* (ITV 1972–73), the animated *Jeannie* (CBS 1973–75), and the unsuccessful ABC series *You Wish* (1997).

The Aladdin and brass bottle narratives also dovetail in the most successful of all *Arabian Nights* movies, Walt Disney's *Aladdin* (1992). In this world of minarets but no mosques, genies are *by their nature* bound to their lamps, and they must grant three wishes to whoever controls the lamp. Their servitude is symbolized by the manacles they wear around their wrists. The rules that circumscribe genies are not only a limitation to create greater drama but become the key narrative device on which the plot turns when, at the climax, Aladdin plays on the villainous Jaffar's lust for power to trick him into wishing himself to become a genie—thus gaining unlimited power but losing his agency to do evil.

Global Genies, Regional Jinn

Hollywood is not, of course, the whole of the world's film industry, but it is arguably the most influential. Regional film industries routinely imitate and appropriate elements from successful Hollywood films, inflect them for local tastes, and distribute them in regional markets. If the jinn made a circuitous route to Hollywood film via European literature, the transformed genie has in turn made its way to the Middle East via international circulation of Western media, as well as local productions. One of the first and certainly the most successful of these was the 1949 film '*Afrīta Hanem* (The Lady Genie), written and directed by Henri Barakat.

In '*Afrīta Hanem,* the penniless nightclub singer Asfour (Farid Al Atrache) is in love with the gold-digging dancer Aliaa (Lola Sedki). She is pursuing the foppish, Europeanized Mimi Bey (Abdel Salam Al Nabulsy), who can afford the three-thousand-pound dowry set by her father, who owns the nightclub where both Asfour and Aliaa work. The heartsick Asfour encounters a mysterious old man who tries to convince him that money does not buy happiness and that his poverty conceals a wisdom he cannot fathom. When Asfour resists this message, the old man sends him to a cave where he finds a magic lamp and releases the 'Afrīta Kharamana (Samia Gamal), who can only be seen by him. She insists that he is her lost love, the shayṭān Asfarot, and that she is "a servant in his hand." This line is a direct quotation from '*Alf Layla wa Layla;* it is what the Slave of the Ring (who does not appear in any Hollywood version of the tale) says to Aladdin when he frees him from the Cave of Wonders.

In spite of their initial terror of her, Asfour and his friend Bo'o (Ismail Yasseen) begin to find the *jinnayah* useful. She transforms their home into a palace and allows them to live in luxury. Unlike most Hollywood genies, though, her agency is never fully subordinated. When Asfour attempts to use money she gave him as a dowry for Aliaa, Kharamana transforms the wad of cash into a deck of cards, and Aliaa's father throws Asfour out. With Kharamana's help, Asfour starts his own club. When he tries to hire a dancer, Kharamana summons (or conjures up) a human

Genie from an unidentified Egyptian film ca. 1950.
(Photo from the collection of Muhammed Bakr.)

doppelgänger of herself, a peppery young woman named Semsema, to
fill the job. Asfour begins to fall in love with Semsema, but when his club
prospers, Aliaa returns to woo him. When Kharamana attempts to show
him that marrying Aliaa is a mistake, he sends the 'afrīta away. All the
wealth wrought by her magic vanishes, and Aliaa deserts him. Asfour
struggles to make his club a success without magic and win back the
love of the jilted Semsema.

'Afrīta Hanem offers an instructive example of the way local film
industries imitate and appropriate films in global circulation but transform them as they inflect them for local audiences. While the idea of the

jinnayah bride is an old theme in Arabic folklore, this film seems to have been more strongly influenced by the 1945 Aladdin film, *A Thousand and One Nights*, where Aladdin (Cornell Wilde) enters a spooky cave with his comic-relief sidekick, Abdullah (Phil Silvers), and releases a female genie named Babs (Evelyn Keyes). No one but Aladdin can see Babs, and her amorous crush on him leads her to interfere in his romance with the sultan's daughter. Some of the cave scenes in *'Afrīta Hanem* are near duplicates of the earlier U.S. film, and there is an interesting inversion of the doppelgänger theme where Babs duplicates not herself but Aladdin so that she and the princess can both have him as a lover.[5]

At the same time, there are interesting regional differences. In the U.S. film, Babs is bound to obey the owner of the lamp and thus lacks any real menace. The Egyptian protagonists, however, are initially terrified of Kharamana, and they remain nervous about her throughout the film. Although she is an agent for good, the similarity between jinn and shayāṭīn is played up several times in the film. She is marked as physically different by great arching eyebrows (which also indicate when Samia Gamal is being Kharamana and when she is being Semsema). Islam forms a significant backdrop in the film, not only in the exclamations of the main characters ("Allah!") but in the ways they evaluate the morality of their actions. The old man—who in one scene carries a Muslim rosary—is clearly a divine messenger: an angel, or perhaps a saint. And the complex plot device of doubling Kharamana and Semsema allows the filmmakers to have their love triangle without actually marrying a human to a jinn, an act specifically forbidden by a *hadith*. In spite of these differences, this is clearly a film about a Hollywood-style genie who, freed from her lamp, must serve its possessor. Its success spawned a number of other films, including *Al-Fānūs as-Sahry* (The Magic Lantern, 1954), and *Sirr Ṭaqiyyat al-'Ikhfa'* (Mystery of the Vanishing Cap, 1959).

As the genie entered the Middle Eastern social imagination, it became especially associated with consumer goods making their way into the market. Many new goods carried both high status and steep prices, and the genie was a powerful device for imagining what one would do with such goods if they were somehow within reach. Thus, Kharamana may prefer to put Asfour in a palace, clad in turban and robes, but she is perfectly adept at conjuring well-tailored business suits and late-model automobiles, the kinds of goods Asfour prefers.

Genies and jinn coexist in Middle Eastern media. Where genies appear primarily in comedies, jinn appear primarily in horror films and psychological dramas. In addition to *Ta'wīzahh*, already discussed, examples of horror films include *'Anyāb* (Fangs, 1981). Clearly inspired by *The Rocky Horror Picture Show* (1975), and Britain's Hammer horror films, this movie is essentially about Western-style vampires, mildly indigenized by referring to the master vampire as an *'afrīt* or *shayṭān*. More imaginative are the psychological thrillers like *Al-'Ins wa al-Jinn* (Humans and Jinn, 1985), where a jinn falls in love with the human woman whose house he inhabits, or *Al-Mar'āh Alaty Ghalabat ash-Shayṭān* (1973), where an urbane *shayṭān* follows a woman about, commenting on her life and actions and seductively urging her to put her own needs and desires above those of her family.

Genies and jinn also coexist in children's media. Every issue of the children's magazine *Majid* features an illustration of a genie rising from a lamp and presenting a computer to a delighted Arab boy. The image marks a regular feature in the magazine describing Web sites, in English and Arabic, intended to be fun or educational for children. Elsewhere in its pages, the magazine may well illustrate a traditional folktale featuring a jinn.[6] Jinn and genies cohabit the pages of many other children's magazines as well, including *Bolbol, Al Arabi Alsaghir,* and *Alaa Eldin.* One regular feature of *Alaa Eldin* is a comic strip featuring the adventures of a contemporary Egyptian Aladdin—in blue jeans and a red button-down shirt—and his genie Morgan, who watches television and sometimes drives an enchanted Model T Ford. The connection between the genie and consumer commodities is a crucial theme.

Speaking of Jinn

Global folklore cannot be considered folklore if it remains purely a product of international and local culture industries. But it does not. Once media texts are in circulation, people borrow from them, interpolating elements from popular media into their own oral performances (Peterson 2005b). If stories about genies become syncretic with local beliefs about jinn in Middle Eastern film, oral tales of jinn are also influenced by genies. This is well illustrated in a story recorded by Farha Ghannam:

> One day in 1994, Amal, a five-year-old girl, sat on my lap to tell me a story. "Praise the Prophet. Once upon a time there was an old woman who used to live in an apartment that was as small as that table [Amal was pointing to a small table in the living room]. Each time the old woman swept the floor, she found either one pound or fifty piasters that she kept hidden in a place by the window. The old woman was saving to buy a larger apartment. But one day a thief stole all the money she had saved. She was very sad.

An *'afriit* [demon or ghost] appeared and asked the old woman what she would like to have. She asked for a larger apartment. The 'afriit asked her, 'Would you like an apartment with a balcony?' She answered 'yes.' He asked her, 'Would you like a television set, a fan and a bottle of water?' [Amal was describing some of the things that were in front of us in the living room.] The old woman said yes. Then he asked her, 'And would you like some pictures of Samira Sa'id and Latifa?' [These are two popular female Moroccan and Tunisian singers whose posters are decorating the wall of the living room.] The woman again answered yes. The 'afriit brought all these things to the old woman. She was very happy and cried out with joy. That same day, however, she smelled the birshaam that was hidden behind the television set [this birshaam is a type of drug that is often believed to be produced and circulated by the United States and Israel; it is a pill that is taken orally and not sniffed as Amal implies]. This caused her heart to collapse [*gham ala albaha*], and the old woman died." (2002 43–44)

Amal's 'afrīt has the agency of a jinn and the desire to reward the goodness of the believer. Like a genie, he is the provider of consumer goods. And like the genie, his incompetence in dealing with the complexities of global society makes his gifts unreliable. There is, literally, a "poison in the gift" of consumer goods (Douglas 1990). Amal's tale is therefore not one where the genie ultimately cures things through magic, or even by simply undoing his spell. As often occurs with jinn, their dealings with mortals are a matter of life and death.

Conclusion

Every text is shaped by its immediate context of production and the historically produced political, social, and economic conditions circumscribing that context. Amal's tale is contextualized by her family's unsuccessful search for a larger apartment than the one-bedroom flat where they currently lived and into which her parents had been relocated by a government urban-renewal project. Her fantasies are shaped by the movies and soap operas she loves to watch but that "contradict the material realities of Amal's life and create desires that cannot be satisfied even through some magical means" (Ghannam 2002, 44). *'Afrīta Hanem* is shaped by postcolonial efforts to imagine an Arab modernity that helps mediate contradictions among nationalism, modernity, and Arabic classicism (Armbrust 1996). Disney's *Aladdin* is structured in part by America's changing attitudes toward Iran and Iraq in a post-cold war world (Nadel 1998).

At the same time, texts are comprised of elements drawn from a larger intertextual matrix. Through a series of choices made by text producers in different times and places, the lamp-bound jinn of Aladdin has come to stand, metonymically, for all jinn. As the genie, it has undergone a series of transformations as it is reproduced in different texts. Bereft of personal agency, set loose from its religious underpinnings, and tied to the notion of unlimited human desire that is at the heart of modern economic concepts about human nature, the genie has become an increasingly universal tool for exploring the contradictions between consumer desire and moral values, contradictions that are everywhere different and yet, in an increasingly globalized world, everywhere the same.

Notes

Much of the work for this article was done in Cairo during the summer of 2005. Funding for this trip was provided in part by the Philip and Elana Hampton Fund. I would like to thank Mustafa Abdel-Raman for his hospitality and generosity, which itself sometimes bordered on something out of *The Arabian Nights*. I must also thank Wesam Younis for his time and enthusiasm in helping me track down obscure videos and for sharing his own experiences with movies as well as jinn. This article benefited from reading and suggestions by Humayun Sidky, Sharon R. Sherman, and Mikel J. Koven.

1. Jinn is both the singular and plural form, although jinn*i* as singular occurs in some colloquial dialects.

2. Westermarck records that among Moroccans it is commonly believed that every place has its resident jinn (1930, 280).

3. In his essay on the translators of *The Arabian Nights*, Borges (2000) points out that what is interesting and important about all of them is the "displacements" between their texts and those that preceded them. While claims of fidelity to a putative original text are important to every translation, it is the infidelities that make each version interesting and successful. Moreover, Borges emphasizes, every translation is an adaptation to a context. A faithful translation would necessarily be a scholarly, philological work. Burton's intention was to "interest nineteenth-century British gentlemen in thirteenth-century Arabian serialized stories" (Waisman 2003); Lane's was to make them appropriate for those gentlemen's wives and children to read; and so forth.

4. In several interviews, Sheldon has affirmed that the 1964 production of *The Brass Bottle* (in which Barbara Eden played Ventmire's fiancée) was his inspiration for the television series.

5. For another account of this film and its relation to literary appropriations from *'Alf Layla wa Layla*, see Ouyang (2003).

6. *Majid*, published weekly since 1979 by Emirates Media, Inc., is probably the most popular children's magazine in the Gulf region, with a total circulation of about 150,000 per month. For more on *Majid*, see Douglas and Fedwa Malti-Douglas (1994) and Peterson (2005a).

Filmography

'Afrīt am 'Abdu [The ghost of Abdu] (1953). Hussein Fawzy
'Afrīt Mirātī [My demon wife] (1968). 100 min. Faṭīn Abdel Wahāb
'Afrīt Samārah [Samarah's ghost] (1959). Hassan Reḏa
'Afrīta Hanem [The lady genie] (1949). 97 min. Henri Barakat
Aladdin (1992). 90 min. Ron Clements and John Musker
'Anyāb [Fangs] (1981). Muhammad Shebl
Bernard and the Genie (1991). 70 min. Paul Weiland
The Brass Bottle (1914). Sidney Morgan
The Brass Bottle (1923). 60 min. Maurice Tourneur
The Brass Bottle (1964). 87 min. Harry Keller
Al-Fānūs as-Sahry [The magic lantern] (1954). Faṭīn Abdel Wahāb
Ga'ana al-Bayan at-Tali [We have just received the following report] (2001). Sa'id
    Hamed
Genie from Down Under (1996). ABC [Australia] / BBC
Genie from Down Under 2 (1998). ABC [Australia] / BBC
I Dream of Jeannie (1965–1970). NBC
The Incredible Genie (1997). 90 min. Alexander Cassini
Al-'Ins wa al-Jinn [Humans and jinn] (1985). Muhammad Rāḏī
Jeannie (19973–1974). CBS
Kazaam (1996). 93 min. Paul Michael Glaser
Al-Mar'āh Alaty Ghalabat ash-Shayṭān (1973). Yehya Al-Al'amy.
Pardon My Genie (1972–1973). ITV
The Rocky Horror Picture Show (1975). 100 min. Jim Sharman.
Sirr Ṭaqiyyat al-'Ikhfa' [Mystery of the vanishing cap] (1959). 96 min. Niyazi
    Mustafa
Ta'wīzah [Talisman] (1988). Muhammad Shebl
The Thief of Bagdad (1940). 106 min. Ludwig Berger, Michael Powell, and Tim
    Whelan
A Thousand and One Nights (1945). 93 min. Alfred E. Green
Three Arabian Nuts (1951). 16 min. Edward Bernds
Where Do We Go From Here? (1945). 74 min. Gregory Ratoff
Wildest Dreams (1990). Chuck Vincent
Wishmaster (1997). 90 min. Robert Kurtzman
Wishmaster 2: Evil Never Dies (1999). 96 min. Jack Sholder
Wishmaster 3: Beyond the Gates of Hell (2001). 90 min. Chris Angel
Wishmaster 4: Prophecy Fulfilled (2002). 90 min. Chris Angel
The Wizard of Bagdad (1960). 92 min. George Sherman
You Wish (1997–98). ABC

Works Cited

Anstey, F. 1900. *The brass bottle.* New York: D. Appleton and Company
Armbrust, Walter. 1996. *Mass culture and modernism in Egypt.* Cambridge: Cam-
    bridge University Press.

Beaumont, Daniel. 1998 'Peut-on…': Intertextual relations in *the Arabian nights* and Genesis. *Comparative Literature* 50 (2): 120–35.

Borges, Jorge Luis. 2000. The translators of the *Thousand and one nights*. In *The translation studies reader*, ed. Lawrence Venuti, 34–48. London/New York: Routledge.

Burton, Sir Richard. 1885. *The book of the Thousand Nights and a NIght: A Plain and literal translation of the Arabian Nights entertainments*. London: The Burton Club.

Coote, Henry Charles. 1880. Folk-lore the source of some of M. Galland's tales. *The Folk-Lore Record* 3 (2): 178–91.

Doubleday, Veronica. 1999. The frame drum in the Middle East: Women, musical instruments and power. *Ethnomusicology* 43 (1): 101–34.

Douglas, Mary. 1990. Foreword: No free gifts. In *The gift: The form and reason for exchange in archaic societies*, by Marcel Mauss, i–xv. Trans. W.D. Halls. London: Routledge.

Douglas, Allen, and Fedwa Malti-Douglas. 1994. *Arab comic strips: Politics of an emerging mass culture*. Bloomington: Indiana University Press.

El-Aswad, El-Sayed. 2002. *Religion and folk cosmology: Scenarios of the visible and invisible in rural Egypt*. Westport, CT: Praeger.

Foucault, Michel. [1977] 1995. *Discipline and punish: The birth of the prison*. Trans. Alan Sheridan. Repr., New York: Vintage Books.

Galland, Antoine 1921. *Les mille et une nuits: Contes Arabes*. Paris: Garnier Fréres.

Ghannam, Farha. 2002. *Remaking the modern: Space, relocation, and the politics of identity in a global Cairo*. Berkeley: University of California Press.

Gingrich, A. 1995. Spirits of the border: Some remarks on the connotation of jinn in north-western Yemen. *Quaderni di Studi Arabi* 13:199–212.

Hammad, Adnan, Rashid Kysia, Raja Rabah, Rosina Hassoun, and Michael Connelly 1999. *Guide to Arab culture: Health care delivery to the Arab American community*. Dearborn, MI: ACCESS Community Health Center.

Hamori, Andras. 1971. An allegory from *the Arabian nights*: The city of brass. *Bulletin of the School of Oriental and African Studies* (University of London) 34 (1): 9–19.

Irwin, Robert. 1994. *The Arabian nights: A companion*. London: Allen Lane.

Izutsu, Toshihiko. 1987. *God and man in the Koran*. Salem, NH: Ayer Co.

Latham, Rob. 2002. *Consuming youth: Vampires, cyborgs, and the culture of consumption*. Chicago: University of Chicago Press.

Larzul, Sylvette. 2004. Further considerations on Galland's *Mille et une nuits:* A study of the tales told by Hanna. *Marvels & Tales: Journal of Fairy-Tale Studies* 18 (2): 258–71.

Lightman, Alan, Daniel Sarewitz, and Christina Desser, eds. 2003. *Living with the genie: Essays on technology and the quest for human mastery*. Washington, DC: Island Press.

Malti-Douglas, Fedwa. 1997. Shahrazad feminist. In *The thousand and one nights in Arabic literature and society*, ed. R.G. Hovannisian and Georges Sabagh, 40–55. Cambridge: Cambridge University Press.

Marcus, George. 1995. The problem of the unseen world of wealth for the rich:

Toward an ethnography of complex connections. In *Ethnography through thick and thin*, 152–60. Princeton, NJ: Princeton University Press.

Martin, Richard. 1982. Understanding the Qur'an in text and context. *History of Religions* 21(4): 361–84.

Matar, Nabil. 2000. Two journeys to seventeenth-century Palestine. *Journal of Palestine Studies* 29 (4): 37–50.

McDonald, D. B. 1924. The earlier history of *the Arabian nights. Journal of the Royal Asiatic Society* 3: 353–97.

McGregor, Richard J. A. 1997. A Sufi legacy in Tunis: Prayer and the shadhili-yya. *International Journal of Middle East Studies* 29 (2): 255–77.

McLean, Sheila A. 2001. The gene genie: Good fairy or wicked witch? Part C of *Studies in History and Philosophy of Science: Biological and Biomedical Sciences* 32 (4): 723–39.

Nadel, Alan. 1998. A whole new (Disney) world order: *Aladdin,* atomic power and the Muslim Middle-East. In *Visions of the East: Orientalism in film,* ed. Matthew Bernstein and Gaylyn Studlar, 184–206. New Brunswick, NJ: Rutgers University Press.

Najmabadi, Afsaneh. 2000a. Reading—and enjoying—"Wiles of women" stories as a feminist. *Iranian Studies* 32 (2): 203–22.

———. 2000b. Reading "Wiles of women" stories as fictions of masculinity. In *Imagined masculinities: Male identity and culture in the modern Middle East,* ed. Mai Ghoussoub and Emma Sinclair-Webb, 147–68. London: Saqi.

Negus, Steve. 2002. Egypt: The genie in the bottle. *Middle East International* 685 (October 11): 16–17.

Ouyang, Wen Chin. 2003. Metamorphoses of Sheherazade in literature and film. *Bulletin of the School of Oriental and African Studies* (University of London) 66 (3): 402–18.

Padwick, Constance. 1924. Notes on the jinn and the ghoul in the peasant mind of Lower Egypt. *Bulletin of the School of Oriental Studies* (University of London) 3 (3): 421–46.

Peterson, Mark Allen. 2003. *Anthropology and mass communication: Media and myth in the new millennium.* New York: Berghahn Books.

———. 2005a. The jinn and the computer: Consumption and identity in Arabic children's magazines. *Childhood* 12 (2): 177–200.

———. 2005b. Performing media: Toward an ethnography of intertextuality. In *Media anthropology,* ed. Mihai Comans and Eric Rothenbuehler, 129–38. London: Sage.

Pinkerton, Frederick E., and Brian G. Wicke. 2004. Bottling the hydrogen genie. *Industrial Physicist* 10 (1): 22–26.

Vaz, Paulo, and Fernanda Bruno. 2003. Types of self-surveillance: From abnormality to individuals 'at risk'. *Surveillance & Society* 1, (3): 272–91.

Waisman, Sergio. 2003. *The thousand and one nights* in Argentina: Translation, narrative, and politics in Borges, Puig, and Piglia. *Comparative Literature Studies* 40 (4): 351–71.

Walker, John. 2003. The digital imprimatur: How big brother and big media can put the Internet genie back in the bottle. *Knowledge, Technology & Policy* 16 (3): 24–78.

Wall Street Journal. 2003. The genie is out of the bottle. Eastern edition 242 (112), Dec. 8, A14.

Westermarck, Edward. 1930. *Wit and wisdom in Morocco*. London: Routledge and Sons.

Younis, Yahia O. 2000. Possession and exorcism: An illustrative case. *Arab Journal of Psychiatry* [Al-Majalla al-`Arabiya li-l-Tibb al-Nafsi] 11(1): 56–59.

6

"Now That I Have It, I Don't Want It"

Vocation and Obligation in Contemporary Hollywood Ghost Films

JAMES A. MILLER

WHAT MAKES *HAMLET'S* ghost so memorably disturbing, for audiences as well as its unwilling interlocutor? Jacques Derrida has pointed out in *Specters of Marx* that the ghost's inscrutable form and ambiguous provenance are crucial to its power. We grasp, with Hamlet, the familiar lineaments of a demanding father, yet "that does not prevent him from looking at us without being seen: his apparition makes him appear still invisible beneath his armour" (1994, 7). We "do not see what looks at us," and this "spectral asymmetry" grants the ghost's implacable gaze the power to judge the living (1994, 7). In the end, then, the haunting figure's forceful and commanding voice remains with us. "Pity me not," it intones, "but lend thy serious hearing to what I shall unfold" (1.5.5–6). The ghost's words imply an ethical imperative: they demand that Hamlet must attend to its message, interpret its exhortations, and act decisively on that knowledge. This obligatory dimension of Hamlet's spectral encounter makes it a locus of unease for viewers. Whatever we may think of the Prince of Denmark and his troubles, we are also encouraged to consider what, if anything, the past demands of us.

Hamlet's ghost poses a question about obligation that is both profoundly traditional and deeply resonant in our contemporary popular culture. It may at first appear difficult to hear the question in today's haunted media, where not all ghosts are taken so seriously. Two of the most memorable ghost films of the 1980s—Ivan Reitman's *Ghostbusters* (1984) and Tim Burton's *Beetlejuice* (1988)—even treat the ghostly with parodic levity. No "pity" or "serious hearing" for Reitman's ghost-troubled urbanites; instead, they simply call on paranormal professionals, whose work has all the banality of pest extermination. Somewhat similar in tone, *Beetlejuice* reverses the usual genre formula by having put-upon ghosts appeal to a spectral bureaucracy for help with their invasive "living family" situation. As is typical when one has to deal with bureaucratic red tape, the solution turns out to be more trouble than the original problem.

In both films, the supernatural event presents an ideal occasion for ostentatious displays of special effects. Linda Bradley has commented on the striking prevalence of *ectoplasm*—concretely visualized spectrality—in 1980s ghost cinema. In this period, she argues, "ghosts became inconceivable unless embodied" (1995, 44–45), thus diminishing their discursive potential in favor of self-consciously visualized spectacle. The ghosts in *Ghostbusters* are a famous example of this trend because they are explicitly objectified as phenomena (or special effect) without roots in history or memory. And while Burton's *Beetlejuice* is more complex because the ghosts have recognizable human desires, there is an ironic undertow to its repetition scenario. In one sense, as Katherine Fowkes has shown, the Maitlands (the primary ghost figures here) can be read psychoanalytically as masochistic figures that return "after the fact...to repeat the original fantasy of the birth of the subject" (1998, 83). Yet their repetition/return evokes only a circumscribed and private history, one that can make no demands on the present.

Several critics have argued that seemingly innocuous films like *Ghostbusters*, along with more conventional horror fare including *The Changeling* (1980), *Ghost Story* (1981), *Poltergeist* (1982), or *The Lady in White* (1988), all articulate a disturbing message about political quietism. Alan Nadel's analysis of the political construction he calls "Reagan's America" is the most detailed explication of this position. For Nadel, Reagan's political vision was the worst kind of dishonest Hollywood confection, a debasement of the materiality of historicized experience into pure escapist narrative, abstracted from the unpleasant details of everyday life that the Hollywood engine works overtime to obscure. Given this, Nadel argues that the real corporate Hollywood products of the time, including popular ghost films like *Field of Dreams* (1989) or *Ghost* (1990), line up to parrot the illusory promises of the administration (1997, 48–85). In these films, the emphasis on spectacle displaces more troubling historical questions by visualizing the past as a mere inconvenience (or an active threat) to be diverted or defeated. With the unwelcome pressures of history conveniently removed, Hollywood's victorious heroes return to the "business as usual" of consumer-culture complacency and implicitly authorize their audiences to do the same.[1]

This model is too monolithic. Several ghost films resist the tendency toward ahistorical cynicism by attempting to reanimate the far older folkloric idea that the spectral encounter may be seen as a conversational dialectic between claimant and interlocutor, obligation and resistance. Popular films like *Field of Dreams* and *The Sixth Sense* (1999) evince serious interest in an ancient fixture of ghost tales: the man or woman set apart, an intermediary between the living and the dead. They explore a "vocational crisis," portraying the ambivalence of the priestly figure as a person whose responsibility to the past is necessary for cultural survival yet may require a disturbing sacrifice of the self. Viewers are encouraged to ask, "What does it mean to live *now*, during this particular moment in history? What, as a human being, do I owe my fellow audience members and the dead who have made my existence possible?" The vocational or priestly figure attempts—not always with great success—to answer these questions by acting as a physical representation of the viewers' necessary attention of self to "other."

Literary scholars today are probably most familiar with a ghostly tradition emerging out of eighteenth- and nineteenth-century Gothic aesthetics, and later, twentieth-century psychoanalysis. From Horace Walpole and Friedrich Schiller to Elizabeth Gaskell and Charles Dickens, from Henry James's *The Turn of the Screw* (1898) to the late stories of Edith Wharton and Shirley Jackson's *The Haunting of Hill House* (1959), literary ghost fiction has developed toward a fatalistic sense of powerlessness and isolation. Twentieth-century tales, in particular, tend to depict the ghost as the precipitant of an intense individual crisis of psychological and spiritual nature and reveal a world where neither institutional nor marginal social structures can offer solace. This tradition presents a parallel to modernist literary themes of isolation, anxiety, and despairing secularization. Unlike the Sartrean leap of faith that authorizes productive individual choice and self-generation out of the void, these narratives underline the essential helplessness of human agents at the mercy of an indifferent universe.

The idea of spectral encounter as impetus for existential crisis is already implicit in Sigmund Freud's conception of the *uncanny*. Freud theorizes that the uncanny feeling inherent in repetition compulsion leads us back to an ancient, supposedly rejected, animistic worldview:

> Our analysis of instances of the uncanny has led us back to the old, animistic conception of the universe, which was characterized by the idea that the world was peopled with the spirits of human beings, and by the narcissistic overestimation of subjective mental processes (such as the belief in the omnipotence of thoughts, the magical practices based upon this belief)....It would seem as though each one of us has been through a phase of

individual development corresponding to that animistic stage in primitive men, that none of us has traversed it without preserving certain traces of it which can be re-activated, and that everything which now strikes us as "uncanny" fulfils the condition of stirring those vestiges of animistic mental activity within us and bringing them to expression. (1995, 141)

Freud implies that the spectral encounter is one with the problem of being itself—that to engage with the ghostly is to question all social, psychological, and ideological order. The radically decentering potential of his thought has been widely influential. Indeed, Freudian conceptions of the supernatural are so entrenched that it is difficult for some people to perceive anything *other* than existential dread in today's ghosts.

In this spirit, it is possible to construct, as R. C. Finucane has done (1996, 90–116), a unified historical model that can trace the roots of our modernist (or post-modernist) anxiety to a specific historical moment— for example, in the sixteenth-century witch-trials era, when ghosts become a locus of intense existential and political debate. Are they (as Reginald Scot insisted in his 1584 *Discoverie of Witchcraft*) merely the fantastical projections of credulous minds, who behave "as if they were babes frayed with bugges" (quoted in Finucane 94)? Or are they evidence of the malignant influence of demons and devils, according to none other than King James' *Daemonologie* (discussed in Finucane 95–96)? Both Scot and James associate ghosts with deception, anxiety, and exploitation: the traditional sense that the spectral is part of intelligible communal experience is nowhere in evidence. The danger of this sort of historical analysis is that it can imply an evolutionary trajectory from tradition to modernity, leaving older experience of the spectral behind.

Unsurprisingly, folkoristic discussions of the ghost often take quite a different approach. Indeed, one of the most striking features of the ghost in traditional societies, in the West and elsewhere, is its functionality. From this perspective, the spectral is not a threat to society but a problem to be addressed through communally sanctioned action. Further, the ghost may be grasped as a rhetorical tool, a mechanism through which pressing localized social issues may be articulated and debated. Timothy Tangherlini has explored this pattern from a folkloristic point of view in his study of nineteenth-century Danish ghost legends, wherein the haunted turn to ministers, folk healers, or others with experience of the supernatural. In the Danish folk tradition, Tangherlini argues, competing claims to ghostly expertise express different attitudes regarding institutional social power, and ghost legends emerge as oral performances that concretize political debate (1998, 155). Some tales support the cleansing powers of the local ministerial elite and, by extension, the nineteenth-century Lutheran church, and behind that the Danish crown and legitimate state power (1998, 160–61). Other tales perform an explicitly subversive function: when religious leaders *fail* to deal with ghostly threats, the culturally marginal folk healer or beggar steps in, thus creating a critique of authority (1998,164–65).

Tangherlini's observations are echoed by Gillian Bennett's study of contemporary ghost memorates from the 1980s in *Alas, Poor Ghost* (1999). She outlines the competition between two cultural traditions, one of "rationalist disbelief" and the other of "belief." Crucially, both traditions can be analyzed rhetorically as they draw on oral conventions of performance, argument, and social interaction. Bennett's insights are threefold: first, she understands that both belief and disbelief are historically and socially mediated positions from which emerge individual performances (conversations, social interactions, and artistic productions like films). Her ethnographic research establishes that both traditions are vibrantly active in contemporary Western, urban, everyday life. Second, Bennett shows that both traditions produce positive cultural results: in folkloristic terms, they serve the psychological and social needs of individuals (1999,31–38). And finally, she points out that many contemporary oral ghost narratives emphasize the continuity and effectiveness of the community and literally *embody* that continuity through the act of storytelling itself. These oral performances describe a world that *works*. Life and death are grounded in an intelligible order of creation, rather than being mere accidents of biology. Human intimacy is remembered and cherished, and justice emerges as the comforter of the weak and bereft (1999, 25–28, 51–66). In the modern era of corporate hegemony, rampant militarism, and widespread political cynicism, the vision of intimate community offered by Bennett's memorates is incredibly appealing and, of course, highly marketable.

In recent cinema, a guarded return to something resembling this traditional model, one that has, after all, never really disappeared in popular folk practice, is also apparent. These films depict a concern with intermediary figures—priests, cunning folk, mediums, converts, and the like. In so many of these films, the grudging admittance of an individual's limits finally results not in existential despair but a discovery of that yearned-for and feared mediating authority within the self. But the key to the vocational theme is that the discovery of secret reserves within, of the ability to mediate between our world and the other, implies a deliberate rethinking of the individual's relationship to the social order. Once the contemporary hero admits the claim of the spectral, an inevitable and ongoing vocation follows, a duty that is understood to continue long after the narrative proper has concluded. The nascent sense of public obligation, and historical consciousness, can be read in implicitly political terms.

These crucial concepts—*obligation, vocation*—are in some ways acutely unfashionable, implying to some people an unwelcome, coercive force. Indeed, they may resemble a strand of Catholic piety that privileges the romance of self-sacrifice. Certainly the Catholic tradition offers a variation on the theme, and as we will see later, several recent films make explicit (if sometimes ironic) use of it. The vocational perspective also has a philosophical inflection, for example, in the work of Emmanuel Levinas, whose sometimes astonishingly extreme claims for interpersonal ethics consistently betray evidence of obligatory thinking. For Levinas, the ethical question is primary and above all others and is grounded in the exchange between self and other: "[It is] as if the proximity of the other man...his face, the expressive in the Other...were what *ordains* me to serve him" (1982, 97). The intensity of this appeal, and the sheer weight of the obligation, are precisely what make the vocational theme so powerful in spectral narratives. Through it, storyteller and listener, filmmaker and viewer can meditate on the ambiguous claims of social order: of a child on its mother, a parent on its child, a community on its people, the past on the present.

Looking back to Nicolas Roeg's 1973 *Don't Look Now*, adapted from Daphne du Maurier's novella (1971), one can see an early expression of a theme that is strikingly common in more recent ghost films: the struggle against vocation. John (Donald Sutherland) and Laura (Julie Christie) are a couple dealing with the recent death of their daughter. Laura, at first the most obviously affected of the two, meets an over-the-top, classic-ghost-story medium, whose assurances of her daughter's happiness allow her to begin taking charge of her life once more. By contrast, John chooses to bury his suffering in his work. As a restorer of old church buildings, he rescues images of the dead, a powerful visualization of sublimated, secularized vocation. He cannot accept the past in any but a purely instrumental sense: as a rapidly decaying legacy of stone monuments and empty symbols that nevertheless pays the bills. But John is also gifted with an unwanted second sight, the ability to see into both past and future—the vocational function articulated in genre terms. His own unconscious quietly insists on the obligatory impact of the past on the present. John absolutely refuses this lesson, and the unwillingness to accept a vocational responsibility leads to his own death.[2]

Don't Look Now may be the most extreme example of the tendency for recent vocational figures to resist their calling, but it is actually a pervasive theme, even visible in the popular *Ghost*. Whoopi Goldberg's Oda Mae, a fake medium, is horrified to discover that she can hear spirits of the dead. Far from legitimating her already-successful spiritualist practice, this unexpected revelation is an unwelcome imposition. At one point she says, "My mother had it, my mother's mother had it. Now that I have it, I don't want it." A reasonable desire, yet the film's titular ghost literally torments her into submitting to her gift. Once she assumes the vocational role, ghosts crowd Oda Mae; her body and identity are subsumed by an unwanted possession not unlike rape.

This element of the film has generated the most criticism, and justifiably so. The narrative, read this way, is essentially about the struggle of a Hollywood, white, middle-class couple to achieve psychological wholeness. They achieve this goal not only through the (initially unwilling) aid of a black woman but explicitly through her possession, or more precisely, her erasure. Yet while it may be true that Oda Mae is eventually enlisted to serve the white patriarchy, at the same time, her struggle— her vocational crisis—is quite genuine. That this is all made comfortably "Hollywood" by the end, and that her struggles against vocation are all played for laughs, do not hide the fact that her gift may be a curse.[3]

Oda Mae's dilemma in *Ghost* is strikingly similar to the situation in *Stir of Echoes* (1999), another ambivalent take on the vocational motif. Tom (Kevin Bacon), the blue-collar hero, is frustrated by the tension between familial expectations and his creative desire to make music. At first the film seems to be about the need to put aside his extended adolescence and shoulder adult responsibilities. Yet Tom's sister-in-law, Lisa (Illeana Douglas), who sees herself as a cosmopolitan, modern person , constantly points out his supposedly bland, unquestioning blue-collar everydayness. In an early scene, she says, "You know, this may come as a surprise to you,...but just because you've knocked around the same six blocks your whole life doesn't mean there isn't a whole larger world out there...doorways you haven't even opened." In the following sequence, Lisa hypnotizes our hero and suggests that he "open up." The result is that Tom becomes uncomfortably aware of ghostly presences and is eventually forced to act as a mediator, righting a wrong that allows a tormented spirit to be appeased. In gendered terms, the repressed male is opened up to the personal in others and acts out the nurturing role he resists in his everyday family life. Conversely, the sequence is an expression of the tensions inherent in the vocational theme.

As in *Ghost*, the mediator's identity, once assumed, is acutely oppressive. Why? The film suggests that the vocational burden is, in part, a threat to the self. This insight is expressed most clearly in the

last shot. As Tom and his family drive away from the familiar neighborhood, their son Jake (Zachary David Cope)—himself on the verge of
vocational crisis—watches the houses flash by, each full of unwelcome
ghostly demands. In a futile gesture of self-assertion, he covers his ears,
unwilling to face the obligatory weight of the past.[4]

Recent films offer more positive resolutions of this vocational ambivalence, nowhere so successfully (or at least economically) as in *Field of
Dreams* and M. Night Shyamalan's *The Sixth Sense*. *Field of Dreams* focuses
on the plight of Ray Kinsella (Kevin Costner), who has spent a lifetime
experimenting with utopian alternatives to mainstream American ideology. Initially he sought refuge from the banal in a mildly rebellious
flirtation with California's 1960s counterculture. Disillusioned with that
experiment, Ray married and bought an Iowa farm, aligning himself
with an embattled agrarian idealism under threat by the economic realities of Reagan's America. But by the time of the film's action in the late
1980s, Ray has matured enough to understand some of the anxieties that
fuel his choices: "I'm 36 years old; I have a wife, a child, and a mortgage,
and I'm scared to death I'm turning into my father....I never forgave him
for getting old. He must have had dreams, but he never did anything
about them....The man never did one spontaneous thing in all the years
I knew him."

The context of the speech is domestic, but it is also a thinly veiled
comment on contemporary social and political complacency. The culture, he seems to be suggesting, has lost the capacity to imagine utopia.
His wife, Annie (Amy Madigan), deals with the same desires and anxieties and is allowed one moment of resistance to the social complacency of
the era. At a PTA meeting, where local prudes have collected to suppress
the work of radical '60s activist Terence Mann, Annie has a chance to
speak out for progressive values. Her utopian ideals are represented in
familiar Hollywood shorthand:"It's like the '60s again!" she enthuses. At
least some sort of (vaguely) political alternative is given a hearing.

Perhaps unsurprisingly, the film's answer to America's social and
political malaise turns out to be patently absurd. While facing fore-
closure of his farm, and by extension the agrarian vision that initially
fueled his embrace of domesticity, Ray hears voices that tell him to
plow under his crops and build a baseball field. The act is irrational,
as Ray, his family, and the community perfectly understand. But critics
like Alan Nadel (1997), Molly Rothenberg (1997), and Thomas DiPiero
(1997) have resisted the sentimental appeal of this gesture. Instead of
confronting honestly the social and economic realities that have led
Ray's farm (and the nation) to the brink of collapse, we are asked to

subscribe to a fantasy of redemption where the failures of the past, of the domestic and political promise of America itself, is assuaged through intense wish fulfillment.

When the film tries to use its fantastical premise to deal with more complex political issues (race, gender, the less co-opted elements of '60s radicalism), the essential confusion of its thinking is revealed, and we are left with sentimentalism verging on materialist cynicism.[5] Yet *Field of Dreams* is also about the possibility that moral and spiritual complacency *can* be transcended through a secular variation on what Flannery O'Connor called *grace,* the voice in the wind that quietly ruptures the surface of everyday life. The film also enacts a traditional conversion narrative, though in thoroughly modern terms. The hero is quite literally called to a vocation, struggles with that calling, and then risks everything to accomplish his mission. This pattern of behavior fulfills the traditional function of the vocational figure: to address the concerns of the dead and, in doing so, to bring history into living communion with the present.

The Sixth Sense, by far the most commercially successful ghost film of recent years, is also the most completely realized example of the vocational theme I have been describing. Shyamalan's tendency to rely heavily on extremely manipulative identification techniques and his preference for gimmicky surprise endings or last-minute twists have tended to obscure his films' more significant content. But just as there is more to Hitchcock's formally experimental *Rope* (1948) than the attempt to make a commercial one-shot film, so *The Sixth Sense* does turn out to be *about* something worthwhile once you get past the tricks. The opening sequence introduces Malcolm (Bruce Willis), a successful child psychologist and recent recipient of a citation from the city of Philadelphia for service to the community. Shyamalan explicitly marks Malcolm as an intermediary figure intent on healing broken children: a committed representative of the community working toward a viable future through the judicious purging of the traumatic past. Yet those he could not help haunt Malcolm, notably Vincent Grey (Donnie Wahlberg), whose psychotic act of violence toward the surrogate father figure who has failed him inaugurates the more explicit structure of the narrative. Malcolm spends most of the rest of the film attempting to assuage his guilt for failing Vincent by helping Cole, a similarly disturbed child going through a parallel experience of divorce, familial breakdown, and resultant psychological collapse.

But in this opening scene, Malcolm's wife, Anna (Olivia Williams), remarks, "They [the city] called you their son." This line hints at the reversal strategy that determines the structure of the rest of the film: the father is also the son. While *The Sixth Sense* may at first appear to be primarily about Malcolm's parental and professional guilt, the more crucial narrative strand emphasizes the child's struggle. The film presents a vocational figure in Cole, the "gifted" child tormented by the unending desires of the dead to be heard and appeased. In the end, he accepts the burden of being a mediator, easing the suffering of both the living and dead and (crucially) explicitly accepting that these acts of kindness are not isolated instances of heroism but the first steps to a lifetime vocation.

Strikingly, most reviews deliberately deemphasized Bruce Willis's star turn in favor of Haley Joel Osment's remarkable performance as the gifted child. I think that this reflects not only the quality of Osment's work but the ideological slant of the film: it focuses unerringly on the *vocational* crisis. When the dubious pleasures of decoding the rather heavy-handed symbolism and clues that set up the surprise ending have begun to pall, there remains a resonant domestic drama with wider sociopolitical implications, one that uses familiar folkloric motifs to do its work.

A close reading of the film with the vocational theme in mind unearths numerous resonances. Can it be an accident that the film first depicts Cole fleeing into a church, echoing the heroes of centuries of ghost legends, who similarly seek the comfort of sacred ground and traditional knowledge? Or that two of the most important encounters between Malcolm and Cole play out in exactly this ancient place of refuge for the desperate? In the first church encounter, Malcolm underlines the traditional meaning of Cole's attraction to the sacred: "You know, in the olden days, in Europe, people used to hide out in churches. They would claim sanctuary." Much later, the two return to the church for a more open discussion, where it is suggested that the surest way to deal with ghosts is to "listen to them." A priestly representative usually, but not always, frames this precise statement of the vocational function. It seems appropriate, then, for the exchange to take place in such a location.

As if to underline the idea that Cole is beginning to grasp his social obligation, the following sequence has him explicitly performing the traditional vocational role. For the first time, he stops running from a desperate ghost and asks it, "Do you want to tell me something?" The film is not so much about clearing up any particular local or domestic trauma, laying any particular unsettled soul to rest, but rather about establishing the need for *commitment* to obligation.

Yet it is not enough to say that Cole, as a vocational figure, simply develops enough maturity to shoulder his social responsibility, an obligation that implicitly belongs to the audience as well. Cole's development takes place through interaction *with* the ghostly past. The relationship is complex: the father, Malcolm, teaches the son, helping him to understand his vocation; the son teaches the father to accept his fate, and thus to embrace social and historical limits. This last insight is quite traditional for ghost narratives. It is a form of exorcism, the insistence of the living that history cannot, and must not, dominate and overpower the present. Malcolm and Cole's evolving relationship (father/son, teacher/student, confessor/penitent) models the sane social organism's dialogue with history.

Shyamalan's work has been incredibly popular, attracting widespread media attention, and even eliciting fairly nuanced academic treatment.[6] And at least three of his major Hollywood pictures—*The Sixth Sense, Unbreakable* (2000), and *Signs* (2002)—are about accepting vocational responsibility, each more explicit than the last. Indeed, the hero of *Signs* is a faith-challenged minister who ends the film with a deliberate and conscious reshouldering of his obligation. I think that the commercial appeal of these films is grounded in their familiar themes and motifs. Behind the pleasures of surprise endings and thriller effects, word-of-mouth enthusiasm and multimillion-dollar marketing campaigns, *The Sixth Sense*, in particular, was successful at least partially because audiences identified with the folkloric traditions it treats so seriously.

But while Shyamalan's vision is undeniably appealing, and powerfully effective when read from a folkloric perspective, it remains politically and ethically problematic. *The Sixth Sense* may gesture toward the necessity of communal obligation as a corrective to ahistorical solipsism, yet its focus on a preadolescent vocational hero conveniently encourages viewers to avoid the larger questions implied by its neat resolution. What would a *mature* vocational attitude look like? How precisely would a sympathetic viewer make practical use of the ethical imperative that animates the film? How, in short, can the obligatory logic manifested by this vocational figure be translated into effective political praxis? Philip Strick's *Sight & Sound* review is the most insightful on this point because it grasps both the intensity and the disturbing implications of the ideas Shyamalan has set in motion: "But what kind of future awaits him in the employment of his now validated gift is left to the imagination" (1999, 54).

Shyamalan's film, like the features he has directed since, is unable or unwilling to answer these questions. It may be that the filmmaker simply lacks the sophistication to think through the implications of his vocational theme. But it may also be that the impasse reached by his films neatly articulates an anxiety characteristic of the current political state. Perhaps, he seems to suggest, a considered reappraisal of the vocational figure can point the way toward a politics grounded in relation to the Other. On the other hand, the overdetermined self-consciousness of his narrative conceits may mask a more disturbing possibility: that Other-centered ethics is literally impossible, that rational sociality is an unattainable phantom.

This possibility is suggested by *The Sixth Sense*'s dark twin, Alejandro Amenábar's *The Others* (2001). The tone of this film is far cooler, even starkly minimalist (for a major studio project), allowing it to capture the bleakness that follows from the vocational opportunity lost, the ghostly crisis made irresolvable. The film refuses Shyamalan's triumph, instead privileging a narrative of vocational absence, which implies a world overwhelmed by absolute political despair.

The Others, significantly focused on wartime experiences on the home front and the battlefield, is a novel variation on the Gothic tradition of the threatened domestic space. Nicole Kidman plays Grace Stewart, an isolated and desperate wife and mother during World War II, literally trapped with her two children inside an imposing, mausoleum-like house overrun with seemingly malignant spirits. For much of the film, Grace deals with both ghostly and earthly threats through denial, rote Catholic piety, and an ever-more obsessive insistence on domestic routine. These conventional avenues of socialized behavior are derived from the home-front tradition exemplified by such popular World War II films as *Mrs. Miniver* (William Wyler, 1942) and *Since You Went Away* (John Cromwell, 1944). But the anxieties that fueled these women's domestic routines are here accentuated to the point of hysteria. And Grace benefits from none of the social networks, neighbors, relief work, and community ritual that cushion Mrs. Miniver's fearful isolation.

In search of precisely that longed-for, but strangely absent, social interaction, Grace eventually gets up the courage to leave the house and seek help from the traditional source: the local parish priest. This gesture, precisely the one that resolves individual trauma and underlines the effectiveness of social institutions in traditional ghost narratives, turns out to be absolutely futile. Grace's aborted appeal to the traditional vocational figure (whom she never reaches) leaves her quite literally lost in a gray, featureless fog, out of which materializes the accusatory specter of Charles Stewart (Christopher Eccleston), her dead soldier/husband. This gaunt, almost-wordless figure recalls the ghostly soldiers in 1940s films like *A Matter of Life and Death* (1946) and *A Guy Named Joe* (1943), but he is bereft of their vivacity and effectiveness. Again, the hopeful spirit of 1940s-era war melodramas is drained away, leaving only longing and regret. Amenábar consistently refuses to give his subjects' narrative authority, foregrounding the frustration of desire at every turn.

The ghostly husband's arrival precipitates the final existential crisis in the film. Eventually we learn that Grace *herself* is a ghost, one who not only took her own life but the lives of her children as well. Pathological isolation is revealed to be absolute, and the maternal domesticity celebrated in an earlier generation's home-front films appears like an illusion. Grace's realization of her guilt is essentially empty because, as she learns from other denizens of the spectral world, she is beyond help from either earthly or spiritual sources. The film leaves the heroine and her family trapped in an eternal loop of domestic suffering and historical trauma.

The Others allegorically imagines a social order unwilling or unable to face its own past, ensuring that the domestic (national, political) landscape will be inhospitable to the living. After all, we learn in the final moments of the film that the household ghosts have ousted the next generation of (living) tenants, reserving this site of collective trauma for their own narratives of abjection. And by the end of the film, Grace has renounced that traditional ghostly appeal to be heard and remembered. *The Others*, remarkably for a commercial film, rejects this possibility. The audience experiences the failure of the spectral encounter from the *inside*, is made to grasp viscerally the possibility that the obligatory ethic is both absolutely essential and tragically unavailable.

Is it possible to live with this bleak possibility: that the committed relation of self to Other can be no more than fanciful abstraction, that history can be grasped only as a mindless violence that inevitably severs us from any meaningful communion with those who share our experience of cinema or the social world outside the theater? Shyamalan and Amenábar offer competing answers to these questions, and also to a more explicitly political one that animates many recent critiques of the "business as usual" of contemporary society: must individuals and local communities accept a passive, powerless role in the developing global economy? *The Sixth Sense* is perhaps overly optimistic on this point and flirts with sentimental dishonesty in its drive to please audiences. But Grace's despairing stasis at the end of *The Others* is more disturbing, echoing an image from Mark Achbar and Jennifer Abbott's 2004 documentary *The Corporation*. A pallid consumer is bathed in the baleful glow of his television, isolated from human contact, mute and unthinking.

The camera circles this virtually spectral figure, revealing the barcode stamped on the back of his neck. The filmmakers suggest that the ahistorical, disengaged passivity of the corporate consumer is not merely a side effect of mediated modernity but the logical endpoint of a society that has lost touch with the idea of social and historical obligation.[7] Without that obligatory relationship allegorized by the spectral encounter, and articulated in social terms through the vocational figure, we can look forward only to a sort of death-in-life, powerless to speak out for justice—to the other, to the earth, and to the memory of those who have gone before us.

Notes

1. Andrew Britton (1985) anticipates Nadel's "Reaganite entertainment" argument. Contemporary reviews of many of these films had already registered unease with their political implications. For representative examples, see Auty (1982), Chanko (1982), Kellner (1983), Sterrit (1989) and (1990), Brown (1990), Gretton (1990), Kelleher (1990), Rainer (1990), and Newman (1991).
2. For discussions of *Don't Look Now,* primarily from a psychoanalytic perspective, see Palmer and Riley (1995), Wilson (1999), and von der Lippe (1999). Only the Palmer/Riley piece, in its concern with the experience of belief, approximates the vocational focus of the present discussion.
3. For discussions of the disturbing implications of Oda Mae's erasure, see Rothenberg (1997) and Modleski (1991, 134).
4. Unsurprisingly, most reviews of *Stir of Echoes* remark on its unfortunate similarity to *The Sixth Sense,* but also its striking depiction of Chicago-area working-class life. Only Atkinson singles out the remarkable final image: "Bacon's spirit-conversant preschool son...sits tiny and implacable before a rising soundtrack storm of needy whispers" (1999, 146).
5. For discussion of the reactionary politics of *Field of Dreams,* see Nadel (1997, 50–53), Holden (1989), and Gretton (1990, 73–74).
6. The weightiest academic treatment of the film so far is La Caze (2002). Meanwhile, mainstream media has consistently treated its director with respect. For example, see Giles (2002).
7. For a discussion of the ethical thrust of *The Corporation'*s argument, see the interview with filmmaker Jennifer Abbott in West and West (2004).

Filmography

Beetlejuice (1988). 92 min. Tim Burton
The Changeling (1980). 115 min. Peter Medak
The Corporation (2003). 145 min. Mark Achbar and Jennifer Abbott
Don't Look Now (1973). 110 min Nicolas Roeg
Field of Dreams (1989). 107 min. Phil Alden Robinson

Ghost (1990). 128 min. Jerry Zucker
Ghostbusters (1984). 107 min. Ivan Reitman
Ghost Story (1981). 110 min. John Irvin
A Guy Named Joe (1943). 122 min. Victor Fleming
Lady in White (1988). 112 min. Frank LaLoggia
A Matter of Life and Death (Stairway to Heaven) (1946). 104 min. Michael Powell and Emeric Pressburger
Mrs. Miniver (1942). 134 min. William Wyler
The Others (2001). 101 min. Alejandro Amenábar
Poltergeist (1982). 114 min. Tobe Hooper
Rope (1948). 80 min. Alfred Hitchcock
Signs (2002). 106 min. M. Night Shyamalan
Since You Went Away (1944). 172 min. John Cromwell
The Sixth Sense (1999). 107 min. M. Night Shyamalan
Stir of Echoes (1999). 99 min. David Koepp
Unbreakable (2000). 106 min. M. Night Shyamalan

Works Cited

Atkinson, Michael. 1999. *Stir of echoes. Village Voice*, September 14, 146.
Auty, Chris. 1982. *Poltergeist. Monthly Film Bulletin* 49: 205–6.
Bennett, Gillian. 1999. *Alas, poor ghost! Traditions of belief in story and discourse.* Logan: Utah State University Press.
Bradley, Linda. 1995. *Film horror and the body fantastic.* Westport, CT: Greenwood Press.
Britton, Andrew. 1985. Blissing out: The politics of Reaganite entertainment. *Movie* 31–32: 2–21.
Brown, Georgia. 1990. *Village Voice*, November 6, 69.
Chanko, Kenneth M. 1982. *Poltergeist. Films in Review* 33: 430–31.
Derrida, Jacques. 1994. *Specters of Marx: The state of the debt, the work of mourning, and the new international.* Trans. Peggy Kamuf. New York: Routledge.
DiPiero, Thomas. 1997. Angels in the (out) field of vision. *Camera Obscura* 40–41:201–25.
duMaurier, Daphne. 1971. *Don't look now.* Garden City, New York: Doubleday.
Finucane, R. C. 1996. *Ghosts: Appearances of the dead and cultural transformation.* Amherst, NY: Prometheus Books.
Fowkes, Katherine. 1998. *Giving up the ghost: Spirits, ghosts and angels in mainstream comedy films.* Detroit: Wayne State University Press.
Freud, Sigmund. 1995. The uncanny. In *Psychological writings and letters,* ed. Sander L. Gilman, 120–53. New York: Continuum Press.
Giles, Jeff. 2002. Out of this world. *Newsweek,* August 5, 48.
Gretton, Viveca. 1990. You could look it up: Notes towards a reading of baseball, history, and ideology in the dominant cinema. *CineAction* 21–22: 73–74.
Holden, Steven. 1989. Today's hits yearn for old times. *New York Times,* Arts and Leisure Section, August 13, 25.
Jackson, Shirley. 1959. *The haunting of Hill House.* New York: Viking Press.
James, Henery. 1898. *The turn of the screw.* London: William Heinemann.

Kelleher, Terry. 1990. *Ghost*. *Newsday*, July 13, sec. 2, 13.

Kellner, Douglas. 1983. *Poltergeist:* Suburban identity. *Jump Cut* 28: 5–7.

La Caze, Marguerite. 2002. The mourning of loss in *The sixth sense*. *Post Script* 21 (3): 111–21.

Levinas, Emmanuel. 1982. *Ethics and infinity*. Pittsburgh: Duquesne University Press.

Modleski, Tania. 1991. *Feminism without women: Culture and criticism in a postfeminist age*. New York: Routledge.

Nadel, Alan. 1997. *Flatlining on the field of dreams: Cultural narratives in the films of President Reagan's America*. New Brunswick, NJ: Rutgers University Press.

Newman, Kim. 1991. *Jacob's Ladder*. *Sight & Sound* 105: 49.

Palmer, James, and Michael Riley. 1995. Seeing, believing and knowing in narrative film: *Don't look now* revisited. *Literature/Film Quarterly* 23 (1): 14–25.

Rainer, Peter. 1990. Casualties of gore. *Los Angeles Times*, October 30, C-1.

Rothenberg, Molly Anne. 1997. The "newer angels" and the living dead: The ethics of screening obsessional desire. *Camera Obscura* 40–41: 17–41.

Shakespeare, William. 1974. *The tragedy of Hamlet, prince of Denmark*. In *The Riverside Shakespeare*, ed. G. Blakemore Evans, 1135–97. Boston: Houghton Mifflin.

Sterrit, David. 1989. Fantasy baseball yarn flounders on sheer niceness. *Christian Science Monitor*, May 2, 11.

———. 1990. *Ghost* provides a second rate showcase for a first rate talent. *Christian Science Monitor*, August 22, 11.

Strick, Philip. 1999. *The sixth sense*. *Sight & Sound* 8: 54.

Tangherlini, Timothy. 1998. 'Who ya gonna call?': Ministers and the mediation of ghostly threat in Danish legend tradition. *Western Folklore* 57: 153–78.

von der Lippe, George B. 1999. *Death in Venice* in literature and film: Six 20th century versions. *Mosaic* 32 (1): 35–54.

West, Dennis, and Joan M. West. 2004. The life and times of *The corporation*. *Cineaste* 30 (1): 28–33.

Wilson, Kristi. 1999. Time, space and vision: Nicolas Roeg's *Don't look now*. *Screen* 40 (3): 277–94.

III.

THROUGH FOLKLORE'S LENSES

7

Märchen as Trauma Narrative

Helma Sanders-Brahms's Film Germany, Pale Mother

MARGARETE JOHANNA LANDWEHR

*"Deeper meaning lies in the fairy tales of my
childhood than in the truth taught by life."*

—Friedrich Schiller, *The Piccolomini*,
3.4.93 (my translation)

Storytelling as a Means of Survival

In GERMANY, PALE *Mother* (1980), Helma Sanders-Brahms depicts her childhood experiences in Germany during and after World War II. The film's tripartite structure consists of the prewar courtship of the film-maker's parents, the wartime tribulations and adventures of mother and child, and the postwar era of domestic misery. In an attempt to survive during the war, mother, Lene (Eva Mattes), and child, Anna (Anna Sanders), form a self-sufficient bond that excludes the father, Hans (Ernst Jacobi), who returns from the war an embittered man. His desperate, sometimes brutal efforts to reassert his authority drive Lene to silence and ultimately to a suicide attempt, which the daughter prevents.

The cinematic narrative represents Sanders-Brahms's attempt to give her mother a voice by telling her story as well as that of the German women who experienced the war. Thus, the film depicts the relationship between national and family history, between the public and private spheres, which is a dominant motif in postwar German (and French) cinema, particularly in films by women. As Helen Fehervary observes, "Whether it be the writer Christa Wolf or the filmmaker Helma Sanders-Brahms reflecting on fascism, women have managed to describe—without all the abstract theoretical paraphernalia—the relationship between history and subjective processes. They show that it is not a matter of grasping the truth in history as some objective entity, but in finding the truth of the experience"(1982, 176).

Although Sanders-Brahms poignantly portrays German women's experience during the war and postwar years, feminists take issue with her use of a melodramatic plot that portrays women as powerless, as victimized. Ellen Seiter argues, "The use of the melodramatic code...creates enormous obstacles to the filmmaker's attempt to historicize the events of the mother's life and to see her suffering in terms of a broader social context....Like the conventional melodramatic victim, Lene is acted upon, but disengaged from her social world. She is assigned to the emotional and psychological, as neither resistance nor participation in history was possible" (1986, 574–78). Seiter claims that the film's central section, which portrays Lene and Anna wandering the German countryside as they attempt to survive the end of the war, transcends political reality. Mother and daughter appear to enjoy an idyllic existence of self-sufficiency separate from the devastation of war.

Not all critics agree, however, that the women are depicted as relegated to a personal realm that is separated from the political one. The juxtaposition of Lene's fictionalized personal story with documentary war footage demonstrates "the intrusion of the historical reality into her mother's life and her entrance into the 'public realm' of history" (McCormick 1993, 191). The women's "idyllic" journey contains not only references to war, such as a dead soldier, but also to the Holocaust. A smokestack of an abandoned factory suggests a crematorium. It appears while Lene recites to Anna the fairy tale of "The Robber Bridegroom," which depicts a "house of murderers." Both the visual and verbal metaphors serve as indirect references to the Holocaust and concentration camps. In an interview, Sanders-Brahms stated that she deliberately inserted the *Märchen* sequence into the film script to represent not only women's fear of men but also German history (Moehrmann 1980, 155).

Thus, as Lene narrates "The Robber Bridegroom" to Anna during their trek through war-torn Germany she presents an apt trope for both her own story and women's experience during and after the war (Sanders-Brahms 1984, 115–16). Although the film depicts the victimization of both mother and country, Lene's act of telling the story portrays women not merely as survivors but also as subjects in history, not as conquerors, as narrators of their own stories. Lene transcends her victim status through the power of storytelling, a means of survival and self-determination that she passes on to her daughter and that is illustrated by the fairy tale's ending, which recounts the triumph of a potential victim over her persecutors.

The Grimms' tale that Lene recites affirms the power of speech, of narration, in overcoming one's enemies. In the story, a young, naïve bride witnesses her fiancé and his cohorts murder a young woman and eat her flesh. When one of the robbers cuts off the victim's finger in order to retrieve her golden ring, it flies into the hidden bride's breast. A friendly older woman dissuades the robbers from searching for it and helps the bride to escape and return home. Claiming her story is merely a dream, the heroine recites it during a feast for her family, the groom, and guests, then suddenly produces the finger, bringing about the capture and execution of the groom and his gang. The director chose to insert the folktale sequence instead of Lene's rape by Russian soldiers and subsequent abortion and regarded the substitution as one of the more successful aspects of the film (Sanders-Brahms 1984, 116). The filmmaker's act thus paralleled that of the bride's: both chose to expose criminals—whether robbers or soldiers—through narrative (Hyams 1988, 49). Through her film, Sanders-Brahms simultaneously broke the chain of silence so pervasive in German women of her mother's generation and demonstrated the power of speech, of story.

Although Lene's silence is ubiquitous in the film's initial and concluding sections, in the central section the director depicts her as both survivor and storyteller. Through a voice-over in the film's initial scene, Sanders-Brahms observes: "My mother. 'I have learned to remain silent,' you said. From you, I have learned to speak. Mother tongue." Just as the elder woman rescues the bride in the Grimms' tale, so too Lene enables her daughter to survive by passing her means of enduring hardship, her storytelling, down to her to retell in her film. Lene's ability to find food and shelter for Anna and her in a war-ravaged landscape provides the backdrop to her repetitious telling of the tale, which underscores the role of storytelling, in particular of folktales, as a survival tactic. Reciting a story about the eventual triumph of victim over perpetrator sustains mother and daughter during their long trek through danger, offering hope that the powerless—women and children—can escape violence and survive through their wits and speech, just as Scheherazade in *The Thousand and One Nights* saved her life by enchanting the sultan with her nightly tales.

As Jack Zipes has noted, *Märchen* were told to "provide hope in a world seemingly on the brink of catastrophe." The hope they fostered was that "miracles involving some kind of magical transformation were possible to bring about a better world" (1996, 370–71). Zipes calls wondrous metamorphosis the key theme of the folktale. Simpletons become princes and lowly maids such as Cinderella become queens. The potential victim of "The Robber Bridegroom" turns the tables on the robbers and brings them to justice. In many folktales, the power of metamorphosis is in the hands of women, as fairies (Zipes 1996, 380). Not surprisingly, the value system of the folktale, including the emphases on compassion and on the hope that the low and meek will triumph, often gives precedence to the powerless. Furthermore, a central message in many folktales is that the weak and oppressed—such as children, women, and members of the working classes—can survive through brains, if not brawn.

Thus, folktales in which lowly heroes or heroines overcome obstacles and rivals and enemies through their wits function as narratives of the dispossessed. In his landmark essay "On the Oppositional Practices of Everyday Life," Michel de Certeau claimed, "Popular cultures, proverbs, tales, folk wisdom, have long seemed to be the place in which such a hero ('the ordinary man') might be sought and reidentified." In distinguishing between strategies, "actions dependent on a space of power," and tactics, "the calculated action which is determined by the absence of a proper place," de Certeau stated that tactics such as narratives found in popular culture constitute "an art of the weak." In particular, "Where dominating powers exploit the order of things, where ideological discourse represses or ignores it, tactics fool this order and make it the field of their art" (1980, 3–7). Moreover, de Certeau claimed that storytelling constitutes theory and practice, both "an art of doing and an art of thinking." In other words, "a tactic [is]... a way of scoring or taking a trick: the narrative does not merely *describe* such a 'hit,' it *effects* one in its own right: ...skill at manipulating, arranging, 'placing' a given utterance and displacing a preexisting set of relations, all are artfully combined" (1980, 33–34). Thus, the young bride's artful telling of her frightening experience as a mere dream and her timely revelation of the narrative's true nature by suddenly displaying the victim's finger aptly demonstrate oral storytelling as a tactic of theory and practice, of narrative and action, of description and effect. As de Certeau observes, the moment of tactics, the moment of art, occurs when opportunities are "grasped, not created" and "the maximum effect is obtained with minimal force" (1980, 37, 40).

A tactic, however, does not achieve permanent change in the existing order: "What it gains cannot be held....It must vigilantly utilize the gaps which the particular combination of circumstances open in the control of the proprietary power. It poaches there. It creates surprises. It is possible for it to be where no one expects it. It is wile. In sum it is an art of the weak" (de Certeau 1980, 6). The conclusion of the Grimms' "The Robber Bridegroom" illustrates de Certeau's description of tactics, literally and metaphorically. Although the bride temporarily upsets the preexisting order of patriarchal power through her narrative, she has not permanently overthrown it. She may have escaped the marriage that her father sought for her, but she has not undermined the patriarchal order in which arranged marriages occur.

Sanders-Brahms's film underscores the temporary character of the dispossessed's victory in the ideal *Märchen* world with the horrific worlds of war and of the postwar period, in which the disparity between powerful evil-doers and helpless victims suggests that not much has changed. Lene's rape by American soldiers abruptly interrupts her narration and depicts the cruel reality of her powerlessness. This shocking scene, witnessed by Anna, contrasts sharply with the bride's triumph over the robber bridegroom. Victimized folktale heroines such as Cinderella rise or return to the ranks of royalty after they have suffered, but Lene suffers without enjoying the fruits of West Germany's Economic Miracle. The bride escapes her ogre of a bridegroom; Lene must endure her husband's harsh treatment. Justice triumphs in the tale; Lene's rapists never answer for their crime. In the postwar period, ex-Nazis advance quickly in their careers while Lene's husband, who never joined the party, is left behind. The bride's story empowers her; Lene and Anna survive, but remain victims of a patriarchal society.

The contrast between the just world of the *Märchen* and the unjust nature of Nazi and postwar Germany supports William Bascom's claim that one of the four functions of folklore is an attempt to escape into fantasy from the repressions and taboos imposed by society (1965, 290). "The Robber Bridegroom" offers the hope that the weak and lowly, specifically women, can survive and overcome stronger and more powerful predators through their wits and speech. Similarly, Lene's narration of the fairy tale allows mother and child to form an idyllic utopia of self-sufficiency sequestered from the horrors of war.

Thus, although the central part of the film, like the *Märchen*, provides a temporary escape from the harsh, violent reality of war, Lene's suffering in the rest of the cinematic narrative reminds the viewer that such a utopia is not sustainable. This juxtaposition of the ideal, just world of the folktale with Lene's real experiences emphasizes the need for a woman's cinematic narrative that can serve as an instrument for real social change. *Germany, Pale Mother* critiques the horrors of war and the repression of a patriarchal postwar society and provides a voice for Lene and women of her generation, but it does not offer an alternative vision for a more egalitarian society.

Folktale as Trauma Narrative

Germany, Pale Mother does not offer a new cinematic narrative that can spur social change; if viewed as a trauma narrative, it does suggest a different sort of transformation: it enables the filmmaker to confront her past, albeit in fictionalized form, and transform suffering into something creative and life affirming. The cinematic retelling of her traumatic child-hood bears witness to the past and enables her to reshape it, create mean-ing out of suffering, and establish a new identity, moving from passive, helpless victim of history to active creator of her and her mother's life stories. These three elements of *Germany, Pale Mother*—reinterpretation of the past, discovery of meaning, and creation of a new self—constitute the central components of successful trauma narrative.

Similarly, the transformation through numerous trials and tribula-tions of a folktale protagonist from a powerless victim to a more mature, effective person constitutes the central plotline in *Märchen*, which con-sequently serve as an appropriate model for trauma narrative. If we consider how and why some western folktales can function as trauma narratives, we can see how Lene's reciting of "The Robber Bridegroom" serves as a microcosm for the Sanders-Brahms's cinematic narrative. Folktales and most films are each products of popular culture—in this instance, German popular culture—and they contain common language and motifs that allow communication between patient and therapist and director and audience alike.

The therapeutic role of reciting and listening to folktales has been acknowledged. by traditional psychoanalysts such as the Freudian Bruno Bettelheim, Carl Jung, and Marie-Louise von Franz and more contempo-rary therapists such as the storyteller Mary Gordon. Gordon has noted that "stories naturally invite us to examine our own lives and choices and then to grow beyond them" and stated further that stories invite us "to envision new possibilities" and "to see that despite the way we feel, and sometimes behave, each of us can sustain losses and yet be generative, caring, and competent" (1993, 266). While stories enable us to confront our own sufferings through empathy with a protagonist, they also draw a boundary between the world of fiction and our reality, establishing a safe distance between the tribulations of protagonists and our world. This dual role of narratives, particularly folktales, in evoking empathy with the characters while also protecting us from direct confrontation with dif-ficult issues provides the effective mechanisms of trauma narrative.

Drawing upon Husserl's philosophy and Pennebaker's clinical experiments, Aaron Mishara explains the therapeutic results of narrating traumatic events. Pennebaker (1990) discovered the healing power of confiding to others. For example, students who wrote about their traumatic experiences showed significant improvement in immune responsiveness, physical health, and remission of psychosomatic symptoms (Pennebaker, Hughes, and O'Heeron 1987). Pennebaker claimed that coping with trauma could be "speeded up" through writing about it and explained that writing is healing because it translates an emotional experience into a cognitive-linguistic one. He and Harber stated that "language brings about the organization and assimilation of traumatic memories and experiences" (1992, 360).

Mishara offered an alternative explanation for the salutary effects of narrating trauma. He claimed that narration enables one to establish distance from and transcend the narrated, traumatized self:

The healing factor in both writing and the talking cure is the changed *relationship* of the subject to his or her own past painful experiencing by virtue of a narrative act. This act brings reflective distance and insight.... From the phenomenological point of view, the narration of an event, even if one's self is the only auditor or witness, makes possible the actively taking up of a new perspective in which the formerly envisioned self, the self that passively suffered the event, is now experienced as "other" to the present self. By means of the narrative act the narrating subject in the present moment of becoming detaches from the subject who experienced the traumatic or painful experience. (1995, 187)

Furthermore, through narration, the traumatic event itself is perceived as past: "The event is experienced as no longer present, or having direct 'affective' connection with the present.... As now past, sealed off from the present, it no longer overwhelms the subject in emotional pain" (Mishara 1995, 189).

Sanders-Brahms's film clearly portrays this split between past and present selves: the director is depicted in the film as a helpless child, yet the occasional voice-over of the filmmaker, which intrudes into various scenes, reminds the spectator of the mature director, who has survived the war and her parents' volatile marriage and now has control over unfolding the plot on both a personal and a political, historical level. Kaja Silverman analyzes the significance of the female voice-over, which is almost completely absent in Hollywood films: "The female subject...is excluded from positions of discursive authority both outside and inside the classic film diegesis; she is confined not only to a safe place *of* the story, but to the safe places *within* the story (to positions, that is, which come within the eventual range of male vision or audition)" (1988, 164).

Thus, Sanders-Brahms underscores her own position of authority as narrator and filmmaker when she not only speaks for her mother in the film and reconstructs their common past together but also offers an alternative account of the war, as a "history from below," that is, as a narrative of the common suffering of civilians, particularly women and children, from a female perspective.

The use of symbols and metaphors constitutes one means of achieving the necessary distance from, transcendence of, a traumatic past (and victimized self) through narrative. The benefits of using metaphor in psychotherapy to treat patients are well known. Jacob Arlow explains, "Because of the element of displacement of meaning, metaphor readily lends itself as a means of warding off anxiety" (1979, 371). Metaphor enables the patient to maintain a safe distance from the traumatic content while also allowing the expression of emotion. In particular, "The themes that cluster around the metaphor during the course of therapy often lead to the discovery of an unconscious fantasy that is usually connected with some trauma" (Arlow 1979, 380).

Some therapists stimulate the patient's associations by using metaphors taken from folklore. They are effective in therapy because patient and therapist are familiar with the plot lines, which strengthens their relationship since studies have shown that sharing a common language and culture enhances the analyst's empathy for the patient. This use of common cultural metaphors in the analyst/patient dialogue resembles the process of aesthetic communication: "The devices that make poetry and enable the poet to transmit to others the emotion he experiences are the same ones which make the patient's material assume configurations that transmit meaning and emotion to the therapist, making empathy possible. Contiguity, repetition, symbolism, allusion, contrast, and, above all, metaphor...are the most important of these devices." (Beres and Arlow 1974, 45)

In Sanders-Brahms's film, Lene's reciting of the Grimms' tale with its allusions to brutality and murder clearly serves as an extended metaphor for the terrors of war, particularly for women, as well as the horrors of the Holocaust that are alluded to in the central scene. For example, just as Lene mentions the ashes that the bride of the tale strews along her path, the factory smokestack reminiscent of a crematorium appears along Lene and Anna's path. Thus, the folktale mirrors the cinematic story itself as trauma narrative. Both are fictionalized representations of suffering, the ultimate survival of the victims, and their power over the past. Both Lene and her daughter, the filmmaker, survive the war, albeit scarred, and Sanders-Brahms creates a work of art from their tribulations.. Both the Grimms' tale and the film incorporate a figure, heroine or filmmaker, who retells the sufferings of a past self that no longer exists but has been integrated into the continuity of the storyteller's life through the act of narrating.

The *Märchen* serves as a perfect paradigm for the trauma narrative in general. Psychoanalysts such as Bruno Bettelheim, folklorists such as Jack Zipes, and writers such as J. R. R. Tolkien have noted the therapeutic effects of narrating folktales. Bettelheim suggested that *Märchen* provide an effective educational tool with which children can come to terms with such dilemmas and fears as anxiety over abandonment by one's parents or feelings of inadequacy. He claimed that folktales externalize inner processes and that "Fairy tales intimate that a rewarding, good life is within one's reach despite adversity—but only if one does not shy away from the hazardous struggles without which one can never achieve true identity" (1977, 24). He pointed out that the use of these tales in therapy had not been limited to western psychoanalysis but had been practiced for centuries elsewhere.[1] Similarly, Zipes has suggested that *Märchen* can disguise common human fears and conflicts through the use of metaphors. He argued that folktale plots externalize in symbolic form universal psychic conflicts such as the fears of being alone and unprotected in a dangerous world, of the loss of love, and of failure and, thus, provide a rich source for metaphors of common human problems.

Some folklorists find Bettelheim's and Zipes' hypotheses problematic, claiming they cannot be verified and noting that they view folktales as depicting universal rather than culture-specific themes. For example, in *The Dynamics of Folklore*, Barre Toelken pointed out that folktales with similar plots may have different connotative meanings that "reside not as manifest content in the item or text or in the denotation of words, but in the feelings and associations people share about the items, situations and words. Since these attitudes are usually culture-specific, the deepest meanings seldom arise openly from the text but need to be extrapolated from ethnographic evidence as well as further discussion from the tradition bearers themselves" (Toelken 1996, 246). Thus, the European and American hero/heroine tales in which the protagonist leaves home and bravely confronts dangers during the journey have a positive connotation whereas a similar plot in another culture, such as the Sun Myth, a Kathlamet Chinook text, portrays the adventurer as egotistical and his actions as destroying the culture (Toelken 1996, 257). If the former tale depicts the western emphasis on the development of the individual, the latter focuses on the well-being of the community, of the clan.

Consequently, it needs to be said that Bettelheim's and Zipes's views of the function of the fairy tale themselves represent not a universal but a culture-specific viewpoint, a traditional western and masculine perspective. It should be assumed, then, that all discussion of folktales in this essay refers to western, European or European-American tales.

Irrespective of Bettelheim's or Zipes' specific interpretations of the therapeutic role of folktales, both folklorists and storytellers have observed that stories trigger in their audiences provocative insights into their own lives. Susan Gordon, for example, discussed her listeners' reaction to her retelling of her version of the Grimms' tale, "The Handless Maiden," noting that those who had been abused as children recognized themselves in the maiden whose father cut off her hands (Gordon 1993, 274). "The Handless Maiden" concludes with the protagonist regaining her hands while saving her child from drowning and then reuniting with her husband, the King, and thereby illustrates the ability to survive trauma and even thrive. Gordon observed "that even handless we are capable of the choices of maturation and development" (1993, 284). Her listeners' identification with the heroine and her tale demonstrated that such Freudian mechanisms as compensation and projection of repressed desires could occur in listeners or readers of folktales.

In a similar vein, Bettelheim believed that *Märchen* provide characters onto which the child, not a society, can project either taboo desires or compensatory scenarios. An evildoer, for example, can embody the child's destructive wishes, whereas the simpleton who makes his way in the world may represent the child's own fears of succeeding on his or her own terms; the simpleton's eventual realization of his goals offers consolation that success is achievable. In *Germany, Pale Mother*, the mother's reciting of "The Robber Bridegroom," which concludes with the bride's triumph over the robbers through a helper and her own wits, clearly provides hope that mother and child will successfully navigate the dangers along their path. The role of folktales in offering hope becomes especially poignant in the scene after the rape. Despite the abuse, Lene does not give into despair but continues telling the tale of the triumphant bride with unexpected resilience.

According to J. R. R. Tolkien, recovery from despair constitutes one of the essential elements of the folktale. The other three are fantasy, escape from danger, and consolation. Except for fantasy, these folktale components are also essential components of successful therapy (1996, 271–86).[2] Indeed Lene's repeated telling of the triumph of the bride over the robber bridegroom clearly serves as a means of consoling Anna and reminding her that ultimately we can triumph over difficulties and survive. As Tolkien pointed out, folktales offer the greatest consolation because they often portray the Great Escape, the escape from death (1996, 284). Lene and Anna's journey through a war-ravaged country, which requires a daily search for food, shelter, and safety, poignantly underscores the need for such consolation. By retelling this tale in her film and contrasting its optimistic message with the harsh realities of life, Sanders-Brahms offers her own daughter a different tale in which the triumphant ending consists in the ability only to survive but also to create meaning out of suffering through narrative.

The positive metamorphosis of the central character of a western folktale from naïve child vulnerable to the manipulations of others during his or her trials and tribulations to a self-sufficient actor on the world stage mirrors the transformation that frequently occurs with trauma victims after they recite their stories. In *Morphology of the Folktale*, Vladimir Propp notes that in most tales the protagonist has to endure a difficult task, whether it is an ordeal by fire, riddle guessing, or a test of strength, endurance, or fortitude. When the task is resolved, the hero or heroine is usually recognized and often undergoes a transfiguration, resulting in a new appearance, and/or gets married, a mark of entering mature adulthood (1968, 60–64).

Similarly, Max Lüthi claims that "the fairy tale depicts processes of development and maturation" (1996, 298). Bettelheim has observed that folktale heroes and heroines often experience a reawakening or rebirth that "symbolizes the reaching of a higher state of maturity and understanding. It is one of the fairy tale's ways to stimulate the wish for higher meaning in life: deeper consciousness, more self-knowledge, and greater maturity" (1977, 214). He further claims that the essential lesson of these tales is "that if one wishes to gain selfhood, achieve integrity, and secure one's identity, difficult developments must be undergone: hardships suffered, dangers met, victories won" (1977, 278). Similarly, trauma narratives enable their tellers to integrate their former victimized selves into their life scripts and make the transition from helpless victims to active, mature participants in life.

In the voice-over narration of her film, Sanders-Brahms clearly states some personal insights that she has gained by retelling her family's story, such as her decision not to marry. Scenes that reenact the discord and anguish that marked her parents' marriage offer a probable reason for this choice. Nevertheless, her decision to bear a child attests to the strength of her bond to her mother and implies the optimistic view that the next generation of women may profit and learn from their mothers' (and grandmothers') suffering.

As Carol Gilligan has repeatedly observed, when women let their voices be heard, the world itself can be transformed: "As we have listened for centuries to the voices of men and the theories of development that their experience informs, so we have come more recently to notice not only the silence of women but the difficulty in hearing what they say when they speak. Yet in the different voice of women lies the truth of an ethic of care, the tie between relationship and responsibility, and the origins of aggression in the failure of connection" (1993, 173). Thus, the bride's escape from her treacherous bridegroom in the Grimms' tale and the subsequent opportunity to reveal his treachery result from female solidarity, from the old woman's assistance in her escape. Similarly, Lene and Anna are able to survive the war years and the postwar domination of husband and father through their close bonds. Lene as a mother feels an obligation to take care of her child and to survive, and in turn her child prevents her suicide by reminding her of their connection. Similarly, the handless maiden in Gordon's tale only recovers her hands when she saves her child. Conversely, as Gilligan notes, the origins of aggression lie in the failure of such connection. Because of his separation from his wife and child during the war years, Anna's father has no intimate link with them, and the only relationship that he knows how to establish is one of dominance and submission.

Finally, the political, subversive aspect of this feminist director's film cannot be ignored. The narratives of "The Robber Bridegroom," the mother's *Märchen,* and Sanders-Brahm's voice-over offer a critique of patriarchal culture and male-dominated narrative. In "Oppositional Practices in Women's Traditional Narrative," Marie Maclean discussed the subversive nature of some seemingly utopian folktales. Drawing upon de Certeau's theory of "tactics," Maclean pointed out that folktales constituted an important aspect of women's subculture and that women have employed de Certeau's "tactics" of the weak with them. Maclean noted that Metis, the divinity of tactics, is the first wife of Zeus and the goddess of nets, associated with the powers of binding and unbinding. Metis, who represents the overcoming of the strong by the weak, is swallowed by Zeus and becomes the hidden mother of the goddess of wisdom, Athena, who springs out of Zeus's head. Observing that folktales were the province of female storytellers until they "became the property" of Monsieur Perrault, the brothers Grimm, and other men, Maclean interpreted Zeus's swallowing of Metis "as the symbol of the constant reterritorialization of popular culture and especially of women's culture by the ideologically dominant" (1987, 40–41). From the subgenre of folktales that depict violence and women's suffering and resistance, Maclean chose "The Robber Bridegroom" as a paradigm of female solidarity and stratagems against violence. She described women's tale-telling as an oppositional practice and cited the bride's revelation of her experiences in the bridegroom's lair as a combination of narrative authority and audience manipulation. She drew plot parallels between the fairy tale and *Germany, Pale Mother* and observed that the feminist filmmaker used the tale to great effect in the film because she knew the hidden messages of women's traditional tales

Thus, Sanders-Brahms's film narrative, which alternates, from a woman and child's perspective, among the pre-war, war, and postwar years in Germany, is an oppositional practice that counters the numerous male versions of the war by depicting women's strength and solidarity. By bequeathing her life story to her own daughter—who also is named Anna, who stars in the film, and to whom the film is dedicated—the filmmaker belongs to a long tradition of women telling folktales to their daughters. For, as Marie Maclean noted, despite the Grimms' assertion that the "vast numbers" of stories and customs were handed down from father to son, in actuality at least eighty percent of their tales were collected from female informants.[3] Cinema, which reaches millions, serves as an effective popular culture medium to communicate not only personal and collective stories but those of nations.

Film as Collective Trauma Narrative

Sanders-Brahms's use of a German *Märchen* with its dual ability to distance the narrator-filmmaker as well as spectators from horrific historical events while also evoking empathy from a German audience that shares the artist's past and cultural heritage, including its folktales, offers a cinematic model for a collective trauma narrative that both remembers and mourns a painful past while also holding out the hope of overcoming it. The criteria for this model come from traditional psychoanalysis as well as contemporary film studies.

Citing Freud's "Mourning and Melancholia" and Alexander and Margarete Mitscherlichs' 1975 study on postwar Germans' inability to mourn the past, Eric Santner (1990) examined the role of art, particularly film, as an instrument of mourning. Believing that the sense of self develops around the child's initial separation from the mother, Freud claimed that the capacity to mourn depends on the child's early ability to regard the (m)other as a separate human being. Thus, if distinct boundaries are established between self and other, there is "space" for empathy that enables one person truly to grieve another's loss. Conversely, melancholy results if this separation is not achieved and the lost love object is regarded as an extension of the self (Freud 1957, 14:244–45). Drawing upon Freud's theory of mourning, the Mitscherlichs stated that *Trauerarbeit* or mourning never took place in postwar Germany, because Germans identified with Hitler and used such defense mechanisms as identification with the victim that prevented guilt from surfacing (1975, 4). Santner focused on Freud's observation that the lack of anxiety, rather than the actual loss, traumatizes the patient. This emotion can be recuperated and overcome only with an empathetic witness present. In the case of a child, a parent could play the role of witness; for a trauma victim, it could be an empathetic analyst (1990, 25).

An artistic endeavor can enable the adult to deal with a past trauma just as the capacity for imaginative play allows a toddler to convert a sense of helplessness at the mother's disappearance into a feeling of power. In "Beyond the Pleasure Principle," Freud stated that the fort/da ("hide-and-seek") game that his grandson played allowed him to overcome his grief at separation from his mother by creating his own game of disappearance and reappearance (1955, 18:14–15). Thus, the game served as a homeopathic means of reenacting the separation and controlling its outcome. Similarly, a creative project enables the artist to transform, to reconstruct, a loss into a work of art and thus allows the creator control over the (fictionalized) event. Moreover, a trauma narrative empowers the narrator/artist to break through psychic numbness, a common reaction to trauma, by allowing an empathetic listener/observer to bear witness to one's past. For example, participants in Yale's Holocaust Survivors Film Project felt empowered by narrating their past suffering in the presence of sympathetic listeners (Hartmann 1996, 152–54).

Santner cited the German director's Edgar Reitz's belief that film is an inherently elegiac medium (1990, 67–72). In *Liebe zum Kino* (Love of Film), Reitz claimed that cinema is the last available site for funerary ritual in a consumer society: "When one looks closely, film always has something to do with parting. Film concerns itself with things and people that disappear from our sensory perception, with this pain that every good frame reproduces and produces. ...Parting is the great theme of film" (Reitz quoted in Santner 1990, 68–69). In a similar vein, Susan Sontag noted, "Photography is an elegiac art, a twilight art. Most subjects photographed are, just by virtue of being photographed, touched with pathos....All photographs are memento mori. To take a photograph is to participate in another person's (or thing's mortality), vulnerability, mutability. Precisely by slicing out this moment and freezing it, all photographs testify to time's relentless melt" (1977, 15).

Because of film's elegiac nature, Santner believes that an audience should be able to experience the mourning process through cinema: "Film invites viewers to overcome a chronic inability to mourn precisely by becoming sensitized to the experience of chronos, that is, the passing of time and the losses and separations that belong to their being-in-time" (1990, 72). Thus film serves as a medium for collective mourning by recounting a country's traumatic past that elicits spectators' empathy.

How can cinematic images elicit this empathy? The seemingly continual onslaught of horrific images of war or other violence in documentaries, feature films, and television news can overwhelm spectators, who may react with horror or helplessness, shock or numbed indifference, rather than sympathy. Such troubling images may even cause secondary trauma in viewers, who may feel a sense of powerlessness when confronting their inability to change the situation (Hartmann 1996,152–54).

Sanders-Brahms's feature film constitutes an effective means to induce public mourning of the past as it elicits from the audience not only emotional involvement but also intellectual distance, two prerequisites for mourning. The film establishes a common human bond in suffering between the fictional characters and audience through melodramatic devices and also creates a distance between spectators and characters through Brechtian disruptions of the melodramatic plot. This distance allows viewers to separate from the film narrative and the characters. As Freud pointed out, this ability to distinguish between self and other enables the audience to empathize, to reflect on the unique suffering of others as well as their own losses, and to mourn.

Although critics of Sanders-Brahms's film such as Seiter claim that *Germany, Pale Mother* constitutes a melodramatic, apolitical narrative of women's role in the war, Richard McCormick has pointed out that the melodramatic plot is undercut with cinematic distancing techniques in the tradition of Fassbinder, a leading director of the New German Cinema (1993, 195).[4] In particular, although the narrative focuses on Lene's excessive suffering and contains such melodramatic plot devices as love and loss, loyalty and betrayal, and the erosion of domestic bliss, Brechtian distancing techniques such as the voice-over narration break the illusion of reality and remind the spectator that the film is a fictional, artificial construct and interrupts emotional identification with the characters. For example, Sanders-Brahms opens her film with a reading of a Brecht poem by his daughter Hanna Hiob, which draws the viewer's attention to the film's discursive nature (McCormick 1993, 195). Other distancing techniques include the intercutting of documentary war footage, such as seemingly interminable aerial shots of bombed-out German cities, with scenes from Lene's life, such as the birth of her daughter. An especially disorienting distancing technique is choosing Eva Mattes, who plays Lene, to also portray a Polish peasant and a French partisan, whom Hans and other German soldiers execute. The voice-over, the splicing of documentary sequences into the fictional narrative, the multiple casting of Eva Mattes, and an occasionally dissonant musical score all remind the audience that the film is a fictional construct, the filmmaker's manipulation of past events into her own personal narrative.

Sanders-Brahms claims that she inserted the *Märchen* because it served not only as an appropriate metaphor for women's war experiences but also as an effective distancing (*Verfremdung*) technique (Moehrmann 1980, 156).[5] The folktale not only interrupts the fictional narrative as a story-within-a-story but also comments on the film's visuals, including a soldier's corpse, a smokestack, an oven, documentary footage of a bombed-out Berlin, and Lene's rape, all of which establish a connection between the folktale and its historical context (McCormick 1993, 201).

Consequently, the *Märchen* sequence works as a distancing technique in both a psychological and an aesthetic sense. As a metaphor, as a fictional construct, it enables the narrator/filmmaker to distance herself from her childhood trauma. As a Brechtian alienation technique, it breaks the illusion of fiction, which allows the spectator to gain distance from the story and the characters and to reflect upon and mourn the losses and horrors of the war. Thus, the folktale and the film function as both a personal trauma narrative and a collective one that elicits empathy for the artist and her mother as well as Holocaust victims and German women and children who suffered in the war.

Some Holocaust narratives such as Jane Yolen's *Briar Rose* (2002; originally published in 1997) or Louise Murphy's *The True Story of Hansel and Gretel: A Novel of War and Survival* (2003) employ or refer to folktales. Conversely, contemporary fairy tales such as Gregory Maguire's *Wicked: The Life and Times of the Wicked Witch of the West* (1995) allude to the Third Reich and the Holocaust.[6] Thus, the fairy tale becomes an appropriate narrative device that enables its creator to grapple with traumas too painful to confront directly. As a genre, it no longer is relegated to the nursery. Whether on the psychoanalyst's couch or the public forum of the stage or cinema, the fairy tale has the ability to depict universal human fears and provide language to express the unspeakable.

Notes

1. "In a fairy tale, internal processes are externalized and become comprehensible as represented by the figures of the story and its events. This is the reason why in traditional Hindu medicine a fairy tale giving form to his [or her] particular problem was offered to a psychically disoriented person, for his meditation. It was expected that through contemplating the story, the disturbed person would be led to visualize both the nature of the impasse in living from which he suffered, and the possibility of its resolution. From what a particular tale implied about man's [or woman's] despair, hopes and methods of overcoming tribulations, the patient could discover not only a way out of his distress but also a way to find himself as the hero of the story did" (Bettelheim 1977, 25).

2. Bettelheim makes a similar observation: "Consolation is the greatest service that a fairy tale can offer a child: the confidence that despite all tribulations that he [or she] has to suffer...not only will he succeed, but the evil forces will be done away with and never again threaten his peace of mind" (1977, 47).

3. For details, see Wilhelm Schoof, cited in Maclean (1987, 37).

4. Angelika Bammer also discusses the use of Brechtian alienation techniques (1985, 102).

5. "Ausserdem setzte ich das Maerchen auch als ein Mittel der Verfremdung ein. Das hatte Hanne Hiob, die Brecht Tochter, auch so gesehen....Das hat mich sehr bestaetigt, denn in der Phase der Herstellung ist sehr darueber diskutiert worden, ob das Maerchen drin bleiben oder rausgeschnitten werden sollte. Manche fanden es viel zu lange und deplaziert. Aber Hanne Hiob hat sich das am Schneidetisch angeguckt und gesagt: Das Maerchen, das ist ja das allerbeste! Das hat mich bestaetigt" (Moehrmann 1980, 156). Literally "I also added the fairy tale as an alienation technique. Hanne Hiob, Brecht's daughter also saw it that way....That also confirmed [my choice] as in the phase of production, it was discussed a lot if the fairy tale should stay or be edited out (of the film). Some found it too long and out of place. But Hanne Hiob looked out on the editing table and said: 'The fairy tale, that is the very best!' That was a confirmation" (my translation).

6. I am indebted to Andrea Leva, whose thesis on adolescent Holocaust narratives mentions the use of folktales in Holocaust literature and cites these works in her conclusion.

Filmography

Germany, Pale Mother (1980). 123 min. Helma Sanders-Brahms.

Works Cited

Arlow, Jacob A., M.D. 1979. Metaphor and the psychoanalytic situation. *The Psychoanalytic Quarterly* 48: 363–85.

Bammer, Angelika. 1985. Through a daughter's eyes: Helma Sanders-Brahms' *Germany, pale mother*. *New German Critique* 36: 91–109.

Bascom, William R. 1965. Four functions of folklore. In *The study of folklore*, ed. Alan Dundes, 279–98. Englewood Cliffs, NJ: Prentice Hall .

Beres, D. and J. A. Arlow. 1974. Fantasy and identification in empathy. *The Psychoanalytic Quarterly* 43: 26–50.

Bettelheim, Bruno. 1977. *The uses of enchantment: The meaning and importance of fairy tales*. New York: Vintage.

de Certeau, Michel. 1980. On the oppositonal practices of everyday life, trans. Fredric Jameson and Carol Lovitt, *Social Text* 3: 3–43.

Franz, Marie-Louise von. 1972. *Problems of the feminine in fairytales*. Dallas: Spring Publications.

Fehervary, Helen, Claudia Lenssen, and Judith Mayne. 1983. From Hitler to Hepburn: A discussion of women's film production and reception. *New German Critique* 82: 172–85.

Freud, Sigmund. 1955. Beyond the pleasure principle. In vol. 18 of *The standard edition of the complete psychological works of Sigmund Freud*, trans. and ed. James Strachey, 7–64. London: Hogarth.

———. 1957. Mourning and melancholia. In vol. 14 of *The standard edition of the complete psychological works of Sigmund Freud*, trans. and ed. James Strachey, 237–58. London: Hogarth.

Gilligan, Carol. [1982] 1993. *In a different voice: Psychological theory and women's development*. Rev. ed. Cambridge, MA: Harvard University Press.

Gordon, Susan. 1993. "The powers of the handless maiden." In *Feminist messages: Coding in women's folk culture*, ed. Joan Newlon Radner, 252–88. Urbana: University of Illinois Press.

Harber, K. D., and J. W. Pennebaker. 1992. Overcoming traumatic memories. In *The handbook of emotion and memory: Research and theory*, ed. S.E. Christianson, 359–87. Hillsdale, N. J.: Lawrence Erlbaum.

Hartmann, Geoffrey H. 1996. *The longest shadow: In the aftermath of the Holocaust*. Bloomington: Indiana University Press.

Hyams, Barbara. 1988. Is the apolitical woman at peace? A reading of the fairy tale in *Germany, Pale Mother*. *Wide Angle* 10 (3): 41–51.

Lüthi, Max. 1996. The fairy tale hero: The image of man in the fairy tale. In *Folk and fairy tales*, ed. Martin Hallett and Barbara Karsek, 295–305. 2nd ed. Peterborough, Ontario: Broadview.

Maclean, Marie. 1987. Oppositional Practices in Women's Traditional Narrative. *New Literary History* 19 (1): 37.

Maguire, Gregory. 1995. *Wicked: The life and times of the wicked witch of the West*. New York: Harper Collins.

McCormick, Richard W. 1993. Confronting German history: Melodrama, distantiation, and women's discourse in *Germany, Pale Mother*. In *Gender and German Cinema: Feminist Interventions*, vol. 2 of *German Film History/German History on Film.*, ed. Sandra Frieden, Richard W. McCormick, Vibeke R. Petersen, and Laurie Melissa Vogelsang, 185–206. Providence, RI: Berg.

Mishara, Aaron L. 1995. Narrative and psychotherapy: The phenomenology of healing. *American Journal of Psychotherapy* 49 (2): 180–195.

Mitscherlich, Alexander, and Margarete Mitscherlich. 1975. *The inability to mourn: Principles of collective behavior*, trans. Beverley R. Placzek. New York: Grove.

Moehrmann, Renate. 1980. "Helma Sanders-Brahms." In *Die frau mit der kamera*, 141–58. Munich: Carl Hanser.

Murphy, Louise. 2003. *The true story of Hansel and Gretel: A novel of war and survival*. New York: Penguin.

Pennebaker, J. W. 1990. *Opening up the healing power of confiding in others*. New York: William Morrow.

Pennebaker, J. W., C. Hughes, and R. C. O'Heeron. 1987. The psychophysiology of confession: Linking inhibitory and psychosomatic processes. *Journal of Personality and Social Psychology* 52: 781–93.

Propp, Vladimir. 1968. *Morphology of the folktale*, trans. Laurence Scott. Publications of the American Folklore Society, bibliographical and special series, vol. 9. 2nd and rev. ed., Austin: University of Texas Press.

Reitz, Edgar. 1984. *Liebe zum kino: Utopien und gedanken zum autorenfilm*. Cologne: Koeln. Quoted in Santner 1990, 67–72.

Sanders-Brahms, Helma. 1984. *Deutschland, bleiche mutter: Film-erzaehlung*. Reinbek bei Hamburg: Rowohlt.

Santner, Eric. 1990. *Stranded objects: Mourning, memory, and film in postwar Germany*. Ithaca, New York: Cornell University Press.

Schiller, Friedrich. 1975. *Die piccolomini*. Stuttgart: Reclam.

Seiter, Ellen E. 1986. Women's history, women's melodrama: *Deutschland, bleiche mutter*. *The German Quarterly* 59: 569–81.

Silverman, Kaja. 1988. Dis-embodying the female voice: Irigaray, experimental feminist cinema, and femininity. In *The acoustic mirror: The female voice in psychoanalysis and cinema*. Bloomington: Indiana University Press.

Sontag, Susan. 1977. *On photography*. New York: Fararr, Strauss, and Giroux.

Toelken, Barre. [1979] 1996. *The dynamics of folklore*. Rev. ed., Logan: Utah State University Press.

Tolkien, J. R. R. 1996. On fairy-stories. In *Folk and fairy tales*, ed. Martin Hallett and Barbara Karsek, 263–94. 2nd ed., Peterborough, Ontario: Broadview Press.

Yolen, Jane. 2002. *Briar Rose*. Repr., New York: Tor.

Zipes, Jack. 1996. Spells of enchantment. In *Folk and fairy tales*, ed. Martin Hallett and Barbara Karsek, 370–92. 2nd ed., Peterborough, Ontario: Broadview Press.

8

The Three Faces in *Eve's Bayou*

Recalling the Conjure Woman in Contemporary Black Cinema

Tarshia L. Stanley

Kasi Lemmons's neoclassical (re)visioning of the conjure woman in her film *Eve's Bayou* (1997) not only reinforces the idea of this archetype as the place where West African and early African American spirituality and consciousness melded to formulate one means of a people's psychical mediation and survival; it also reinvigorates the tendency of black women griots to cling to the past as a means to determine the present and the future. In creating this film, Lemmons joins a distinguished cohort of African American women storytellers who return to the traditional image of the conjure woman to discover and celebrate their unique identity as women of African descent in America.

The conjure woman has long been a source of mystery and mayhem, as well as healing and power, in the African American oral tradition and literary imagination; *Eve's Bayou* introduces her to filmic discourse. In the southern African American literary tradition, the idea of the conjure woman is widespread. She has appeared in everything from folktales and classical black fiction to children's fairy tales (Buckner 2001; Hamilton 1995). The potency of her incarnation traverses the anthropological musings of Zora Neale Hurston, the art of Romare Bearden, and now the film work of Kasi Lemmons. *Eve's Bayou* is the tale of the conjure woman and the way she both safeguards and creates history through memory. She functions in much the same way as the traditional griot, only the conjure woman has second sight along with hindsight, and this second sight enables her to interpret memory as well as document it.

Set in early 1960s Louisiana, *Eve's Bayou* relates the story of the Batiste family. Philanderer Louis (Samuel L. Jackson) is the charming local doctor whose beautiful wife and children are not enough to keep him at home. The film's protagonist is ten-year-old Eve (Jurnee Smollett) who, like her Aunt Mozelle (Debbi Morgan), has the "gift of sight." The story begins when young Eve accidentally witnesses her father involved in an illicit affair. She shares her secret with her older, sister Cisely (Meagan Good), who, like all the women of the town, worships Louis. Eve is placated by Cisely's dismissal of what Eve saw as a bad dream until Louis wounds Cisely. Hurt and enraged by her father's betrayal, Eve uses her gift to seek revenge and sets in motion the destruction of the Batiste family.

Eve's Bayou is evidence of the African American woman's fascination with and simultaneous need to fashion and reclaim her personal identity through revisiting mythic identities. In "African American Literary Criticism as a Model for the Analysis of Films by African American Women," Gloria Gibson-Hudson writes that "throughout the centuries, slave narratives, poetry and novels have exhibited formative power, shaping texts from an interplay of social forces and personal creative expression...black film has continued this same tradition" (1991, 44). *Eve's Bayou* continues this tradition by referencing the image of the conjure woman, specifically as it has appeared within the African American literary tradition.

The Conjure Woman in the African American Tradition

The figure of the conjure woman is a complex part of the African American folk tradition. She was born in the antebellum south, a kind of mediation between African religious and spiritual customs and Christianity (Johnson 1997, 168). Although it was denied for years, it is now quite common knowledge that African captives retained their indigenous spiritual beliefs in various forms in the new world. Even when many of them were converted to Christianity during the Great Awakening, African slaves subscribed to a hybrid of West African and Anglo-American spiritual beliefs of which the conjure woman is one (Hine, Hine, and Harrold 2000, 60–61).

Historian Lawrence Levine warns that an archetype like the conjure woman must be understood as a conglomeration of circumstance, history, and culture: "We must be sensitive to the ways in which the African world view interacted with that of the Euro-American world into which it was carried and the extent to which an Afro-American perspective was created" (1977, 5). If Christianity offered the African slaves salvation and peace in the next world, then the conjure woman represented immediate benefits. She functioned as hope within their present conditions. For a people who had no legal or even moral defense against forced labor and persecution, the conjure woman or "root worker" was the last line of defense. Calling upon memories of African mysticism and magic and combining them with practices rooted in the Judeo-Christian religion, she seemed like a witch to so-called civilized society.

The conjure woman's job was to connect the people to the spirit world to protect them from harm. Drawing from the remnants of the West African traditions of the Igbo and Yoruba people, she made charms and *gris-gris*, root potions and *mojos* (Johnson 1997, 169). Although her powers were not absolute, she was entrusted with everything from keeping the members of slave families from being sold separately to sustaining interest in wayward lovers. The talismans that she created were weapons used to combat the cruel reality of slavery and, later on, the capriciousness of fate.

When slavery ended, the conjure woman continued to be a potent member of southern black society. While she still offered protection, in keeping with the needs of the people, she morphed to also become fortune-teller, spiritual healer, and life advisor. Many in the black community sought her expertise to help them with health problems, financial advice, willful family members, lost loves, and even revenge and retribution. The potency of the conjure woman was directly connected to her clients' faith in her powers. Her abilities were dependent upon her knowledge of the human spirit and her skill at manipulating innuendo and superstition. Carol S. Taylor Johnson writes that the "transformative power of words combined with symbolic acts is at the heart of the 'magic' of conjuring" (1997, 169). In short, the conjure woman's conjuring relied upon her ability to alleviate desperation with prescriptive action. Johnson asserts,

> She is expected to provide a diagnosis, identify the source of the problem, cast a spell upon a selected victim through the use of charms and/or poison for the purpose of avenging the malignant deeds of the enemy, provide conteractants to remove a spell that has been placed maliciously upon a victim, provide a protective "hand" or charm for a client to help him control antagonistic circumstances, give advice on the management of daily affairs, and predict future events. Conjurers assist in matters related to health, love, and social, economic, and personal empowerment. (1997, 168)

People who felt helpless against great odds usually sought out the conjure woman's services. They hoped the conjure woman could provide them with a sling and a stone against Goliaths like slavery, sickness, poverty, unrequited love, uncertain future, and even death.

In addition to all of these duties, the conjure woman in the literary tradition also served as a site of collective memory. In the epic poem "Molly Means" by Margaret Walker, Molly is both a feared conjure woman and the object of the community's collective mimetic force. Tomeiko Ashford, in her essay "Performing Community: Margaret Walker's use of poetic 'Folk Voice,'" writes, "Molly Means's character, however, remains mythic since she becomes forever a part of the community's shared memory" (2001, 151). As such, the conjure woman is a coalescing agent for the community; she is one of the things its members have in common that make them a unique cultural entity, and she is further evidence of the multitudinous ways these women functioned in the African American community.

Calling upon the Image

In keeping with the way that she functioned in life and literature, the image of the conjure woman in *Eve's Bayou* serves several narrative and structural purposes. First, she mimics the role she plays in the African American literary and oral traditions as one who helps to establish identity and define the way the culture works. According to literary critic Karla F.C. Holloway, the very nature of African American women's literature is the writer's desire to script those things that "reflect the community—the cultural ways of knowing as well as the ways of framing knowledge in literature" (1992, 1). The conjure woman's narrative presence establishes a link with the social, historical, and political life of a people. Because her way of healing or hurting, living and dying, defies Western ideological interpretations of space, time, and spirituality, the conjure woman is a marker for differentiating cultural practices. Holloway also maintains that this continued reworking of the conjure woman, or what she calls in her work the "ancestral presence," is purposeful and may be compulsive: "I believe that far from being a coincidental selection of a metaphor, the ancestral presence in contemporary African American women's writing reconstructs an imaginative, cultural (re)membrance of a dimension of West African spirituality, and that the spiritual place of this objective figuration is fixed into the structures of the text's language" (1992, 2).

Holloway is describing not only a tendency in black women's fiction to recall an ancestral presence but the life cycle of conjure-woman iconography. Invoking the conjure woman (whether consciously or subconsciously) bespeaks a desire to reframe knowledge, language, and interpretive practices. In this case, Lemmons's calling forth the conjure woman definitely informs both the narrative and cinematic structure of the film. Since conjure women populate *Eve's Bayou*, we can expect Western ideals of logic and order in textual language to be disrupted or even expanded in keeping with narrative practices by black women writers—and filmmakers.

From Holloway's perspective, black women's texts want to recall lived experiences metaphorically, in all their richness, through what she calls "the screen of language" (1992, 3). Since I'm extrapolating texts to include filmic ones, I can also take liberty with the concept of screen of language and infer it to include the "language of the screen." While Holloway is dealing with written words and concepts, I believe Lemmons is on a parallel mission using cinematography, landscaping, and character presentation as a type of language that also pays homage to the complex and diverse folk experience recalled in *Eve's Bayou.*

Marjorie Pryse and Hortense Spillers write in *Conjuring: Black Women's Fiction and Literary Tradition* "that part of the conjure woman's power is her ability to tell stories" (1985, 14). Thus, not only is Lemmons using film techniques to join the canon of black women writers, but her characters themselves live out the legacy. In addition to their other primordial functions, the conjure women in the film tell stories. Mozelle is constantly weaving the narrative of her life as a gift for Eve. The adult Eve does the same for the audience as she narrates the film. Positioned at her fortune-telling booth in the marketplace even Elzora (Diahann Carroll) is a storyteller.

In addition to following in the footsteps of black women whose texts engage communal identity, Lemmons is also in line with a tradition that seeks to negotiate, reaffirm, and promote individual identity. Whatever the media, black women who tell stories often return to an ancestor image as a way of remembering themselves in a social and political system traditionally designed to disregard and disremember them. In *Conjuring: Black Women's Fiction and Literary Tradition*, Barbara Christian says that, during the 1970s and 1980s, black women fought an inner battle to write about themselves. She surmises that the kind of self-focusing and self-awareness black women writers needed to solidify a literary tradition concerned with naming themselves was often interpreted both inside and outside of the black community as selfishness rather than self-actualization (1985, 233–34).

Yet the concern for self depicted in the texts of black women has rarely produced self-indulgence. In fact, many of the texts are "dynamic, not static, as they communicate and integrate a discourse of African American culture, history and politics" (Gibson-Hudson 1991, 53). Texts by black women often are consumed with identifying their heritage, position, and legacy in actual history and cultural memory. However, the very nature of this anthropological work rightly yields priceless information about the totality of culture, community, and history—both "real" and (re)membered. As Gibson-Hudson notes, "African American women writers and filmmakers are artists interpreting women's experiences with the hope that the readers or viewers will examine their own consciousness and develop a clearer vision for the future. Their work functions as participatory, not escapist art, because the works invite dialogue and activism" (1998, 53). Gibson-Hudson refers here to films by black women whose primary audiences are people of color and those who want to accept the challenge to engage actively with the films. *Eve's Bayou* straddles a strange fence because many of its viewers belong to mainstream audiences.

Lemmons's summoning of the conjure woman may also be read as her endeavor to remember who she is. It may be that *Eve's Bayou* is the filmmaker's attempt to go home, to understand this strange, rich, historical place from which her familial roots spring. In an interview with Ann Brown (1997), Lemmons stated that although she was not reared in the South, her parents, who hail from Louisiana and Georgia, described life there to her. It is clear that Lemmons has an understanding of, and an appreciation for, the iconography of the southern black folk tradition. She does not present the conjure woman as an exoticized Other. She is instead part of the family, part of the landscape, part of the memory—a part of the whole culture. Indeed the conjure woman is the foundation of the culture we see in the town of *Eve's Bayou*. She is not only the founder of the Batiste bloodline but also the progenitor of the ability to conjure in its women. Thus, in watching *Eve's Bayou*, audiences may understand more about the black woman, her art, her community, and the way in which she herself understands all of these. There also exists the potential for mainstream audiences to encounter the continuing complexities of a slave system which begat founding mothers and fledgling daughters like both of the Eve Baptistes.

The Dawn of Eve

In the diegetic space of the town of *Eve's Bayou*, folks still have need of the conjure woman to provide protection and prophecy, insight and inspiration much the same way their ancestors did. They still battle a physical world bent on destroying them or their dreams by engaging an intercessor who has power in the spiritual world. Rather than sculpting a conjure woman who embodies all the various facets of the archetype, Lemmons rather wisely chooses to break the conjure woman into pieces. Like a fractured mind, the conjure woman in this film dwells in the

Young Eve Batiste.

lived experiences of three characters, each of whom plays one or more of the roles of the traditional icon. Through the narrated memories of the young Eve Batiste and the characters of Aunt Mozelle and the witch woman Elzora, we come to understand the conjure woman herself, not only as the site where identity is reclaimed but also as the very process of negotiating myth and memory.

Young Eve Batiste is the film's protagonist. She reconciles both of the contradictory aspects of the conjure woman. She has the same second sight as her Aunt Mozelle and a desire for the darker side of conjuring represented by Elzora, the character who uses the gift to avenge and destroy. Although the story takes place in the Louisiana of the 1960s, the ghost of the slave woman Eve haunts it from the beginning. The original Eve won her freedom and, therefore, the freedom of her children because she used "powerful medicine" to save the life of her owner. The first Eve was a conjure woman, and during the film, we learn the fate of her daughters.

The film begins with a voice-over that establishes the grown-up Eve as both diegetic and nondiegetic narrator. As a principal character, she functions as a diegetic narrator but in the person of her past, young-child self. We do not interact with the adult Eve as a nondiegetic narrator. Eve recounts the history of the town: "The town we lived in was named after a slave....I was named for her." While the film is a reflection on the ability of memories to transform themselves into history and a treatise on the entities that act as bridges between these memories and history, it is also quite obviously a female-centered *Bildungsroman*, a commentary on black middle-class life in the 1960s, and a murder mystery.

At the opening party scene, we see Eve as the middle child. She is jealous of the affection her father showers on her older sister and angry about her mother's obvious favoring of her younger brother. While clearly the daughters are rivals for their father's affection, both Eve and Cisely unite wholeheartedly when their perception of their father is endangered. Shortly after Eve's father chooses to dance with Cisely, Eve runs away to hide in an old carriage house. She is awakened by the sight and sound of her father having sex with Matty Mereaux. Stunned into silence, Eve cannot confront her father. Later in their room when she shares her secret with Cisely, the camera does what it will do throughout the film. It moves the viewers from the diegetic present into the past. Eve and Cisely are suddenly transported into Eve's memory. There we see the two girls as observers in the carriage house, where Cisely rewrites what her little sister has seen. The audience becomes privy to a new reading of the scene; instead of Louis Batiste and Matty Mereaux engaged in the sex act, we see an innocent embrace. While Eve is sure about what she saw, she prefers Cisely's reinterpretation, and this is the way memory continues to be reconfigured throughout the film.

Eve's Bayou is a film that takes advantage of the language of the screen, the cinematic apparatus that facilitates a visual perception of the multilayered storytelling that began orally and then became part of the written tradition. In much the same way that artisans like Zora Neale Hurston, Toni Morrison, and Gloria Naylor capture the essence of the polymorphic word on the page, the technology of film becomes the great catalyst for this newest dissemination of the folk tradition. For instance, *Eve's Bayou* begins with a recollection that sets the precedent for the way that memory (and psychic vision) is juxtaposed with diegetic reality throughout the film. Because the first shot shows us things we have yet to see, or remember, we cannot make sense of it. It only becomes clear as we learn to look through young Eve's eyes that we are sharing her perspective. We are remembering and understanding the story through her.

One of the ways logic and order are expanded in the film is through mirrors and memories. Drawing from the legend and lore of African American literature and culture, the film addresses myth against memory by repositioning them as mirror images of each other and implies that it is in their amalgamation that identity is discovered. For example, because of the voice-over narration, we know that the film depicts a memory. What is the function of a mirror except to reflect what is before it, to make the reflected readable and discernable? The adult Eve is remembering the summer she was ten years old. As the audience enters Eve's memory via the film, we also see the memories of other characters. Often the cinematic depiction of these memories utilizes mirrors or reflections in water.

As already mentioned, the beginning of the film is actually a memory; it is shot in vignettes in grainy black and white to differentiate it from the film's real time. It is difficult to describe the film's time continuum. We hear the adult voice of Eve narrating action that took place in the past. Thus, the audience is never quite sure what time it is because the film is a memory and within it are more memories.

In one of the many memory scenes in the film, Eve brushes Mozelle's hair in front of a large antique mirror. Mozelle's reaction to her reflection makes Eve think her aunt is upset at the distressed way she looks in her mourning. The bond between Mozelle and Eve is strong not only because she is an out-of-place middle child but also because they share the blood and the abilities of the conjure woman. It is Eve who pulls Mozelle from her stupor after Harry's death and reminds her that she has "clients coming" and work to do in the community. It is Eve who says to Mozelle, "It's not your fault they die." However, Mozelle's concern in this scene is otherworldly because she sees the images of all three of her dead husbands reflected in one of the mirrors attached to her wardrobe. "I swear I loved them," moans Mozelle as if she is being haunted by the men she has betrayed by marrying them. The abilities of a conjure woman come at a high price. While Mozelle is able to dole out help and advice to those who come to her, she cannot see clearly into her own life. She seems fated to marry and then bury her husbands.

As Mozelle and Eve continue to stand before the mirror, Mozelle recalls how she lost her first husband. Behind the two, reflected in the mirror, are her first husband, Maynard, and his lover, Hosea. Mozelle tells the story in sync with the action in the mirror's background reflection. As her tale reaches its climax and the lover who has confronted her husband threatens to kill him, Mozelle moves from her position beside Eve into the mirrored image. While the apparent feat is in fact simply Mozelle walking back across the room and cast as the mirror's background reflection, the effect is dramatic. Like Eve and Cisely, who earlier moved into Eve's memory, Mozelle has literally (re)inhabited her

Aunt Mozelle.

recollection of her first husband's death. Eve remains close to the mirror in the foreground of the shot. In this exchange, she learns the power of the conjure woman to reshape interpretation, reinvigorate memory, and rewrite history.

Geta J. LeSeur suggests that the journey that the protagonist in the Western *Bildungsroman* must take to fulfill his or her destiny manifests itself as a break with the family and/or community when the writer and subjects are black (1995, 30). Eve can no longer ignore the painful truth of her father's infidelity against her mother and the family can no longer be ignored when she believes he has assaulted her sister. In the moment of that realization, Eve breaks with her little-girl self, with her dutiful daughter image, and becomes the avenging conjurer. She sets out to right the wrong against her sister and the rest of her family and believes that the affront calls for no less than her father's life. Once she makes the decision to seek out Elzora rather than Mozelle, she leaves her innocence behind and is on her way to becoming a conjure woman.

Eve is clearly the union of Mozelle and Elzora. She is the interme-diary or reconciling figure between the conjure woman as healer and one who can do harm. Not only does she reconcile the two sides of the conjure woman, but she ties this role to the griot as well. Eve is responsible for passing on both the letter and spirit of memory. The problem is that for all her precociousness, she is still a child and one who reacts to her sister's pain and her father's betrayal with vengeance. She cannot yet dispassionately wield the weight and responsibility of the gifts she has been given.

The highest power of the conjure woman in the literary and folk tradition lay not in her charms or gris-gris, her potions or instructions, but her ability to manipulate people—for good or ill. We witness Mozelle and Elzora changing the way their clients interact with the world on the power of their words alone. Eve's conversation with Mr. Mereaux (Matty's husband) is the perfect example. Mr. Mereaux has not allowed himself to hear the rumors or see the evidence of his wife's liaison with Louis Batiste. Eve's words to him and her manner are superficially innocent, but underneath are consequences for which Eve herself is not prepared. She plants a seed in the heart and mind of Lenny Mereaux that will flower in death.

Reflecting the idea that Lemmons's work is an evolutionary movement in black women's texts, Annis Pratt writes in *Archetypal Pattern in Women's Fiction* that among the replicating themes are the "green world epiphany" and the "rape trauma" (1981, 170–78). Each of these themes reverberates with Eve. The green world epiphany theory argues that the female protagonist in women's texts is spurred on in her development by submersion in a luxuriant green land. Lemmons uses the landscape as almost another character in the film. The bayou is represented by marshland and the moss-hung trees; it is lush, green, and fertile. It is also a landscape haunted by the original Eve Batiste because the town bears her name. One of the opening shots of the film depicts an African woman framed by sugar-cane fields as the story of the slave owner, Jean Paul Batiste, and his slave woman, Eve, unfolds. Because Mozelle's visions of the future always appear as reflections on the waters of the bayou, we know that the conjure woman's power and the place where she lives are tied tightly together. Many of the scenes of Eve show her playing in the bayou. We see Eve pushed to her breaking point when she and the other Batiste children are forbidden to leave the house because of one of Mozelle's premonitions. We even see her seek solace in the arms of a huge oak tree as she mourns her father. In the end, it is the waters of the bayou that drown the secret of Louis and Cisely and reflect the surviving daughters, Eve and Cisely.

The green world where Eve thrives is a catalyst for her development and links her to the past. It is significant that the film is set in the

1960s in the Louisiana low country. Eve can embrace herself as a conjurer because she does not live in a time when video games, cell phones, or satellite television could distract her consciousness. In the land where she is free to roam, she is equally free to embrace all that history and mystery allow. Numerous scenes depict her walking alone along country roads, walking alone at night, and having overall freedom to roam the landscape. When Eve takes Cisely's hands at the end of the story to determine what really happened between Cisely and their father, her vision, too, is embedded in the landscape. The moss hanging from the great cypress trees parts and lets Eve into her sister's memory.

D. Soyini Madison asserts the importance of Elzora dwelling in the almost uninhabitable borderland of the green world. She writes, "[Elzora] is not a stereotypical voodoo queen, but a purposeful stocktype. She is a presentational prototype of both ominous black magic and enlivening power. Elzora lives on the swamp, a classic border of outsiderhood and threat" (2000, 326). Eve occupies the beautiful green space of the bayou, while Elzora inhabits the dark, foreboding, and dangerous marshland. Unlike Mozelle's elegant home, Elzora's "office" is a tiny rundown shack perched precariously on the stagnant waters of the swamp. Mozelle sees her clients and does her work in her home, supported by her status as psychic counselor, while Elzora is relegated to the role and accoutrements of a fortune-teller.

The rape trauma element is also present in the film. The two Batiste daughters idolize their father and are particularly troubled by his infidelity. Cisely chooses to see her father's philandering as the result of her mother's inability to please him. She responds by trying to become her mother in Oedipal terms. Eve is not yet sure what to do with her feelings for her father and vacillates between jealousy of Cisely and anger at her father's behavior. Both Eve and Cisely are the woman/child, caught between adolescence and adulthood, memory and truth. As Cisely is on the verge of physical awakening as a woman, Eve is in the process of awakening spiritually, and she will bear the burden, as the conjure woman does, of remaining in the space between memory and truth to mediate it.

The conjure woman can be either an asset or a liability in the community. She can use her powers to help or to harm. Folk tradition does not always recognize the conjure woman as a positive figure in society. Many ideas about her focus on her ability to summon dark magic and work against the community as well as for it (Tucker 1994, 173–88).[1] Charles Chesnutt created one of the first portraits of the conjure woman in African American literature in *The Conjure Woman and Other Conjure*

Tales ([1899] 1993), a collection of short stories that reveal the complex relationships between the conjurer and the community. In most of the seven stories (narrated by Uncle Julius to the white landowner, John, who in turn narrates them to the reader), Chesnutt depicts the way that the conjure woman protects and avenges the black community. For instance, in "Mars Jeem's Nightmare," the plantation master is transformed into a slave. Mars Jeem then suffers firsthand the malice usually perpetrated against the slave community.

This kind of story demonstrates the conjure woman's capacity to engender hope in the slave community. Chesnutt's other stories illustrate the conjure woman battling the dark force of separation as she tries to keep slave families and loved ones together. Yet Chesnutt is careful to draw a picture of the conjurer as a dark force as well. In "The Conjurer's Revenge" and "The Gray Wolf's Ha'nt," the conjure woman becomes a conjure man and exacts revenge when he is crossed. In the first story, a slave is turned into a mule for stealing from the conjurer; in the second, poor Dan is turned into a wolf and tricked into murdering his own wife as punishment for killing the conjurer's son.

Continuing the tradition, Gloria Naylor's *Mama Day* (1988) is a conventional tale of a good and powerful conjure woman, but set in modern times. Like Chesnutt's work, *Mama Day* is written *fin de siècle* and demonstrates the multiple facets of the conjure woman. Miranda (Mama) Day is the quintessential conjure woman. She holds the island community of Willow Springs together in the same way the conjure woman did in slave and postslave African American communities. Miranda is healer, educator, and nurturer. She is the link to the power and history that the citizens of her tiny island need to retain their identity in a world that wants to erase them.

In *Eve's Bayou*, the character of Elzora certainly represents the more sinister facet of the conjure woman. In direct contrast to the beautiful and elegant Mozelle, Elzora appears in white makeup, mimicking a death mask.[2] While Mozelle practices from an elegant home, Elzora works in the marketplace. She tells fortunes in a dilapidated booth, filled with indiscernible mixtures in jars. Elzora is the bearer of bad, albeit truthful, news. She does not soften the impact of her words or offer ways to circumvent them. Elzora is the third member of the conjuring trinity, the side of the gift of sight that can be commercialized and bent to evil.

It is no wonder that Eve is both frightened by, and drawn to, Elzora. Eve chooses this quality of the conjure woman when she feels she must punish her father for what he has done to Cisely. Although Eve commissions Elzora to kill her father, audiences are invited to draw their own

Diahann Carroll as Elzora.

conclusions. Was it the twenty dollars and the bit of hair from his comb that began Louis's demise, or was it the words Eve deposited into the psyche of Mr. Mereaux? We are left to wonder whether it is Eve or Elzora who casts the spell that kills Louis Batiste. Perhaps it is the combination of the two. Or perhaps it was Louis who, as Elzora predicted, "fell on his own sword."

In Louis's death scene, the three faces of the conjure woman meet. Lenny Mereaux forbids Louis to speak to Matty again and threatens to kill him for his betrayal. Louis, who cannot bear to be anything less than the hero, insists upon saying good night to Matty. As Mereaux fires his gun and Louis pushes Eve to the ground to prevent her from being shot, we see Mozelle's previous vision come to pass. Earlier in the film, Mozelle had a vision of a local child being hit by a bus, but when the body fell, it was near a railroad track rather than on the street. Since Mozelle did not complete reading her vision—she stopped when the bus hit the child— she does not understand that she has also foreseen Louis's death. Thus, the audience is devastated along with Eve. We are all unprepared for the legacy of memory. As Eve lies on the ground screaming for her father,

her work and Elzora's come to fruition. Eve has gotten what she paid for, and Louis has paid for what he was.

Inheritances

At the end of the film, while rummaging among her father's effects, Eve finds a letter that seems to absolve him of his purported crimes against Cisely. During Eve's confrontation with Cisely, she must use her second sight to learn the truth. Eve takes Cisely's hands the same way that Mozelle does with her clients. The mantle has been passed to Eve. She does not use the truth of what she learns to condemn either Cisely or her father. Rather, in healing conjure-woman fashion, she buries Louis's letter and takes Cisely's hand. As the two girls stand mirrored in the waters of the bayou, no definitive answers emerge. We hear the grown-up Eve resume the soliloquy she started at the beginning of the film:

> Like others before me I have the gift of sight, but the truth changes color depending on the light, and tomorrow can be clearer than yesterday. Memory is a selection of images, some elusive, others printed indelibly on the brain. Each image is like a thread, each thread woven together to make a tapestry of intricate texture, and the tapestry tells a story, and the story is our past.

The story of Eve and the Batiste family is one thread in the long history of conjure women in the African American oral and literary tradition. Celebrated for its stunning cinematography and brilliant casting, *Eve's Bayou* is a film that stirs memories and invokes traditional narrative roles. It is also a testament to the ways that the African American female storytelling tradition wrestles with identity. Black women have established a pattern of (re)membering themselves, their community, and their history. Black female texts often exhume their ancestors even if they existed primarily as types. There is little tension between the ancestor and the archetype because these writers understand the ability of memory to (re)present and to (re)create. In truth, memory can be history, and for a people long stripped of history, it is a justifiable retrofit.

This pattern began in oral tradition and then found its way into writings by black women. Lately, this (re)membering takes place in such films as *Eve's Bayou*. We see the conjure woman in various stages of her existence. We see how she was born, how she has survived, and what happens when she must reconcile all the aspects of her nature. In addition to all of her façades, the conjure woman is a figure for (re)claming and (re)inventing the African American female self. In *Eve's Bayou*, the black woman is Mozelle the mediator and Elzora the menace. Finally, she is Eve, the intermediary bridge between the two. The conjure woman is one expression of the power black women writers and now filmmakers invoke to (re)member history and (in)script it for generations to come.

Notes

1. Lindsay Tucker examines the ominous presentations of the conjure woman. Tucker frames her critique of Ruby (who is the antithesis of Mama Day—the good conjure woman) in Naylor's work with Zora Neale Hurston's analysis of the conjure tradition in her autobiography *Mules and Men* ([1935] 1978). Tucker sees Naylor and Hurston as having to work against negative images of the conjure woman "distorted by European Eurocentrism" and "Christianity" (1994,175).
2. In the director's commentary, Kasi Lemmons says that Diahann Carroll was too beautiful as Elzora. She made the decision to cover her face with the makeup as a way of distinguishing Elzora's brand of conjuring from Mozelle's.

Filmography

Eve's Bayou (1997). 109 min. Kasi Lemmons

Works Cited

Ashford, Tomeiko R. 2001. Performing community: Margaret Walker's use of poetic "folk voice." In *Fields watered with blood: Critical essays on Margaret Walker*, ed. Maryemma Graham, 148–63. Athens: University of Georgia Press.

Brown, Ann. 1997. Bayou spirits on-screen. *American Visions* 12 (5): 39.

Buckner, B. Dilla. 2001. Folkloric elements in Margaret Walker's poetry. In *Fields watered with blood: Critical essays on Margaret Walker*, ed. Maryemma Graham, 139–47. Athens: University of Georgia Press.

Chesnutt, Charles Waddell. [1899] 1993. *The conjure woman and other conjure tales.* Ed. Richard H. Brodhead. Repr., Durham, NC: Duke University Press.

Christian, Barbara. 1985. Trajectories of self-definition: Placing contemporary Afro-American women's fiction. In *Conjuring: Black women's fiction and literary tradition*, ed. Marjorie Pryse and Hortense J. Spillers, 233–34. Bloomington: Indiana University Press.

Gibson-Hudson, Gloria J. 1991. African American literary criticism as a model for the analysis of films by African American women. *Wide Angle* 13 (3–4): 44–54.

Hamilton, Virginia. 1995. *Her stories: African American folktales, fairy tales and true tales.* New York: Scholastic, Inc.

Hine, Darlene Clark, William C. Hine, and Stanley Harrold. 2000. *The African-American odyssey.* Upper Saddle River, NJ: Prentice Hall.

Holloway, Karla F. C. 1992. *Mooring and metaphors: Figures of culture and gender in black women's literature.* New Brunswick, NJ: Rutgers University Press.

Hurston, Zora Neale. [1935] 1978. *Mules and men.* Repr., Bloomington: Indiana University Press.

Johnson, Carol S. Taylor. 1997. Conjuring. In *The Oxford companion to African American literature,* ed. William L. Andrews, Frances Smith, and Trudier Harris, 168–69. New York/Oxford: Oxford University Press.

Levine, Lawrence W. 1977. *Black culture and black consciousness: Afro-American folk thought from slavery to freedom.* London: Oxford University Press.

LeSeur, Geta J. 1995. *Ten is the age of darkness: The black bildungsroman.* Columbia: University of Missouri Press.

Madison, D. Soyini. 2000. Oedipus rex at *Eve's Bayou* or the little black girl who left Sigmund Freud in the swamp. *Cultural Studies* 14 (2): 311–40.

Naylor, Gloria. 1988. *Mama Day.* New York: Vintage Press.

Pratt, Annis. 1981. *Archetypal patterns in women's fiction.* Bloomington: Indiana University Press.

Pryse, Marjorie, and Hortense J. Spillers, eds. 1985. *Conjuring: Black women's fiction and literary tradition.* Bloomington: Indiana University Press.

Tucker, Lindsay. 1994. Recovering the conjure woman: Texts and contexts in Gloria Naylor's *Mama Day. African American Review* 28 (2): 173–88.

9

Allegories of the Undead

Rites and Rituals in Tales from the Hood

Carol E. Henderson

Ed Guerrero argues in *Framing Blackness,* "Hollywood's unceasing efforts to frame *blackness* are constantly challenged by the cultural and political self-definitions of African Americans, who as a people have been determined since the inception of commercial cinema to militate against this limiting system of representation" (1994,3). Guerrero's comments point up the systematic continuums that create discursive battles that shape and inform national and international discussions about not only African American people's subjectivity but also their woundedness. Because of the volatile nature of race, African Americans have had to represent the brutality of their historical experiences in ways that amplify the literary, social, and oral replications of these themes expressed in America's collective memory.

In the 1995 horror film *Tales from the Hood,* director/screenwriter Rusty Cundieff reworks the textures of these traumas by eerily refashioning the cultural dynamics that shape our understanding of the bitter reality that haunts the psyches of three urbanites in the film. Of key concern in my discussion are the refigurings of folk culture that shape the dialogue in these tales and recontextualize the basis for examining the unresolved issues of racism and self-hatred embedded in the African American urban experience. As Ralph Ellison and Toni Morrison have argued elsewhere, folklore or *vernacular art* (as it is also known) is black America's legacy of self-awareness, often communicated in harsh and honest terms (O'Meally 2004, 4). The self-reflexivity of the art is its enduring quality because it functions not only as a vehicle of change but also a portal into the way the past is evaluated, remembered, and used by its contemporaries. Cundieff "conjures up" some of the remnants of this past in his film as he reconsiders the psychological and metaphysical costs of hauntings that mar the African American racial memory and prevent reconciliation in the present. In the end, these tales tell the stories of the undead in ways that reflect the material reality of violence and ritual in the urban community.

Tales of the Undead

In reassessing the cultural and political consciousness of Cundieff's art, we may be tempted to rename the film *Tales of the Undead* because of the narrative intimacy Cundieff uses to reclaim the past—a past that is haunted, as Toni Morrison states elsewhere, by "signs, visitations, and ways of knowing that [encompass] more than concrete reality" (McKay 1983, 414). The overall approach of *Tales* reflects this twining of life in the here and hereafter, stressing, in particular, the spiritual and psychic wrangling of spirits who have died unceremoniously and remain restless. Their unsettling appearances throughout the film—some appear as dead men walking the streets of Los Angeles after an unjustifiably brutal murder by corrupt police officers; others manifest themselves as little dolls whose souls have been spirited into archeological figures painted in a mural at a former plantation—point up Cundieff's parodic riffing of ancestral reckoning and spiritual retribution.

Cundieff's film directs attention to a long line of cultural narratives that have considered the impact of death on the African American community. From the imposing phototexts of the deceased by photographer James Van Der Zee to the conjure stories of reincarnation by writer Charles Chesnutt,[1] African American artists have measured the continuous cycle of life, charting with painstaking acuity the imaginative ingenuity African Americans have used to preserve themselves, their families, and their human dignity in the face of overwhelming odds.

Still, the didactic nature of these narratives stresses the iniquitous follies of those in the African American community who, like the flying Africans, lose their wings "owing to their many transgressions..." (All God's Chillen 2004, 132). Their inability to "find their way back" to a cultural or spiritual center shapes the tenor of many of the conjurer or trickster stories intended to prick the consciousness of their listeners. The structure of *Tales* encourages this interpretation. Through a series of interfacing vignettes and subplots, the film conveys the conundrum of a group of young gang members whose insatiable appetite for a missing drug shipment leads them to the premises of Mr. Simms (Clarence Williams III), an eccentric mortician. Simms's role in the film is evident from the beginning: he is the trickster, the storyteller whose connection with the dead gives him omniscient power. While the three hold a gun to

Simms's head, he weaves his moral tales of revenge and reprisal, using the enchanted objects and twisted corpses in his mortuary.

There is the body of a rookie police officer, Clarence Smith (Anthony Griffith), whose failure to intercede on behalf of Martin Ezekiel Moorehouse (Tom Wright), a promising African American civil-rights activist, results in the beating and death of Moorehouse, who is then framed as a heroin addict by three white police officers. The sullying of Moorehouse's name ensures that the press will taint his activist legacy. Yet, as this vignette makes clear, it is Clarence's job to make sure history is *re*written. Clarence's culpability in *allowing* Moorehouse's death to go uninvestigated creates a mental and spiritual dilemma for him. He descends into a personal hell—becoming an alcoholic and recluse. We are led to believe that Moorehouse's ghost coerces Clarence into bringing the three officers to his grave. There, revenge is enacted, and the three officers die a brutal death. In the end, Clarence is seen strapped into a straitjacket in a ten-by-ten-foot cell. We are never told how he gets from the cell to the coffin. But the master narrative fills in this gap: more than likely, Clarence is executed because he is charged with the death of the three officers.

Simms's next tale revolves around the twisted corpse of a professional domestic batterer, Carl (David Alan Grier), whose soft-spoken and calm exterior (he obsessively wears a shirt and tie) masks the grotesque monster within. Carl's constant abuse is obvious on the body of Walter (Brandon Hammond), the son of the woman Carl is dating. Despite the pleas of his teacher and the school nurse, Walter cannot find words to express the brutality he witnesses each night. Subsequently, Carl's comeuppance comes at the hands of this fragile young boy, whose enchanted childhood drawings give him the power to destroy the monster who beats him and his mom nightly.

The third tale centers on an enchanted object, a wooden doll. As Simms explains, this doll once held the soul of a slave who was massacred at a plantation by a master who did not want to free his slaves after the Civil War. He, along with hundreds of other men, women, and children, was lynched and burned. Their restless spirits were then housed in wooden dolls made by dollmaker Miss Cobbs (who is also a conjurer). A former Klansman turned politician, Duke Metger (Corbin Bernsen),[2] moves into the house as a political stunt to garner votes. He even employs as his public-relations expert an up and coming young buppie named Rhodie (Roger Smith), who, as his name suggests, will go along with just about anything as long as the price is right. Rhodie dies in the house of his ancestors after tripping over one of the dolls that lies unseen at the top of the stairs. The ironic nature of his death, along with that of Metger (who is eaten alive by the dolls while draped in the American flag he tries to hide behind), serves as a reminder of the reprisal exacted from those who desecrate the memory of the ancestors.

Simms's final anecdote leads the three young men to the coffin of a young man they know as Jerome (Lamont Bentley), aka Crazy K. Jerome's life unfolds through a series of flashbacks that parallel his violent gang life with his days in prison and his inability to be rehabilitated through an experimental program run by Dr. Cushing (Rosalind Cash). Through a visual montage that interweaves shots of historical violence against blacks with those depicting gang violence, Cushing hopes to persuade the hardened Crazy K into changing his evil ways. Her motherly wit, reminiscent of the African *griots* of the past, manipulates time and violence becomes the language reinvented and translated in the "chamber chair" of her makeshift laboratory. As her name suggests, Cushing attempts to mitigate the nefarious effects of poverty and nihilism on Crazy K's psyche, but her hopes to negotiate a treaty between him and his hood prove futile. Even the ghostly apparitions of those Jerome has killed in the past (including a young girl of ten) do not move him.

This arrogance leads to his subsequent death at the hands of other gang members (the three who hold Simms hostage at his funeral home) who, likewise, lack the power of discernment. And in a marvelous twist that demonstrates the preeminence of karma and the *intra*cultural power of the trickster, these three young men meet their own perverted fate at the hands of the demoniacally transformed Simms when the last three coffins in the basement of the mortuary contain mirror images of themselves.

The eerie appearance of Mr. Simms masks the interrogative relationship between his character and role in the film. While Simms's *behavior* (i.e., character) seems based on the perceptions of an old "crazy" man who appears to have lost touch with his surroundings and his people, his *role* as an elder foreshadows the ingenuity he uses to outwit and condemn his captors. As Elizabeth Ammons reminds us, the essence of tricksterism is "change, contradiction, adaptation, surprise" (Ammons and White-Parks 1994, xii). Simms's eccentric and seemingly loony demeanor signals a return to the southern trickster, whose tales of revenge against obstinate slave masters peppered the plantation literature of the previous century. Simms's character extends this paradigm, directing attention to the socioeconomic elements of deprivation and cynicism that enslave so many young black men in urban centers.

Simms's inability to reach the moral center of these young men points up the self-reflexive nature of folk culture, which warns, "You will reap what you sow."

In addition, the inability of Stack (Joe Torry), Bulldog (Samuel Monroe, Jr.), and Ball (De'aundre Bonds) to recognize that they too are the "walking dead" presupposes toward the end of the film that certain urban dwellers are *sleepwalkers* (borrowing a term from Ralph Ellison's *Invisible Man*), unaware of their own blind moral ambition and spiritual deprivation. That the boys do not recognize Simms as the devil further demonstrates their own disconnectedness from the lore of folk culture that teaches youngsters to "beware of the boogeyman!" As Simms states in the opening dialogue of the film, "Death...comes in many strange packages." Yet in the spirit of ancestral forgiveness that grounds *Tales*, Stack, Bulldog, and Ball are given chance after chance to redeem themselves through the telling of the tales. But because of the arrogance and ignorance these young men display toward an elder (they hold a gun to Simms's head at one point and hit him with the butt of the gun at another), their fate is sealed.

As a trickster, Simms's character blurs the boundary between enforcer and healer of the cultural wounds in the hood. That he takes the time to tell his tales to these gang members suggests the didactic quality of his role. Critics such as Jacqueline Fulmer have argued that Simms is both trickster and conjurer because "in folklore, the conjurer performs two ways: by conjuring or tricking someone and by curing those who have already been conjured" (2002, 431). I think that the *order* in which the tales are told suggests that the trickster Simms knows Stack, Bulldog, and Ball have been "conjured" by the circumstances of life in the hood: the cyclical repetitiveness of oppression, hatred, poverty, and violence. Analogously, Simms's folk character exposes the irony of contemporary slavery—an enslavement bound by ignorance of purpose and linked to the past by the painful normalcy of violence against African Americans.[3] Simms's eccentricitieshis madness—are a direct result of what he witnesses on a daily basis in the hood: the unreconciled striving of a people "with an almost morbid sense of personality and moral hesitancy which is fatal to self-confidence" (Du Bois [1908] 1989, xxi) and human decency.

Cundieff's allusions to two industries fueled by urban life—mortuaries and illegal drug activities—do not go unnoticed. Because these characters (Simms, Bulldog, Stack, and Ball) constitute the structural link that joins each of the additional stories to the film, the overarching plot of *Tales* links African and African American folklore to the horrific internalizations of people trapped by the temperament of the oppressor. Each of the subplots concretizes the complex interrelationships of fleeting eruptions of social discontent. The overlapping effect—the interrogation of the causes of racism and violence that vex the community—is seemingly contained in the frame story and its characters. Their guises (one aspect of folklore's continuing influence in the film) coincide with the structure, principles, imagery, and reversals that shape the horror genre, whether in film, literature, or television. The rites and rituals performed in the film (in one instance, each of the gang members takes a hit off a joint in a ceremonial attempt to gain courage to enter Simms's funeral home; in another, corrupt policemen desecrate the grave of a well-respected fallen black political hero by urinating on his headstone) render these abusers of cultural norms impotent and sanction the retribution of ancestral violations.

Because the wounds of the past do not disappear easily, characters such as the corpse Moorehouse[4] and the conjurer, Miss Cobbs (the ghost of the dollmaker), invite contemplation of race and gender within the context of the film, as American history serves as a parallel text to folk history. Liberation comes from telling these stories because both approaches question the benign depictions of white domination in American culture and, more importantly, underscore the tumultuous influence race exerts on identity formation in these various communities. As the mortician Simms aptly states, "Reality is a matter of perception...; perception is a cornucopia of clashing and divergent ideas."

As it stands, *Tales from the Hood* references most of the traditional folkloric elements in popular culture. *Scream* (1996), *Urban Legend* (1998), and *I Know What You Did Last Summer* (1997) are just a few of the recent movies that reveal the hedonistic disregard for moral character exhibited by white suburban youth. Their egregious coupling of sex and violence lays the groundwork for a more extensive investigation of the connections between sexuality and physical or economic dominance. These movies, along with *Tales from the Hood,* weave an interesting tapestry of cultural "punishment" enacted against the young who ignore the wisdom of the elders.

In a similar way, the monsters who dole out retribution to those who fail to turn away from their selfish ways serve as a warning to sojourners. According to Mark Kermode, the slasher film and the urban legend known as "The Hook" are similar because they revolve around the morally archetypal character of sexual promiscuity. Mikel J. Koven extends Kermode's paradigm, arguing that the enduring power of both these films and the legend rests in their "close call with death" (Koven 2003).

That is, in meeting death head on, either consciously or unaware, the surviving protagonist lives to tell the tale as a moral warning to others, thereby creating a "hook" that resonates with the other characters and audience alike (2003). In this context, *urban legend* acquires broader meanings because it becomes not only a reflection of society's hopes and fears but also an indigenous account of America's social history.

To this end, the fantastic—defined as the world where we live by Tzvetan Todorov (2000)—distinguished from the uncanny—the world that is likewise known and unknown—transcends common ways of knowing because it encodes a pedagogical and epistemological system of storytelling that reaffirms the uncommon occurrence in understandable terms. Likewise, this text—displayed in visual signs—speaks the unspeakable in cognitive categories that challenge our understanding not only of horror but also history within the confines of the horrific. Thus, the social-script is interrogated and the cultural text reified through a process of oral/visual literacy.

These allegories codify the unifying myths and dreams that the dominant culture revisits through mass culture. The dismantling of social and political ideologies worshipped in certain strata of society fuels the renegotiation of folk traditions in American culture. Ideological primers such as materialism, vanity, and compulsive sexuality reappear as rhyming didactic elements whose effectiveness stems from the influential reality of existing norms. The cover of the video case for *Tales from the Hood* depicts a skull with sunshades that cover the sockets of its empty eyes. If the eyes are indeed the windows to the soul, the emptiness of the nihilistic deprivation that pervades many urban centers is reflected back to the viewer of this film in a self-reflexive form of the monstrous Other—an Other historically affirmed in the mythologies of racism that undergird the representations of poverty so prevalent in Hollywood screen images. By incorporating and adapting these representations, narratives, and images, Cundieff reinscribes the filmic language of horror so that these images can now be read in a distinctly black voice that simultaneously frames and reformulates the genre. Moreover, the hood, in this sense, becomes its own reflective center, straddling the borderlands of the imagined and real elements of this space. If the hood is indeed the site "where nightmares and reality meet on the streets" (*Tales'* tagline), then the architects of this nightmare become the progenitors of an urban legacy that is replicated in the communal traditions of a people whose inheritance is siphoned away by the everyday realities of city living.

The Paradox of Horror

The paradox of horror is that we must revisit, more often than not, the origin of our fear. The production of *Tales from the Hood* coincided, eerily, with the barely repressed fears of an American society grappling with the resurgence of blatant acts of racism that demonstrated a reckless disregard for black life. The 1990 videotaped beating of Rodney King and the spectacle of the O.J. Simpson trial loomed large in American popular culture. So, too, did the 1989 Charles Stuart case and the 1994 Susan Smith case, which exemplified the national perception of African Americans as venal and inhumane.

The murder of Martin Moorehouse, the first tale in the film, reflects the angst of this cultural vortex and reveals the ever-present fear of "high-tech" and "low-tech" lynching that permeates the African American male psyche. This "racial ritual of keeping the Negro 'in his place'" (Ellison 1964, 276) has played itself out in repetitious formulations centered on maleness—images that continue to define power relationships in American society. According to Sandra Gunning, the image of the black man has continually functioned as an ever-evolving metaphor in our national discourse of power (1996, 3). History has demonstrated that whenever mainstream power is threatened, reconfigured, or socially realigned, violence—literal or rhetorical—is the method of defense. If the rope or gun used in these acts of domination represents low-tech lynching , high-tech lynching encompasses the repressive actions implemented against black males whom society has deemed "strange fruit" within America's infrastructure of privilege and politics. Moorehouse's death at the hands of corrupt racist white cops who deem him a political agitator can then be viewed as a reflection of this interracial wrangling. His beating and subsequent death (which stems from a routine traffic stop) underscores the vulnerability black men feel in the presence of the law. Racial profiling is the cause of this angst. That Cundieff and coproducer and coscreenwriter Darin Scott chose Billie Holiday's version of Abel Meeropol's song "Strange Fruit" as background music while Moorehouse is savagely assaulted emphasizes the black man's vulnerability: the past and present become one in the battered physical frame of the "prophet" Martin Ezekiel Moorehouse.

Cundieff's savvy in weaving fact with fiction in this scene enables him to rewrite the cultural narrative of lynching. As Fredric Jameson argues in *The Political Unconscious*, we must foreground the interpretative frameworks or codes through which we receive and read texts: "texts come before us as the always-already read" (1981, 9). It is the goal of folklore, then, and its accompanying devices, tricksterism and resistance, to "mess up the order...," to disrupt what is normal (Ammons and White-Parks 1994, vii). *Tales* accomplishes this feat. Where in the historical record, the victim is castrated, disembodied, dismembered, and silenced, *Tales* provides a forum for the victim to "talk back" to his aggressors in horrific fashion, in acts of retaliation that seldom occur in public circles. The brutal deaths of these rogue cops—one has his head completely severed from his body; another is killed by flying hypodermic needles from a crack alley that nail him to a muraled wall emblazoned with an image of a crucifix (flipping the script if you will)—suggest that spiritual law will right the wrongs in the end.

So the film simultaneously reworks the historical master narrative of lynching that found many African American men and women killed by "parties unknown." Because these lynchings were more often than not public ceremonies carried out in the presence of white judges, attorneys, and law-enforcement officials, *Tales* confronts the larger issue of social accountability for historical wrongs in American history and foregrounds the anonymity of passive compliance with racist ideologies.

That the dead exact revenge against the living in this film underscores the narrative of lynching. Moorehouse's spiritual return in the psyche of the young black rookie who witnesses his beating reveals that *witnessing* such an act carries with it the burden of genealogical transference. In "Can you be BLACK and look at this?" Elizabeth Alexander poses a central question concerning African American racial memory and the paradoxical nature of witnessing, which includes recognizing yourself in what you see. She asks, "What do the scenes of communally witnessed violence...tell us about the way that 'text' is carried in the African-American flesh?" (1994, 77) Embedded in Alexander's probing analysis is a series of cultural touchstones—mnemonic wounds—that return the reader to the repressed racial subtext associated with the national failure to recognize black communal pain. As Alexander rightly determines, "African-Americans have always existed in a counter-citizen relationship to the law; how else to contend with knowing oneself as a whole human when the Constitution defines you as 'three-fifths'?"(1994, 77). This fact alone *re*aggravates the cultural wounds evident in the African American racial memory. What is less clear, however, is the damage done to individuals subjected to daily assaults upon their persons. The four central characters and subcharacters in *Tales* suggest that these assaults leave fissures in the troubled minds of their sufferers.

That films such as *Candyman* (1992), *Bones* (2001), and *Tales from the Hood* pose these and other questions concerning the impact of urban decay and economic and social disenfranchisement upon the African American community means that the national consciousness is being pricked and cannot continue to exist in the comfort of its amnesiac haze. But as Audre Lorde reminds us, "...we have no patterns for relating across our human differences as equals" (West 1993, 93). The horror of this inability to reach across developing patterns of human communication points to a more troubling paradox associated with human nature and the effects that witnessing has on the seer. As Ellison so poignantly illustrates, the "sleepwalkers" are those with the most power—to see or not to see. They can choose to acknowledge the character of a man or hide it under the myths of distorting glass insidiously created by American society ([1947] 1994, 1). The potency of these myths and the unyielding power they have over those individuals who create and use them freely is movingly embodied in the mental and spiritual breakdown of the black rookie cop Clarence Smith. His descent into a mental and spiritual hell is as much a result of his naïveté (he really did believe that his fellow officers would take Moorehouse to the hospital) as his disillusioned belief that his blue uniform will help him make a difference. As Elizabeth Alexander aptly points out, "African-American viewers have been taught a sorry lesson of their continual, physical vulnerability in the United States, a lesson that helps shape how it is we understand ourselves..." (1994, 78). It is this feeling of angst that frames the context for understanding the undercurrent in *Tales*, a film that asks the question: "Where do we go from here?"

Allegorical Returns

Kelly Oliver argues in her study *Witnessing* that your ability to bear witness to trauma involves a working through of your own feelings of inadequacy to avoid the repetitive compulsion of "recalling the ways in which you were made into an object" (2001, x). In short, bearing witness to torture or enslavement recalls the trauma of that original experience. In depicting the overlapping actions of Smith and gang member Crazy K, Cundieff and Scott act as elders themselves by creating a continuum that extends from the previous centuries of black male existence to the present. Viewed through the lens of African American folklore, this conversion narrative refigures the dynamic of the ritualized and tortured black male figure through a psychic rememorialization that allows the living to re-member him and demonstrates the community's responsibility to educate, recall, and reach out to those who have forgotten how to fly. As the folk tale "The Parable of the Eagle" states, "My people of Africa, we were created in the image of God, but men have made us think that we are chickens, and we still think we are, but we are eagles. Stretch forth your wings and fly! Don't be content with the food of chickens!" (Aggrey 1971, 135). The goal of the listener, the reader, and critic alike is to remind others—through written, oral, or visual means—to look beyond the first story and absorb the second story, that narrative that lies below the surface. If we fail to examine this morphological structure of storytelling—its legends and subtexts—we will be condemned to a psychic hell of disremembered rememberings as we perpetually engage in vain rhetorical strivings where no one knows how "to fly." But more chilling is the realization that if we do not reach back, we will have no one to tell our stories to or left to hear them.

Notes

1. James Van Der Zee (1886–1983) is best known for his portraits of black New Yorkers during the Harlem Renaissance. His portraits of the dead, however, have solidified his place in African American folk culture. Writer Toni Morrison states that Van Der Zee's work in *The Harlem Book of the Dead* (1978) helped to shape her character Beloved. Along those same lines, African American writer Charles Chesnutt (1858–1932) made African American hoodoo beliefs and practices available to the reading public in his collection *The Conjure Woman and other Conjure Tales* ([1899] 1993). Chesnutt's tales of reincarnation and retribution helped revitalize the culture of folklore in the late nineteenth and early twentieth centuries, and both Chesnutt and Van Der Zee's artistic works suggest that African Americans have long used death to investigate social injustice and cultural immorality in the past and present. This folk culture of death is what Cundieff engages with in *Tales*. The significance of this approach is brilliantly displayed in Karla Holloway's *Passed On: African American Mourning Stories* (2002) and Sharon Holland's *Raising the Dead: Readings of Death and (Black) Subjectivity* (2000), where Holland suggests that staying black and dying may be twins of the same lived experience in America.
2. His name resonates with two known Klansmen whose prominence in political circles has always caused alarm—David Duke, the former Grand Wizard of the Ku Klux Klan in the 1970s (who also ran a hotly contested race for the Louisiana House of Representatives in 1989), and Tom Metzger, grand wizard of the California Ku Klux Klan and leader of the White Aryan Resistance. Metzger's organization took a major hit in the mid-1980s when Morris Dees, a prominent Jewish attorney, sued and won millions of dollars in a wrongful death suit lodged against Metzger's group for the lynching death of a sixteen-year-old African American teen.
3. Simms's folk-character persona also includes his memorable role of Linc Hayes in the cult television series *The Mod Squad* (ABC, 1968–73), which was

a permanent fixture in the late 1960s and early '70s. The show stressed the notion of achieving justice "by any means necessary"—that is, through non-conventional means.

4. Moorehouse's name suggests Morehouse University—an institution that grooms strong black male leaders; his middle name, Ezekiel, reflects his prophet status in the hood—a valley of "dry bones."

Filmography

Bones (2001). 96 min. Ernest R. Dickerson
Candyman (1992). 99 min. Bernard Rose
I Know What You Did Last Summer (1997). 100 min. Jim Gillespie
The Mod Squad (1968–1973). ABC
Scream (1996). 111 min. Wes Craven
Tales from the Crypt (1989–1996). HBO
Tales from the Hood (1995). 98 min. Rusty Cundieff
Urban Legend (1998). 99 min. Jamie Blanks

Works Cited

Aggrey, James. 1971. The parable of the eagle. In *Tales and stories for black folks,* ed. Toni Cade Bambara, 135. Garden City, New York: Zenith Books.

Alexander, Elizabeth. 1994. "Can you be BLACK and look at this": Reading the Rodney King video(s). *Public Culture 7*: 77–95.

All God's chillen had wings. 2004. In *The Norton anthology of African American literature,* ed. Nellie McKay and Henry Louis Gates, Jr., 132–34. 2nd ed. New York: W.W. Norton & Company.

Ammons, Elizabeth, and Annette White-Parks, eds. 1994. *Tricksterism in turn-of-the-century American literature: A multicultural perspective.* Hanover, NH: University Press of New England.

Chesnutt, Charles Waddell. [1899] 1993. *The conjure woman and other conjure tales.* Ed. Richard H. Brodhead. Repr., Durham, NC: Duke University Press.

Du Bois, W. E. B. [1908] 1989. *The souls of black folk.* Repr., New York: Bantam Books.

Ellison, Ralph. 1964. *Shadow and act.* New York: Random House.

———. *Invisible man.* [1947] 1994. Repr. New York: Vintage Books.

Fulmer, Jacqueline. 2002. "Men ain't all"—A reworking of masculinity in *Tales from the hood* or Grandma meets the zombie. *Journal of American Folklore 115*: 422–42.

Guerrero, Ed. 1994. *Framing blackness.* Philadelphia: Temple University Press.

Gunning, Sandra. 1996. *Race, rape, and lynching: The red record of American literature, 1890–1912.* New York: Oxford University Press.

Holland, Sharon. 2000. *Raising the dead: Readings of death and (black) subjectivity.* Durham, NC: Duke University Press.

Holloway, Karla. 2002. *Passed on: African American mourning stories.* Durham, NC: Duke University Press.

Jameson, Fredric. 1981. *The political unconscious: Narrative as a socially symbolic act.* Ithaca, NY: Cornell University Press.

Koven, Mikel J. 2003. The terror tale: Urban legends and the slasher film. *Scope: An on-line journal of film studies,* April. Institute of Film Studies, University of Nottingham. http://www.scope.nottingham.ac.uk/ (accessed July 12, 2005).

McKay, Nellie. 1983. An interview with Toni Morrison. *Contemporary Literature* 24 (4): 413–29.

Oliver, Kelly. 2001. *Witnessing: Beyond recognition.* Minneapolis: University of Minnesota Press.

O'Meally, Robert G. 2004. Introduction to *The Norton Anthology of African American Literature,* ed. Nellie McKay and Henry Louis Gates, Jr., 3–8.

Todorov, Tzvetan. 2000. Definition of the fantastic. In *The horror reader,* ed. Ken Gelder, 14–19. London: Routledge.

Van Der Zee, James. 1978. *The Harlem book of the dead.* Ed. Camille Billops. New York: Morgan & Morgan, Inc.

West, Cornel. 1993. *Race matters.* New York: Vintage Books.

IV.

DISRUPTION AND INCORPORATION

10

The Virgin Victim

Reimagining a Medieval Folk Ballad in The Virgin Spring
and The Last House on the Left

K. A. LAITY

Two FILMS COULD not be executed more differently than Ingmar Bergman's crisp, black-and-white *Jungfrukällan* (*The Virgin Spring*, 1960), and
Wes Craven's boldly bloody *The Last House on the Left* (1972), yet both
ultimately spring from the same source: a ballad of tragedy and revenge
dating to at least the sixteenth century. The plot of the ballad details the
murder of a daughter by robbers. Seeking shelter, the robbers unknow-
ingly ask hospitality of the girl's parents and then display her belong-
ings. The parents, realizing what has occurred, kill the killers. The two
filmmakers share not only this story but also a strict religious upbringing
against which both rebelled; yet their interpretations of the tale suggest
very different conclusions about the ballad's significance. For Bergman,
the landscape rests uneasily between two harsh father gods: Ingeri's
Odin and the Christian God of Karin's father. For Craven, the absence of
moral certainty permeates the lives of the parents as well as the killers,
and authority appears either nonexistent or ridiculous. The flexibility
of the ballad tradition easily encompasses both interpretations despite
major changes in details and different production choices.

This should come as no surprise. As G. Malcolm Laws, Jr., noted in
his study, *The British Literary Ballad*, the most successful modern practitioners of the ancient form are those who combine "timeless subject
matter and contemporary idiom" (1972, 94). While Laws focused on the
effect of the broadside on contemporary ballad tradition, it is easy to
argue that film provides an even more immediate re-visioning of ballad motifs. The ballad "Herr Truelses døtre" (the English title, "which is
descriptive of the narrative content of the type" [Jonsson, Solheim, and
Danielson 1978, 20], is "Sisters murder by brothers avenged by Father")
proves to be a perfect springboard for these filmmakers. The ballad tradition across Scandinavia shows much variety, yet also considerable

similarities, largely due to the language congruence during the Middle Ages. While many examples may be younger (or older) than this time, "Scandinavian ballads are usually regarded as a medieval genre" because of their oral formulaic qualities (Rossel 1982, 11). While Danish practitioners of the *rímur* maintained this oral tradition, throughout much of Scandinavia (and Sweden, in particular), the ballads eventually became a part of literary tradition (Ker 1909, 18). Thus, Bergman came to the film version of the ballad by way of the novelist Ulla Isaksson, screenwriter for the film. New packaging for the Criterion rerelease, however, implies a more direct link by including a copy of the ballad in the companion booklet.

Ballads based on anonymous martyrs often feature motifs known throughout Europe, specified by locations familiar to regional singers and audiences. Religious stories in Scandinavia often center on particular figures: St. Olaf in Norway and St. Stephen in Sweden (Rossel 1982, 9). "Herr Truelses døtre" does not follow this pattern, however; it is listed as B21 among the legendary ballads in *The Types of the Scandinavian Medieval Ballad: A Descriptive Catalogue* (Jonsson, Solheim, and Danielson 1978, 55). This comprehensive catalogue gives a definitive outline of the B21 ballad type, but we should keep in mind the authors' caveat that "a ballad is an 'idea' in the Platonic sense...every text is as *good* as another" (Jonsson, Solheim, and Danielson 1978, 14). Indeed this particular narrative appears in Danish, Faroese, Icelandic, and Norwegian as well as Swedish in more or less comparable forms. Jonsson, Solheim, and Danielson summarize the story this way:

> Sir Truels' sons are...stolen away by robbers or...sent away by Truels (because they are told that they will harm their own sisters). Truels' (two or three) daughters oversleep one morning. They...put on their best clothes and hurry off to church. In the wood they meet robbers (one, two or three). When the girls reject their erotic advances the robbers kill them...(Miracles appear at the place where they die). The robbers go to the Truels' house and display the possessions of the murdered girls. Truels understands what has happened...Truels has the robbers executed or kills them himself...Truels comes to understand that the robbers were his own sons...he commits suicide or...does penance by building a church. (1978, 55)

The ballad certainly offers a macabre tale. Though the two filmmakers decided to abandon the motif of the final revelation of the robbers as sons, for the most part, they kept the major elements intact. We might expect more radical changes, given the date of the source. Robert Stam argues, "The greater the lapse in time, the less reverence toward the source text and the more likely the reinterpretation through the values of the present" (2000, 57). However, both filmmakers seem to want to maintain the folkloric ambience of the tale while updating the setting and reflecting the "values of the present." Bergman does so by maintaining the authoritative setting of the medieval past; Craven instead capitalizes on the salacious appeal of the urban (or contemporary) legend, a phenomenon Jan Harold Brunvand identified several years after the film's release. As Brunvand puts it, "Urban legends gain credibility from specific details of time and place or from reference to source authorities" ([1979] 1989, 3). Craven sets the ballad narrative in the present day to provide specific and believable details, while Bergman invokes the ballad itself as an authority. Both make changes but often with the same aim: connecting the audience emotionally to the narrative.

Rossel argues that "a study of such changes in the ballad text...which create[s] the variants is extremely valuable in order to map out and analyze the tradition of a certain text" (1982, 14). Changing the robber sons to robber strangers seems appropriate to reflect the complexities of the modern world and proves typical of the appropriation of medieval stories in general. As Greta Austin writes, medieval-themed films "usually tell stories not about the Middle Ages, but about modern Western life in a period dress" (2002, 137). Bergman takes this tack, using the medieval setting to express his ambivalence about the role of divinity in his life, while Craven discards the pretence of the medieval setting altogether to depict a world bereft of divine influence.

Both use the miraculous tale to question the role of and attention to the divine in their characters' lives, while maintaining the horror of the original ballad. The folkloric inclusion of the transformative forest, where significant action takes place in both films, strengthens the overlap between the two narratives and creates a sense of verisimilitude. As Jack Zipes argues, "The forest *allows* for enchantment and disenchantment, for it is the place where society's conventions no longer hold true. It is the source of natural right, thus the starting place where social wrongs can be righted" (1987, 67). Because of the ballad, we have these transformative expectations in mind, but both filmmakers use the chthonic power of the forest to destabilize society, not to right wrongs. Thus, as Zipes also argues, the forest encompasses all possibilities for it is "unconventional, free, alluring, but dangerous" (1987, 67). For Bergman, the divine power of the father god must impose his will upon the freedom of the forest; for Craven, the absence of that power assures that the forest remains a dangerous place.

The moral choices presented by the filmmakers provide the sharpest contrasts between their films. According to Philip Strick, Bergman had apparently been searching for the right material to recapture a sense of certainty. Bergman himself noted, "I needed a severe and schematic conception of the world to get away from the formless, the vague and the obscure in which I was stuck. So I turned to the dogmatic Christianity of the Middle Ages with its clear dividing lines between Good and Evil" (2002, 2). The screenplay by Ulla Isaksson mirrors that stark morality, just as the black-and-white imagery of the film reflects it. The harsh father god, whether Odin or Yahweh, maintains an iron rule without sympathy. There are no doubts about the rules, just as there are no doubts about the consequences of breaking them, whether the crime is lust, pride, avarice, or anger.

If Craven lacked Bergman's desire for moral certitude, it was no doubt due to his upbringing: "I wasn't allowed to see movies when I was a child. It was against the religion I was raised in, Fundamentalist Baptist. I didn't go into a commercial movie house until I was a senior in college, and that was on the sly. It wasn't until I was in graduate school that I immersed myself in films. Then, I went to see all the films by Bergman, Fellini, etc." (Lofficier 1999). Beginning filmmaking at the bottom as a messenger boy, Craven found modest initial success working with producer Sean Cunningham. The two were offered fifty thousand dollars by Vanguard, a small film company, to make a horror film. Craven describes their guiding principle: "Our agreement was that we would just hold nothing back. We would do the most outrageous things we could think of" (Lofficier 1999). Craven's recollection on the commentary of the DVD release is that the film was based "roughly on *The Virgin Spring*, where you had a girl who was middle class and her father was a doctor and she went off on a pilgrimage, and there was a serving girl who was a friend of hers and actually knew much more about the world and helped her get through the rougher parts of the world when disaster started to strike."[1] His recall of Bergman's film is, of course, wildly inaccurate. Karin and Ingeri are far from friends, and Ingeri certainly does not help Karin when disaster strikes, but rather watches from afar. The girls are not really on a pilgrimage in the medieval sense, more of an errand. Töre is not a doctor but a farmer.

Unlike Bergman's film that begins with the hopefulness of spring, *Last House* takes place in autumn as if the world itself is dying. The voice of authority is at once ever present in the voice of the radio and TV news and the uniforms of the postman, sheriff, and deputy, but also distant and usually ineffectual. Craven's aim was not to seek an absolute moral victory; rather, he "wanted to show violence how it was, nasty and ugly and protracted," capturing the reality where you "didn't have a cutaway or a fade to black." In essence, he wished to deconstruct any notion of true authority or morality, to problematize the categories of good and evil, and to leave the audience adrift in a shaky conundrum. He explained later, "My whole intention was to show murder in a film that was as I would imagine it to be, rather than as it was depicted in films normally at that time. That is, the person delivered the killing blow, and the victim died, maybe with a few gasps, but not always. They would never fight a protracted fight, and would [never] suffer clearly in front of the camera" (Lofficier 1999). Craven hoped the ugliness would make viewers acknowledge their participation and complicity in the process, asking them "Were you hoping to be amused?" by all the violence in the film. He says it was the "academic in me" that made him want to compel the audience to consider all the violence in the past, the background against which history to date has unfolded.

The daughters form the center of the moral questioning. For Bergman, the split is particularly poignant. Not only are the two girls stepsisters but they are also openly hostile to one another. The family has taken in pregnant Ingeri (Gunnel Lindblom), while the favored daughter Karin (Birgitta Pettersson) glows in pampered luxury. Bergman's stark black-and-white palate, aided by the preternaturally beautiful cinematography of Sven Nykvist, seems always to cast shadows upon Ingeri while bathing Karin in light, even in her small, close room. She assumes her status as special and beloved and also assumes that no one is immune to her charm. The antagonism between the two girls goes beyond simple sibling rivalry—they are representatives of the warring gods, Odin and Christ. Bergman uses the girls to reflect the lingering hold of paganism within the Christian realm of late medieval Sweden. Ingeri's knowledge that it is the family's Christian charity that gives her a place on their farm only magnifies her resentment. Her furtive prayer to Odin that opens the film calls curses down upon her benefactors, particularly the privileged Karin, whom Ingeri later admits to hating because she has become pregnant. She secretes a toad within a loaf of bread for Karin's trip as a silent curse upon her privileged state, unaware that she will accompany her to the distant church to take candles for the virgin.

In *Last House*, the two young women are best friends rather than sisters. The friend, like Ingeri, is considerably more morally ambiguous than the virtuous heroine. The free-spirited ambience of the 1960s infuses the opening of the film with a deceptively lighthearted tone, as nostalgia inducing as Mari's peace-sign necklace. Our first view of Mari

Collingwood (Sandra Cassel) is through the frosted glass of her shower, then nude from the waist up before a fogged mirror. She clears it with a towel and then smiles at her reflection. She is openly proud of her figure and comfortable with the image of her naked body. In the previous scene with the postman, he comments upon her "pride," saying, "she's not the first girl to turn sixteen." Even when dressed, Mari is transparent: as Craven remarks, "This was still the time when going without a brassiere was considered incredibly risqué." Doubling the scene in *The Virgin Spring* when Karin's mother frets about the beating she would have received if she had had Karin's stubbornness, Mari's mother tries to talk about how different things were when she was her daughter's age, but neither daughter wants any curbs on her enthusiasm. In Craven's film, the friend, Phyllis Stone (Lucy Grantham), is the more experienced of the two, taking the lead in their conversations and adventures and, eventually, attempting to shield Mari from the worst assaults. Yet despite her edge of world weariness, it is presumably Phyllis who suggests they stop in the city for an innocent ice cream before the concert. Though Phyllis and Mari are not actual sisters, the bond between the two is stronger and more sustaining than the blood between Karin and Ingeri.

The parents in the two films are likewise contrasted against their respective moral backdrops. The ever-anxious Märeta (Birgitta Valberg) in *The Virgin Spring* first appears before her giant crucifix. The shot cuts directly from Ingeri's call to Odin to Märeta, thereby emphasizing her piety. Märeta suffers, but it is not immediately clear from what. Prayers are insufficient to slake her guilt, though. Despite her husband's protesting reaction, she pours hot wax from her candle onto her wrist to mortify her flesh. We later discover that Märeta's other children have all died, and consequently understand better why she spoils Karin. She "is all I have," Märeta repeats. Together the two dress Karin in her finest for the journey: the shift embroidered by fifteen maidens, the white stockings, and the blue shoes with pearls. While Märeta cannot help worrying about all the boys Karin danced with the night before, her daughter is unconcerned. Karin knows her fate is not to marry a mere farmer and ignores the prophecy in her mother's "evil dream." Yet Märeta's distress suggests that, in reward for her faith, her God seeks to warn her of impending doom.

Her husband, Töre (Max von Sydow), seems to have tired long ago of Märeta's painful mortifications despite his concern for her pain. He has dealt with their losses by becoming stern and withdrawn. He makes his pronouncements with the gravity of an Old Testament prophet, except when it comes to scolding lazy Karin. In a rare moment, he lifts her in his arms, and amidst their joshing banter, we see the child she no longer is and the man he can no longer be.

The Collingwoods in *Last House*, in contrast, are themselves sensual and affectionate with one another. The lighthearted scenes of the couple at home, both with Mari before she and Phyllis go off to the concert and while preparing for Mari's birthday celebrations, show their intimacy and genuine affection; the fact that these shots are intercut with the increasingly tense scenes of the girls in the thugs' apartment heightens the contrast. Unlike Bergman, Craven only sketches in the characters. While the two films run nearly the same length, Bergman uses much more of his time setting up the characters' positions across the moral spectrum; Craven, on the other hand, stretches out the violent episodes. The running time of *The Virgin Spring* is eighty-nine minutes, while *The Last House on the Left* (depending on the cut) runs anywhere from eighty-two to ninety-one minutes, but these running times are close enough to be comparable. We know that John (Richard Towers) is a doctor and that Estelle (Cynthia Carr) is not a professional baker (as the lopsided birthday cake demonstrates), but other than the fact that they are loving, permissive, and middle class, they are not given any moral standing. John gives Mari the important peace-symbol necklace, but the focus seems to be on his affection, negating the symbol's original meaning. Although Estelle and John seem a little surprised by their daughter's "new" ideas, they are not at all alarmed. That complacency, though, is precisely what Craven hopes to attack: their assumption that a moral structure guides behavior, yet there is no need to invoke it, explain it, or maintain it. While Bergman examines the effects of harsh morality, Craven dissects the results of the all-too-vague morality of the early 1970s.

The other important characters are, of course, the robbers. In *The Virgin Spring*, they initially claim to be goatherds, which potentially aligns them with demonic forces according to Christian mythology and Thor on the pagan side, as he drove a pair of goats which remain popular as the omnipresent Swedish holiday decoration, the Julbok. (The goats also prove to be their downfall—Karin recognizes the mark on one goat as her neighbor's and begins to grow suspicious.) The folkloric number of three remains; one is mute (Tor Isedal), but his companion (Axel Düberg) makes up for his inability to express himself by having a tongue more than ready to deceive with volubility. The third, however, is a small boy (Ove Porath) that again suggests the possibility of brothers: given their ruthlessness, why else would the two others allow him to tag along? The child's innocence offers the audience the possibility of sympathy and hope. Of all the characters in *The Virgin Spring*, the robbers are the least well developed. They seem to stand for the ideas of hunger and aimlessness, lacking sustenance and direction both literally and spiritually.

We see a lot more of the robbers in *Last House*, in part due to Craven's stated intent to problematize our notions of good and evil. While they are initially presented as types, we come to recognize—if not sympathize—with them as individuals. Most disturbingly, the leader "Krug [David Hess] was based on my father," Craven claims, "who always scared the shit out of me." Although his father died while Craven was young, he used the film to explore the frightening father figure, commenting, "So I guess Junior [Marc Sheffler] is a little bit of me, too." Rather than brothers, we have the father and son play out a painful Oedipal dynamic. As if to emphasize this archetypal relationship, Krug is almost always chomping on a phallic cigar. The third robber, Weasel (Fred J. Lincoln), initially resembles another stereotypical tough guy but gradually reveals some surprising nuances. Craven adds a fourth—Sadie (Jeramie Rain), a female, as if in ironic recognition of the strides women were just beginning to make during the growing second wave of feminism in the early seventies. In Craven's film, women's equality extends to violent criminal activities. When Krug and Weasel converge on her for a sexual encounter, she fights them off with "I'm my own freakin' woman" and demands that they get "a couple more chicks" to handle the sexual burden. It is Sadie who points out the phallic symbolism, although in a nod to her criminal ignorance, she pronounces it "p-hallus." Craven and Cunningham acknowledge that they exploited the issues of the time like emerging feminism and sexually explorative films.[2]

Key to both narratives are the rape scenes. In *The Virgin Spring*, Ingeri sees the encounter as fulfillment of her prayer to Odin. The slap Karin delivers just before they reach the river seems to have sealed her fate. A cut to a cawing raven brings a dark ambience to the journey of the wrangling girls. If the raven is an ambiguous sign of Odin, the immediate cut to the one-eyed bridge keeper (Axel Slangus) is far less so. The man under the cloak is unmistakably Odin, and a terrified Ingeri recognizes him at once. As if to assure our connection between the god and his familiar raven (Huginn or Munin), a longer shot frames both as the raven continues to cry. Karin blithely takes no notice, but Ingeri's gaze is fixed and suspicious. Impulsively, she runs across the river and begs Karin not to go on because "the forest is so black," but Karin, unafraid, dismisses her sister's fears and convinces Ingeri instead to remain behind "to rest."

The bridge keeper begs Ingeri to enter his home, claiming he can help her. Asking his name, Ingeri receives the typically noncommittal answer of gods in human disguise: "These days, I have no name." He continues answering her direct questions with prevarications: "I hear what I will, and I see what I will. I hear what mankind whispers in secret…" He suggests that Ingeri can share his power, and she hears a thundering sound which he declares to be "three dead men rid[ing] north." His mocking laughter frightens Ingeri, and she seeks to avoid his apparently amorous intentions. His bench is carved with likenesses of the gods, and he displays before her amulets with various powers. When she accuses him of blood sacrifice, he growls, "I recognized you at once" and promises to give her strength if she is not afraid. Yet she cannot bear his embrace and rushes off in time to witness—but not prevent—Karin's rape and murder.

While Ingeri struggles with her god, Karin plays the princess. Intrigued by the jaw harp one herder plays, she stops to talk, then decides magnanimously to share her meal with the hungry travelers. Clearly the mute robber is ready to forcefully take her wealth immediately, but his partner seems to be looking at the long-term possibilities, and they sit down to eat, somewhat annoyed by Karin's insistence on prayer first. Her bragging about her wonderful (and imaginary) wealth and prominence whets their other appetites, and Karin begins to fear for her safety, capturing a kid in her arms as if to shield her innocence with another's. The reappearance of the toad presages the sudden attack by the two men, which is stark and violent, the two fighting even between themselves to be the one to rape her first, while the wide-eyed boy looks on. Ingeri, watching from a distance, picks up a rock but helplessly lets it fall. It is what she wished for. The despoiled Karin clutches her torn shift and staggers toward the camera as if to seek aid from the audience, then gives up and turns away. Frightened by their own actions, the robbers panic, and the mute robber strikes her down with a single blow from a branch, causing the blood on her forehead to mirror the shadows of the branches above her. Recovering from the shock, the robbers hastily strip her body of its finery. They leave the boy behind to gaze mutely upon her body as a light snow falls.

The encounter between the robbers and the girls in *Last House* lacks all innocence because the two are in search of marijuana on the Lower East Side, the place where Craven says he "lost his virginity" and became "cynical." Mari seems somewhat reluctant to wander the city streets, calling the area "dirty." Phyllis avers that it is only "funky," and thus no threat, because she remains determined to buy some drugs. Spotting Junior, they decide to ask him where they can score some drugs. Initially he repulses their question, then seems to remember Sadie's desire for a "couple more chicks" and brings them back to the flat. The turn to violence here is also sudden and scary. The rape scene is drawn out in full horror, extended as if to prolong the hope that something, anything, will happen to stop the final outcome. Phyllis is raped first to force us to watch Mari's initial loss of innocence and denial. The tender scenes between the Collingwoods offer a stark counterpoint to the violence of the thugs, ganging up on Phyllis and punching her in the stomach to subdue her. The couple's fond embrace, between civilized tumblers of scotch, fades to black in a genteel recognition of propriety, and then cuts to stark daylight outside the crumbling building where the thugs dwell. The harsh morning light highlights the removal of one body down the fire escape, leaving the viewer initially in suspense as to both the fate of innocent Mari and the state of both girls, who wind up in the trunk of the Cadillac. Recalling once more the ballad narrative, the car happens to break down just in front of the Collingwood house.

The narrative should move at that point to the revenge scenario, but instead we get a prolongation of the rape and murder. One focus is humiliation: "piss your pants," Krug demands of Phyllis, which she does, then unconsciously tries to shield herself. Next they demand that the two girls perform lasciviously before the eager onlookers. Phyllis tries to protect and comfort Mari, repeating, "It's just us," as if she can ignore the horror surrounding them. Phyllis's escape attempt proves a dead end, but Craven manipulates the audience expectation that, so close to home, the girls will survive the ordeal and get away. Mari's frantic bargaining with Junior—whom she rechristens Willow, perhaps in the hope that he will bend to her weeping—offers momentary hope and allows the passing of the symbolic—and telling—peace-symbol necklace. Weasel shows concern for the injured Sadie, which is "one of the set of mindfucks of this movie," Craven remarks; "these people doing horrible things, somehow, in their perverse way cared about each other so that the audience had to feel their humanity." He notes, "People hated you for it," but his aim was to throw the "whole moral compass...out the window." He deconstructs the moral absolutism of *The Virgin Spring*. Even the use of handheld cameras mirrors the omnipresent (in 1972) handheld camera footage of Vietnam, the war that still divides Americans into opposing factions more than thirty years later.

The carnage continues. The sound of a car nearby encourages Phyllis, but she is betrayed by the sight of a grim cemetery. Its dappled sunlight breaks with the sudden thrust into the frame of Krug's machete. Her murder is the realism Craven sought to reproduce, the desire to "hang on to life, try to crawl away," while the brutal flat expressions of the killers, as we now know them to be, surround her. In contrast to Karin's death, there is no single blow of violence. Instead, we have an orgy of blood on the victim's body and the killers. Interspliced with the gore are shots of Phyllis's exposed underwear as she is once more stripped before her tormentors, who all take pleasure in penetrating her flesh. As if afraid we may not be flinching sufficiently, Sadie reaches into Phyllis's gut and caresses a length of bowel. Even the killers seem shocked by their daring. Without boundaries, they seem uncertain and cowed before the awesome universe opening before them.

The subsequent rape of Mari becomes a necessity because, as Craven argues, "they [the robbers] don't have any authority anymore" and need to reestablish it. This action is punctuated by Junior/Willow's single tear, his last vestige of humanity. It remains "a powerful depiction of rape," Craven acknowledges, with man as animal while the woman "has more dignity than he will ever have in his life." Her captors exchange looks of—if not guilt—confusion. Mari retches behind them, then launches into the whispered prayer of a child: "Now I lay me down to sleep." The ineffectuality of their bid to reclaim power shows as they attempt to wipe the blood off their hands, then follow Mari as she shambles down the water's edge as if to wash the horror off herself. The killers at last resort to shooting her submerged body, unable to bring themselves to once more meet her flesh to flesh.

Vengeance for his daughter's death seems destined already in *The Virgin Spring* when we see Töre, fully dressed and standing implacably before his door. It almost seems a surprise that he graciously offers the robbers sanctuary from the storm and, later, the possibility of work. But we believe much more easily in offered hospitality because of the medieval setting of Bergman's film; much of northern Germanic literature eagerly applauds the man who gives freely of gifts and readily offers hospitality. It is telling that in the midst of their anxiety—Märeta can only wring her hands wistfully and repeat, "She's all I have"—they hold firmly to their views of Christian charity and allow the killers at their table. When the boy, still sickened by the violence, cannot eat the food put before them, both Märeta and Frida (Gudrun Brost) suggest helpful healing remedies for the child. A fallen priest (Oskar Ljung) even makes an attempt to heal the boy's soul with warnings about hell and stories about the power of faith.

In *Last House,* credibility is stretched thin by the desire to stick close to the ballad's plot for the first time, not so much by the bizarre coincidence of the robbers finding Mari's home but by their seeking sanctuary there. It is telling that the most antiquated aspect of the film is the offering of hospitality. Craven mentions the original scene in *The Virgin*

Spring, noting how a storm forces the robbers to take shelter in "the house of the parents of one of the girls that they've just killed." He also gives the killers his own remembered awkwardness in dealing with a more sophisticated lifestyle. In a reversal, it is the robbers who discover first that they have fallen upon the home of Mari, pondering aloud (as Craven says, no doubt echoing the viewer's incredulity), "Wonder what the odds are on that?" He is conscious, too, of using the "*Psycho* technique" (having the main characters killed off in the middle of the film) to leave the audience at sea without a clear trajectory.

While in *The Virgin Spring* Märeta receives Karin's torn shift from the hands of her killer, John the father puts together some of the clues in *Last House*, noticing the bite mark on Krug's hand, the bandage on Sadie's head, while the spaghetti sauce reminds the uneasy audience of the bloodbath barely completed. The increasingly ill Junior, fighting withdrawal, moans aloud, tortured by the crimes in a series of flashbacks. It is Estelle's compassion for Junior's late-night retching that leads to the revelation about Mari's fate, when her mother catches sight of the peace-sign necklace around Junior's neck. Suspicious, she surreptitiously examines the robber's suitcase and finds the girls' bloody clothes, which Craven notes "is what happens in *The Virgin Spring*, too."

The reactions of the parents differ, though, because of their entirely separate moral universes. When the truth becomes plain, Töre prepares ritually to extract his revenge; while Märeta locks the robbers inside, Töre puts the guilty Ingeri to work stoking the bathhouse fire while he goes out to gather birch whisks. His only break in composure during this ordeal comes as he struggles with the birch; unable to contain his rage, he knocks down the entire tree before chopping off small branches. After he ritually cleanses himself, he orders Ingeri to get his butcher knife. Although he has originally removed a sword from a trunk in their bedroom, Töre now seems to realize that this is no duel but a slaughter. There is no moral ambiguity here; Töre seems assured that he is doing his God's work. Bergman's narrative harks back to the roots of the ballad and signals a decision in favor of Märeta's God, despite the apparent power of Ingeri's father god.

Armed with the knife and covered by a butcher's apron, Töre goes to work. He first sits at his immense chair, which displaces the image of the bridge-keeper's pagan bench, and glowers like a god in judgment at the three thieves. As if to signal his decision, he throws down the knife, awakening the doomed men. They are quickly and efficiently dispatched, even the boy, despite Märeta's attempt to shelter him from the vengeful Töre. The aim is not revenge but dispassionate judgment.

The mute robber ends up splayed cruciform upon the chair, the voluble one stretched across the hell-like fire, and the boy crushed by Töre in a parody of the priest's promise of a hand of salvation reaching out. Only when the family has carried out divine justice do they seek Karin's body.

The impulses are reversed in *Last House*. Here the parents' first compulsion is to find their daughter. Unlike Karin's parents, who take it on faith that their daughter is dead (a faith that is rewarded by the miracle at the end), Mari's parents want tangible proof and quickly locate their dying daughter for one final tearful reunion. Craven seems to suggest that the audience needs to see the family reunited on the physical plane, for neither he nor the parents trust in an afterlife. The simultaneous dream sequence, where Weasel imagines the pair operating upon him with chisel and hammer, reveals the very human remorse even the monsters feel—and consequently forces the audience to flinch in sympathy with the metallic hammer blow. Craven relates that he learned from his lover of the time, a Ph.D. student in anthropology, that "having your teeth broken" is "one of the most primal dreams." Whether Craven sees the current cultural climate as a movement beyond the era of faith, or a reversion to a more primal and primitive era, is difficult to tell.

In contrast to Töre's ritualistic preparation, Mari's parents surreptitiously ransack their home for possible weapons. Their actions are devoid of the sureness of divine judgment. John proceeds to booby-trap the house against the sleeping robbers, using techniques, Craven reveals, taken from a Green Beret handbook on improvised battle. Estelle convinces Weasel to stroll outdoors, presumably for a passionate encounter, leading him away from the barely concealed body of Mari on the couch. Once outside, the shy housewife convinces the criminal of her hidden desire for bondage. So eager is he for the encounter that Weasel insists that she tie him up, assuming the house's neat suburban exterior is incapable of concealing malicious intent. Craven expects the early 1970s audience to identify with the reality of this early "desperate" housewife, having been awakened to the sexual desires of the "girl next door" by porn star Marilyn Chambers, star of the contemporaneous *Behind the Green Door*.

Craven plays upon the expected sexual politics in his attempt to show the reality of violence in all its true ugliness. Turning the tables of sexual violence on men seldom happened in films at this time. The first warning of Estelle's vengeful objective comes when she manages to catch Weasel's trouser zipper on his delicate flesh. "How did I do that?" the seemingly innocent, but calculating, housewife asks her suddenly regretful paramour. "Aw, poor little fella," she comments as she sees his no-longer-proud member. Weasel responds to the humiliating criticism with an avowal that "you just scared it, that's all," and predictably doubles his determination to continue despite the warning signs. Our next clear signal of the coming violence is Estelle's hand tearing up the grass as she clamps down upon his penis with her teeth. The spectacle of revenge has become as elaborate as the initial orgy of rape and murder. Craven equalizes the crimes in our eyes and dares us to look away.

Similarly, when John and Krug meet at last, skin to skin, they exchange blows, but there is no decisive victory—if anything, it appears that the guilty killer will not succumb to the vengeful father. Craven overturns the expected revenge scenario and the resolution it would offer. Without the clarity of a moral connection to a powerful father god, John lacks the ability to wield his weapon in judgment. All that saves John is the interruption of Junior, who fires a pistol at his father, whose only response is to taunt and ridicule his son in what Craven calls "my worst nightmare of a father." He adds, "My father was not that bad, by the way. I didn't kill myself." But this is exactly what Krug convinces his son to do. His horror is not the one the audience shares; according to Craven, Krug's true horror is that his own son disappoints him by actually committing suicide. The earthly fathers have the final say in Craven's universe. The denouement continues the unpredictable moral reversals. There is no one to save the family from their attackers; there is no one to offer an ethical compass. All the trappings of the righteous have disintegrated in Craven's moral vacuum.

The final return of authority, in the person of the sheriff, ineffectually seeks to hold back the "good" parents from the brink of murder. Arriving on the bloody scene, the police officer shouts, "John! For God's sake, don't!" but there are no gods in authority here. Accompanied by the whine of the chainsaw, Estelle charges across the lawn, phallic knife in hand, while John's face freezes in a rictus grin. Sadie falls into the pool, blood streaming from her mouth. The impaling of Krug spurts blood even across the face of the sheriff. No one remains unsullied, presumably even the audience, whom Craven notes should be left "completely enraged and befuddled, and not knowing who they are or what they can do, except to try to go out and kill the filmmakers," he adds sardonically. Moral certainty has been erased and authority questioned; morality has become dumb.

The Virgin Spring, of course, ends with the title miracle. Töre, in despair, wonders how he can ever be reconciled to his murderous hands and offers to use them to build a church on the site of Karin's murder. During his wrenching appeal, his back is to the audience, but when the miraculous spring is revealed, he turns and rejoins his remaining family and, in so doing, seems to heal the disruption caused by his angry outburst. All are reconciled, including the priest, who had lost his faith, and even Ingeri, who, bathed in sunlight, seems to have changed gods and been received into the Christian light. No such reconciliation is possible in *Last House*; the parents are left without a method to appease their suffering or guilt, with blood literally on their hands. There is no one even to avenge Phyllis, no one to claim her body. We are adrift in a world where both technology and authority (such as the sheriff or deputy) are mostly absent or ridiculed, mocked by teens and defied by the sole person of color. For Craven, there is little to hope for and nothing to hold onto in this world of uncertain morality.

The medieval ballad offers a stable form. The rhyme, the rhythm, the tune all work to maintain the story's shape and impact, although the world around it continues to change. Reimaginings are inevitable. Yet the variety of interpretations tells us more about the adapters than it does about the original ballad. While both filmmakers strayed from the original ballad, both also used it to define a moral center from which they diverged. Just as Umberto Eco describes, the general appropriation of "the Middle Ages as a *pretext*...a sort of mythological stage on which to place contemporary characters" operates here, too (1986, 68). Bergman remains closer to the ballad's origins but creates a narrative of (then contemporary) religious questioning. Craven uses the ballad structure and audience expectations to show the malaise of American culture in the 1970s and the void created by the absence of the father god(s). This characterization fits neatly into Arthur Lindley's second type of medieval film: "the Middle Ages as shorthand for the-spirituality-missing-in-our-lives" type (1998, 17). Craven's vision focuses upon a deficiency in contrast to Bergman's uncertainty.

Certainty is the key: Bergman simply does not know and wishes he did, while Craven seems sure that there are no gods, no rules. His use of the horror genre highlights this loss. If we agree with Bruce Kawin that "one goes to a horror film in order to have a nightmare—not simply a frightening dream, but a dream whose undercurrent of anxiety both presents and masks the desire to fulfill and be punished for conventionally or personally unacceptable impulses" (1999, 680), Craven knows that members of his audience expect a final moral solution. They can vicariously enjoy the horror but anticipate a resolution that restores balance, just as the medieval audience knew the ballad would restore balance through divine control. Craven, however, denies them the expected comfort and restoration of order. His film mirrors the malaise and moral uncertainty of his time, just as the ballad reflected the known universe to the medieval Christian audience. Unlike Bergman, he cannot bring himself to offer the illusion of order in a chaotic world. While Bergman clings to the ballad's world of black-and-white morality, Craven resigns himself to a stark, disordered planet where the ballad and its morality have been forgotten.

Notes

1. All quotes from Craven are from the director's commentary on the DVD unless otherwise noted.
2. This period marked the advent of the "new" pornographic features like *Deep Throat* and *Behind the Green Door,* both made in 1972.

Filmography

Behind the Green Door (1972). 72 min. Artie and Jim Mitchell
Deep Throat (1972). 61 min. Gerard Damiano
Jungfrukällan [The Virgin Spring] (1960). 89 min. Ingmar Bergman
The Last House on the Left (1972). 85 min. Wes Craven

Works Cited

Austin, Greta. 2002. Were the peasants really so clean? The Middle Ages in film. *Film History* 14: 136–41.

Brunvand, Jan Harold. [1979] 1989. *The vanishing hitchhiker.* Repr., New York: W.W. Norton and Co.

Eco, Umberto. 1986. *Travels in hyperreality.* New York: Harcourt.

Jonsson, Bengt R., Svale Solheim, and Eva Danielson. 1978. *The types of the Scandinavian medieval ballad: A descriptive catalogue.* Oslo: Universitetsforlaget.

Kawin, Bruce. 1999. The mummy's pool. In *Film theory and criticism,* ed. Leo Braudy and Marshall Cohen, 679–90. New York: Oxford University Press.

Ker, W.P. 1909. *On the history of the ballads 1100–1500.* London: Oxford University Press.

Laws, G. Malcom, Jr. 1972. *The British literary ballad.* Carbondale: Southern Illinois University Press.

Lindley, Arthur. 1998. The ahistoricism of medieval film. *Screening the Past* 3. http://www.latrobe.edu.au/screeningthepast/firstrelease/fir598/ALfr3a.htm (accessed August 15, 2005).

Lofficier, Randy. 1999. Interview with Wes Craven. Perfect world: Official Web site of Randy Lofficier. http://www.perfectworldusa.com/craven.htm (accessed August 15, 2005).

Rossel, Sven H. 1982. *Scandinavian ballads*. Wisconsin Introductions to Scandinavia 2. Madison: University of Wisconsin Press.

Stam, Robert. 2000. Beyond fidelity: The dialogics of adaptation. In *Film adaptation*, ed. James Naremore, 54–76. New Brunswick, NJ: Rutgers University Press.

Strick, Philip. 2002. Film Notes for *The virgin spring*. Tartan DVD. Released October 28, 2002.

Zipes, Jack. 1987. The enchanted forest of the Brothers Grimm. *Germanic Review* 62 (2): 66–74.

11

Beyond *Communitas*

*Cinematic Food Events and the Negotiation of Power,
Belonging, and Exclusion*

LuAnne Roth

Many classic studies of foodways by folklorists and other scholars have effectively shown the sophisticated ways that food functions to foster *communitas*, a heightened sense of group cohesion. Owing to the ethnographic tradition of representing cultures in a decidedly celebratory manner, as well as the tendency for individuals and groups to perform self-consciously, it follows that most depictions of food within communities adhere to this paradigm of communitas (cf. Humphrey and Humphrey 1988). Recently, a few studies have moved beyond this positive function of food behavior to consider how food may be employed simultaneously to reinforce hegemonic or patriarchal structures as well as punish, cajole, or otherwise negotiate power relationships.

Looking at cinematic portrayals of food events may be particularly revealing because, as mimetic devices, they represent aspects of food behavior not generally included in extant ethnographic and autoethnographic representations of foodways. Indeed "scenes which suggest happiness, comfort, or fulfillment are exceptional among Hollywood productions," observes film critic Parley Ann Boswell. "In American movies, food and dining are most often associated with crisis, frustration, conflict, or emptiness. No matter what the food, or what the meal being presented to us, Hollywood shows us not how Americans celebrate an abundance of food, but how this very abundance of food exposes other yearnings and other needs of American culture" (1993, 9). Approaching popular American films through an ethnographic lens, I rely on folkloristic, feminist, psychoanalytic, and postcolonial theories for insight. Beyond the obvious examples of "food films," those employing food as a central thematic device, I examine mainstream popular films for the brief, subtle, yet powerfully resonant moments when food symbolizes racial and cultural identity and, more significantly, negotiates power, belonging, and exclusion.[1]

In this schema, the foreign Other—like the "disgusting" foods the Other is presumed to eat—manifests as the *abject*. Presented cinematically as defiled and polluting, the Other must be expelled, a process painfully evident in Tony Kaye's *American History X* (1998). In this and other films, there exists a simultaneous desire to consume the Other. A negotiation of this conflict is exemplified in Joel Zwick's *My Big Fat Greek Wedding* (2002) and John Hamburg's *Along Came Polly* (2004), where the Other is confronted (and confined) safely at the *ethnic* restaurant—a mediating site that, in the final analysis, reinforces colonialism and complicates traditional approaches to foodways.

Abjecting the Other in *American History X*

People being equated with the food they eat, of course, is not a new idea. In light of the worn adage, "we are what we eat," most people can quickly rattle off a number of foods associated with their own families and communities; food in this sense clearly functions to create communitas and ethnic identity. The flip side of creating communitas through food is that it often does so by defining alterity—what is outside, what is foreign—we are what we don't eat. Hence, people can also, if asked, recall stereotypes about the food of other groups, especially that of "foreigners" (Kalčik 1984).

Historically, food has been one of the primary means by which the other is posited as inferior, and it constituted an integral part of the social construction of race during the early colonial period. Africans, for example, were seen first and foremost as bodies, and perceived bodily functions differentiated the traveler from the native (see, for example, Fanon [1952] 1967, 111–14; Pratt [1992] 1998, 52; Spurr 1993, 22; and Turner 1993, 9–32). The construction of the Other, above all, as a body positions it as an embodiment of filth, something that needs to be abjected. The more "foreign" people are considered, the more likely their food behavior will be considered repulsive, immoral, or barbaric. The reverse is also true: the more a group's food is perceived to be repulsive, immoral, or barbaric, the more likely the people who eat (or are presumed to eat) it will be seen that way. Whether it involves rumors about "man-eating" Africans (e.g., Fanon [1952] 1967; Turner 1993) or endogamic, cannibalistic Asian American immigrants (Kalčik 1984), real or imagined food behavior has been used to justify the colonization of many nations and cultures and otherwise express racism and hatred.

Several processes of othering via food and the mouth are exposed in *American History X*, a powerful film that reveals the world of Derek

Vinyard (Edward Norton), who is trying to salvage his ruptured family after serving a three-year prison term for involuntary manslaughter. Employing a flashback narrative structure, the film traces the ripple effects of Derek's racism and the tangled web of the neo-Nazi movement in Venice, California, which have now spread to his younger brother, Danny (Edward Furlong).

The movie opens with the nondiagetic sound of a sorrowful trumpet playing over a sunset beach. The solo gradually becomes a duet and then choral vocals and an occasional snare drum roll. The peaceful moment ends as the next scene unfolds. We see three Caucasian characters—Danny trying to sleep while his brother Derek and girlfriend Stacey have loud sex beneath a swastika flag in the room next door. Outside the window, three African American men conspire to steal Derek's pickup truck. Alerted by Danny, Derek grabs his gun and shoots without hesitation, killing one man, wounding another, and firing repeatedly at the fleeing getaway car. The choral music swells resplendently, creating a powerful counterpoint to the slow-motion images of Danny's horrified reaction and Derek—proud and almost radiant—sporting his swastika and barbed wire tattoos. After several scenes that take place in the present, the film returns to this flashback scene. The brutal manner in which Derek murders the already-wounded man (Antonio David Lyons) is significant. At gunpoint, Derek orders the man to place his open mouth—the oral cavity that becomes a preoccupation in later scenes—on the curb's edge. "Now say 'good night,'" Derek exclaims, as his boot stomps down on the man's head. The next image is withheld; we can only hear a ripping sound as the camera cuts to Danny's stunned expression and then returns to Derek, who spits in disgust on the dead man and walks away. "The sound of the kid's head splitting open on the curb went right through me," recalls Danny.

Most of the film's story, in fact, unfolds via either Danny's recollections, shown in black-and-white flashbacks, or events in the present. For submitting a history paper that proposed Adolf Hitler as a civil-rights hero, Danny has a makeup paper assignment that requires him to analyze the events surrounding his brother's incarceration. Through stream of consciousness, he recalls several food-related moments. For example, at a basketball game—between the white guys and the black guys—a black player (Antonio David Lyons) "plays the dozens" on a morbidly obese white-supremacist player, Seth Ryan (Ethan Suplee), calling him a "fat, pale, pasty, pastrami-eating, cracker motherfucker." The same player, who is later killed, knocks Derek down during the game, giving him a bloody lip. In the Vinyard family living room shortly after, Seth crashes in a chair, complaining loudly about starving as he reaches for handfuls of jelly beans, throwing a black one, as if repulsive, onto the floor. These scenes, though brief, draw attention to connections between food and race.

In her analysis of the conflicting discourses surrounding soul food, Doris Witt confronts "the discrepancy between filthy 'matter' and filthy 'actions'" (1998, 260), theorizing where the "disorder" of nonwhiteness is situated in terms of food. Is it in the person (who eats the food)? In the act (of eating)? Or in the object of action (the food itself)? (265). Exploring such key "ontologies of blackness," Witt finds that those stigmatized elements "have been thought to reside not in black bodies but instead in foods said to nourish those bodies" (260). This problem of where filth and foreignness are located manifests itself several times in *American History X*.

Accounting for the way Derek became *the* Skinhead, one scene shows a flashback of him holding a pep rally for his white followers in a parking lot across from a neighborhood supermarket, now owned by "some fucking Korean." Calling immigrants "social parasites," "criminals," and "border jumpers," the charismatic leader preaches about the way "they" have taken over "our" country and "our" jobs, giving "decent, hard-working Americans...the shaft." The supermarket becomes the battlefield. The terrorist group, wearing stocking and ski masks as disguises, rushes into the market, shouting and smashing everything in sight, including the workers (who appear to be Latino) and food, with baseball bats, fists, and feet. Forty-pound bags of pinto beans are slashed open with knives as if they are human bodies; the gutted bags pour their contents onto the floor "like a fucking piñata"— a symbolic display threatening further brutal acts.

A dark-skinned female worker (Francine Morris) cowers behind the cash register as the vandals tear the place apart. When they discover her, three masked men hoist her screaming and struggling body onto the counter, separating her legs and otherwise positioning her as if to gang-rape her. One of the men says soothingly, "It's okay, sweetheart...I'm not going to hurt you." We hear the other men saying things such as, "This bitch stinks," "Get some cleaning products on her," and "She smells like fish and chips and guacamole." The camera cuts quickly back and forth between the scenes of food items being destroyed and the men's degrading treatment of the woman. The men force what we take to be Mexican food items (hot sauce and salsa) into her mouth, followed by what appears to be applesauce and cow's milk, which they also smear over her face. The camera lingers uncomfortably in a close-up of the viscous whiteness, dripping in slow motion from the woman's mouth, then cuts to Seth standing at the door, clutching a nightstick in one hand and what appears to be a large plastic hamburger in the other while the gang runs out of the store.

This rape-by-food scene is ripe for analysis. In addition to the willful destruction of the Other's food, symbolizing the Other's body, is the suggestion that the consumption of certain "stinky" foods is associated, however erroneously, with foreignness. Following Joel Kovel ([1970] 1988), Richard Dyer writes, "Non-white people are associated in various ways with the dirt that comes out of the body, notably in the repeated racist perception that they smell...,that their food smells, that they eat dirty foods—offal, dogs, snakes—and that they slaughter it in direct and bloody forms. Obsessive control of faeces and identification of them as the nadir of human dirt both characterize Western culture: to be white is to be well potty-trained" (1997, 75–76). Focusing on the connection between the color of excrement and skin, Kovel explains "the central symbol of dirt throughout the world is faeces, known by that profane word with which the emotion of disgust is expressed: shit...when contrasted with the light colour of the body of the Caucasian person, the dark colour of faeces reinforces, from the infancy of the individual in the culture of the West, the connotation of blackness with badness" ([1970] 1988, 87).

The men's insults to the female grocery-store clerk employ food names, particularly those deemed smelly and disgusting. Thought to eat disgusting cultural foods, the woman becomes disgusting herself and must be purified before she can be safely approached. Threatening to pour cleaning products on her (we do not see whether they actually do so), the men force into her mouth first Mexican foods and then various "white" foods, smearing them on her face. We hear the attackers saying, as they rub in the liquids, "Hey, this is a great color on you," "You could get a white woman's job, bitch," and "Moving up in the world, huh?" Such comments reveal their attempt to make her more white and graphically illustrate how the Other's perceived stinkiness, filthiness, and badness may be countered, symbolically at least, with pale/white/American foods because "to be white is to have expunged all dirt, faecal or otherwise, from oneself: to look white is to look clean" (Dyer 1997, 76).

In contrast to the handful of male workers attacked, the woman is the only one violated on such a personal and degrading level. In the sad reality of war, women are often raped and sexually abused by members of the conquering group as a symbol of their dominance. Even in the postwar period, the violation of women symbolizes the West's penetration of foreign markets. Traise Yamamoto argues, for instance, that the "unstated structure of heterosexual mastery reveals itself if we look at what are frequent descriptions of the present economical need to *'penetrate* the Japanese market'" (1999, 22; emphasis in original). Common American phrases, such as "the opening of Japan," contain images of "forced penetration" that are repeatedly utilized in such American institutions as the military, government, and media, all of which employ the "language of rape in the postwar period" (23). On the battlefield of the supermarket, therefore, the men penetrate the woman through her oral cavity as a way of expressing anger and hatred over the nonwhites in America. And if the connection to rape still eludes the viewer at this point, the inescapable allusion to male ejaculation is underscored as the white fluids drip out of the screaming, gagging woman's mouth.

Like the food on which the woman gags, this scene is hard to swallow. What makes it particularly intriguing are the attackers' statements about the need to *clean* the victim. The more I reflect on this scene, the more I cannot escape Julia Kristeva's theory of abjection as an analytical tool. Abjection is the primary form of repression, according to Kristeva, that occurs prior to ego development. Before abjection, the infant exists in a state of *chora*, where the child "experiences itself...as being one with all" (1982, 13). Abjection is the moment that makes the dichotomy between the ego and the object possible. It is the infant subject's initial attempt to establish a corporeal schema separate from the maternal body, first enacted by the infant spitting out the mother's milk. This moment is "a violent, clumsy breaking away" from the state of undifferentiated chora with the maternal prior to the formation of the "I" (1982, 13). Having established the self via this expulsion, the abject then comes to threaten the "clean and proper body" and thereby becomes loathsome and disgusting. The process is complicated, though, by the concomitant experience of dread and attraction. If we could just expel the abject and "get it over with," that would be one matter. But because we must continually live with the abject, because we cannot escape it completely, "the abject is fascinating, bringing out an obsessed attraction" at the same time it creates "dread of the unnameable" (Young 1990, 145).

While the primal Other for Kristeva is the maternal, her theory leaves room for positing the foreigner (or racialized Other) as abject as others have done, for "defilement is what is jettisoned from the symbolic system" (1982, 65).[2] Kristeva argues, by implication, that the constitution of Western hegemonic identity, the "symbolic order," requires abjection in some form. Something must be "othered" in constructing the hegemony's identity. If, as Kristeva claims, "abjection is coextensive with social and symbolic order," then wherever a social system exists, we can expect to find abjection (1982, 68), and we see this idea illustrated in *American History X* through the murder-by-mouth scene and two rape-by-food scenes. Like the primal abjection Kristeva describes, the threat of the foreign Other's presence, resulting in the possible disintegration of the boundaries of the nation-state self, is experienced as frightening. The supermarket no longer offers comfort as the white gang's neighborhood store because foreigners now own it. While foreigners are recognized as a threat to subjectivity, they are simultaneously desired and feared, and necessary for the preservation of the nation-state self.

It is no accident that, in films such as *American History X*, this process of abjection manifests itself so frequently via alimentary images, considering that "food loathing is perhaps the most elementary and most archaic form of abjection" (Kristeva 1982, 2). Although the abject is associated with filth and disgust, Kristeva reminds us, "It is...not lack of cleanliness...that causes abjection but what disturbs identity, system, order. What does not respect borders, positions, rules. The in-between, the ambiguous, the composite" (1982, 4)—like the border-jumping, foreign woman in the grocery store. Hence, the woman becomes the abject—desired by the men, yet standing outside the white colonial system, making that desire disturbing. To survive this psychological crisis, the men transform her into filth, allowing them to "clean" her so they can then "consume" her without risk of defiling themselves.

This rape-by-food scenario becomes especially poignant when a similar one occurs in the following scene, taking place during a family meal. Thanks to food scholars, we understand how the family meal—a microcosm of family dynamics— socializes, educates, expresses and plays out relational and power dynamics. James Bossard suggested long ago that the family meal is the family "at ease" (1943). Just as often, though, it is the family battlefield (Belasco 1989; Roth 2005). As a symbolically charged occasion, the family meal manages to operate—like other family dynamics—largely unself-consciously until a change is introduced. Boswell challenges the assumption that "in American films...,home cooking should tell us that all is well in these American homes." This is rarely the case, she notes: "When we see entire families sitting around a table eating a home-cooked meal, we are almost never made to feel comfortable. In Hollywood productions of the last 20 years, home-cooked food and family dining scenes have been used to highlight unhealthy aspects of the American family" (1993, 17).

In this particular disrupted family meal at the Vinyard home, the attending family members include the recently widowed mother, Doris

(Beverly D'Angelo), oldest brother Derek, middle sister Davina (Jennifer Lien), and younger brother Danny. They sit around a formal dining-room table the evening before Derek commits murder. Joining the family are two nonfamily members: the mother's new boyfriend, Murray (Elliott Gould), who, we quickly learn, is Jewish, and Stacey (Fairuza Balk), Derek's skinhead girlfriend. Here the family meal serves as a judicial court where people evaluate and judge each other, debate contemporary issues, make important decisions, and negotiate relationships. The already tense table conversation quickly becomes heated with the highly charged issue of race—the Rodney King case—being debated. We see Derek expressing his racist doctrine, cheered on by his sycophantic girlfriend; Davina becoming increasingly shocked and frustrated by the racist attitudes; and newcomer Murray trying to be the mediating voice of reason but clearly disturbed by the direction of the conversation. As the tension between the "liberals" and the "racists" rises, Doris touches Murray's hand several times in comfort, but then she explodes briefly, slamming her open hand on the table and saying, "Can we just drop this Rodney King thing?" She pauses, takes a deep breath, then forces a smile and asks sweetly, "Who'd like some dessert?"

But the arguing resumes immediately. When it becomes heated again, and Stacey begins to rant, Davina interrupts to ask desperately, "Can I please be excused?" Her mother quickly answers yes to forestall further escalation. But Derek, having stepped into his deceased father's shoes, immediately overrides his mother, asserting his presumed patriarchal dominance. "No, you cannot," he commands Davina; "You need to stay until you learn some fucking manners!" Davina retorts, "Who the hell do you think you are?" and stands to leave. Derek physically blocks Davina; when she attempts to get around him, he grabs her by the hair, yanking her back and forth. Grabbing a handful of roast beef from the table, he shoves it into her mouth, yelling, "You need to learn some fucking manners" until she cries and chokes, gasping for breath.

After this explosion, Derek turns triumphantly to Murray, ripping off his shirt to expose his white-power tattoos and yelling,

> My family...my family....You're not a part of it, and you never will be....You don't think I see what you're trying to do here? You think I'm gonna sit here and smile while some fucking kike tries to fuck my mother? It's never going to happen, Murray, fucking forget it; not on my watch, not while I'm in this family. I will fucking cut your shylock nose off and stick it up your ass before I'll let that happen. Coming in here and *poisoning my family's dinner* with your Jewish, nigger-loving, hippie-bullshit. Fuck you, fuck you, asshole.

Fucking Kabala-reading motherfucker. Get the fuck out of my
house![3] (*emphasis added*)

Like the black jelly bean and the supermarket workers, the Jewish boyfriend threatens the "clean and proper" body of the Caucasian American family and is considered, therefore, to be filthy and disgusting. The
boyfriend is abjected from the sanctity of the family, just as the foreign
woman and African American man were abjected in prior scenes. Family systems theorists Michael Nichols and Richard Schwartz explain,
"Family structure involves a set of covert rules that govern transactions
in the family...altering the basic structure will have ripple effects on all
family transactions....Whatever the chosen pattern, it tends to be self-
perpetuating and resistant to change" ([1984] 1998, 244). If one group
member shifts within the family structure (in this case, because of the
father's death), the others fill in the absent space and/or pressure devi-
ating members to return to earlier roles—hence, Derek steps into the
space left by his father. Note, for instance, that after this violent eruption,
Derek stops calling his mother Ma and begins calling her Doris instead.

The change in family roles also affects Davina. When she does not
obey Derek's orders, he asserts his patriarchal authority by disciplining
her. With physical force and food, he teaches her manners. Dyer explains,
"There are special anxieties surrounding the whiteness of white women
vis-à-vis sexuality. As the literal bearers of children, and because they
are held primarily responsible for their initial raising, women are the
indispensable means by which the group—the race—is in every sense
reproduced" (1997, 29). By attacking his sister, Derek proves his dominance not just over Davina but also over Murray, and Derek's verbal
attack on his mother, "How could you bring him to my father's table?...
You disgust me" follows suit.

Significantly, Derek uses roast beef to choke his sister, instead of
green beans, dinner rolls, or dessert. Recently, feminist scholars have
addressed the more than metaphorical connection (at least in Western
cultures) between killing animals and raping women. As several scholars have argued, meat eating inherently involves sexual politics—meat is
identified with maleness, masculinity, virility, and strength (see Adams
1994; Twigg 1983). Therefore, meat symbolizes male dominance in this
cinematic scene, becoming a celebration of patriarchy itself. And in light
of Dyer's observation about white women reproducing "the race," it
is no accident that Derek penetrates his sister/daughter's mouth with
meat—a hypermasculine symbol that powerfully communicates his
dominance. That he exerts his power by penetrating her oral cavity is
also not accidental. Near the end of this scene, the mother, in despair,

crouches over the curb in front of the house—foreshadowing the place where Derek will enact the brutal murder-by-mouth later that night.

Mary Douglas has discussed that the oral cavity is believed to be highly vulnerable, especially during times of stress. Explaining why certain groups of people approach foods more cautiously than others, she suggests that minorities are more likely to be suspicious of food cooked by outsiders and more protective of their body orifices. "Food is not likely to be polluting at all," in fact, "unless the external boundaries of the social system are under pressure" (1966, 126; see also Angyal 1941; Turner 1987, 1993). Moving beyond the either/or of Douglas's model, in *American History X*, we see members of the minority being violated but also members of the dominant group (white males) feeling threatened and fearing defilement and poisoning by nonwhite outsiders. By tying together these three parallel incidents of people being violated through the oral cavity, Tony Kaye's *American History X* blatantly portrays how this perceived vulnerability relates to processes of othering and abjection. As I will show, these dynamics are at work in other forms as well.

Othering, Abjecting, and Continuing Colonialism in *My Big Fat Greek Wedding* and *Along Came Polly*

Beyond the explicitness of race relations in *American History X*, abjection and processes of othering play out in other recent popular films, albeit in more subtle forms. I turn next to Joel Zwick's *My Big Fat Greek Wedding* and John Hamburg's *Along Came Polly*, both romantic comedies where food functions as the main vehicle to express difference (and otherness). However, if the Other's food is initially viewed with suspicion, it is eventually embraced in ritual spaces (i.e., ethnic restaurants) as a sign of adventurousness and cultural capital.[4]

My Big Fat Greek Wedding is a love story narrated in the first person by Toula Portokalos (Nia Vardalos), the second-generation daughter of an extended Greek family. Toula recollects her childhood in Chicago fairly quickly through food scenes in a way that parallels the overall narrative structure of *American History X* (e.g., flashbacks and voice-overs). All of the early food events depict Toula being embarrassed and othered because of her family's "weird" Greek foodways. For instance, Toula describes how her family celebrates a traditional Christian holiday:

> Christmas...? What's it like? Well...I'm Greek, right? Okay....My mom makes roast lamb; my dad and uncle fight over who gets the lamb brain; my Aunt Voula forks it with a fork and chases me around, trying to get me to eat it because it will make me smart....

My whole family—is big and loud, and everybody's always in each other's lives and business. Like you never have a minute alone to just think because we're always together, just eating, eating. The only other people we know are Greeks...because Greeks marry Greeks, to breed more Greeks...to be loud, breeding Greek eaters!

Toula recounts other memories of ways her family foodways have caused her to feel othered. "When I was growing up," Toula explains, "I knew I was different. The other girls were blond and delicate. And I was a swarthy six-year-old with sideburns. I so badly wanted to be like the popular girls...all sitting together, talking...eating their Wonder Bread sandwiches." Here we see the young Toula (Christina Eleusiniotis) at school, resignedly eating her lunch of moussaka at a table by herself, while at the next table, the popular girls—white, blond, thin, pretty—are eating sandwiches, the all-American food. The girls make fun of Toula's lunch; one deliberately mispronounces it "moose ka-ka" (feces), establishing the boundaries between self and Other by associating the Other's food, and therefore the Other, with filth. This is similar to what happens in *American History X*, except that in *My Big Fat Greek Wedding*, we share Toula's awareness of the ways her family's foodways help to constitute and maintain her as Other.[5]

Like Danny in *American History X*, Toula also recalls being socialized over family meals. For example, Toula sits at the kitchen table with her siblings while her mother, Maria Portokalos (Lainie Kazan), prepares food. "My mom was always cooking foods filled with warmth and wisdom," Toula says in the voice-over, "and never forgetting that side dish of steaming guilt." At this, her mother chastises Toula's baby brother, "Nikko, don't play with your food. When I was your age, we didn't have food." Next, we see Toula as a twelve-year-old (Marita Zouravlioff), sitting at the kitchen table while her father, Gus Portokalos (Michael Constantine), lectures to the children about the history "of our people" over breakfast. "Nice Greek girls," Toula is told regularly throughout her childhood, "are supposed to do three things in life: marry Greek boys, make Greek babies, and feed everyone until the day we die."[6] Destined to have her future as a woman determined this way for the rest of her life, Toula despairs. Moreover, members of her family repeatedly point out that, at thirty, Toula is virtually unmarriageable.

We can read some feminist coding into Toula's character at this point, perhaps a strategy of feigning incompetence (Radner and Lanser 1993), because we never actually see her demonstrating traditional forms of "female competence" (e.g., preparing food). Given the stated purpose of Greek women, Toula's failure to cook is significant. "It's like she don't want to get married," remarks Toula's bewildered father.[7] But this incompetence does not save her from a life of serving food: "Nice Greek girls who don't find a husband work in the family restaurant...day after day, year after year." Toula desires a career and a life outside her overly determined Greek identity. In the restaurant, she stands behind the counter, lifeless, wearing thick glasses and a drab brown waitress smock that matches her equally drab hair. "I wish I had a different life," she laments. "I wish I was braver or prettier or just happy. But it's useless to dream because nothing ever changes."

Of course, things do change. To achieve the heterosexual resolution that classic Hollywood cinema demands, Toula's narrative leads her to meet Ian Miller (John Corbett), a Caucasian –American, vegetarian, literature professor. Ian walks into the restaurant one day, past the Greek landscape painting that covers one entire wall, and sits down with his professor friend, Mike (Ian Gomez), who is examining a photo of a woman. "You set me up with her already—I already met her," Ian says dismissively, confusing this woman with others. "They look the same—They're all the same, Mike." As he finishes, he notices Toula, standing—like his "own private Greek statue"—to take his order. This brief encounter between Toula and Ian unwittingly inspires Toula's metamorphosis from frumpy to beautiful, a transformation that occurs virtually overnight (even without a fairy godmother). The rest of the film, as the title promises, traces the hilarious ordeal of planning a wedding amid two very different families where the Greek side more or less dominates.

Because this film is not *My Big Fat Anglo Wedding* (there are already plenty of those), we do not learn much about the Miller family's foodways, but we do glean that Ian's parents, Harriet and Rodney Miller (Fiona Reid and Bruce Gray), are Caucasian, upper-middle-class members of the North Shore Country Club and exemplify the classic sense of Victorian aesthetics. The first introduction of Toula to the Millers is awkward, to say the least. At the formal dinner table, during strained, albeit polite, conversation, the Millers reveal they are unfamiliar relating to nonwhite people in such a personal setting without a servant/employee relationship existing: "So you're Greek then?" Mr. Miller asks. Then Mrs. Miller turns to her husband and asks, "Rodney, didn't you have a receptionist who was Greek?" "No, Harriet," he answers, "she was...." They ponder this for a moment, considering Armenian, until they come to the conclusion the receptionist was not Armenian or Greek; she was, in fact, Guatemalan. They smile smugly at having recalled this detail, and we see Toula recoiling at the implication that, as far as the Other goes, "They're all the same."

Foodways theorist Lucy Long sets up a model for establishing difference and othering based on the boundaries of what is considered edible versus palatable: "The difference between the realms of edible and palatable is perhaps most clearly seen in how we use them to evaluate other eaters. The eater of the 'not edible' is perceived as strange, perhaps dangerous, definitely not one of us, whereas the eater of the unpalatable is seen as having different tastes" (2004, 33). While we do not know exactly what the Millers consider edible or palatable, we can observe the outer boundaries of their food system by what they refuse to eat and by what they find unpalatable or disgusting about the Portokalos family's food system.

When Ian's parents first meet the Portokalos family, over what is supposed to be "a quiet dinner" with Toula's parents, the entire extended family is present (twenty-seven first cousins plus aunts and uncles), along with a lamb roasting on a spit on the front lawn (from which people take meat with their fingers), amid hearty drinking, dancing, and laughing. What is normal and celebratory for the Portokalos family completely inverts the Victorian restraint that the Millers consider normal behavior. As the Millers are led to a love seat in the Portokalos living room, Aunt Voula (Andrea Martin) sits down beside them and proceeds to tell a story about a lump that grew on her neck, had to have a biopsy, and was found to contain the teeth and spinal cord of her twin. As these last words leave her mouth, a tray of food is thrust in front of the Millers—"Spanakopita! You hungry?" Their disgusted response is triggered by the close proximity of the twin-bearing-lump story to the food offered them inside the Portokalos home. They are soon intoxicated by the countless shots of the liquor ouzo being pushed upon them by their future in-laws, who are eager to liven them up. The subjective camera reveals the Millers' dizzy and confused point of view while Mr. Portokalos brings another tray of food to them: "You like some meat? Some *Greek* meat, very good, very good." The Millers look away in disgust as if the thought of eating the meat makes them want to vomit..

We see several alimentary scenes in *My Big Fat Greek Wedding* when the Other is aware of being othered, as well as the inverse—when the Other is *othering* members of the dominant culture. For instance, when Mrs. Miller nervously presents an elegant, but restrained, bundt cake as a gift, Mrs. Portokalos receives it politely, asking, "What is it?" After several attempts, she ultimately is incapable of correctly pronouncing the name of this strange item from the Miller food tradition.[8] Furthermore, Mrs. Portokalos fails to identify the symbolic significance of the gift because she is unfamiliar with the larger system of food traditions which explain it. "There's a hole in this cake," she whispers to a female relative, interpreting the gift as flawed, and she later emerges proudly with the cake, which she has "fixed" by filling the hole with a flowerpot.

That night after the party, Mr. and Mrs. Portokalos discuss the disastrous first encounter between the two families. Exasperated, Mr. Portokalos says to his wife, "They look at us like we're from the zoo. This no work. This no work, Maria. They different people. So dry. *That family is like a piece of toast. No honey, no jam, just dry.* My daughter... my daughter gonna marry *I-an Miller. A xeno, a xeno with a toast family. I never think this can happen to us. I try to put a little marmalade. Oh no, they don't like. They like themselves all dry and crackling*" (emphasis added). Here we see the Other aware of being othered—like animals in a zoo—and also talking back with his own characterization of the Millers. As with the American schoolgirls eating Wonder Bread sandwiches, we see American food and Caucasian Americans themselves being compared to foods that are bland and dry, and so entrenched in their blandness that even Mr. Portokalos's charming efforts to sweeten them up with "a little marmalade" fail miserably. They like being that way, Mr. Portokalos concludes; they like being plain and dry—"a toast family." One can make a great deal, therefore, of how the Millers are characterized by the Portokalos family—through *absence* (e.g., the hole in the cake, the rejection of meat, the lack of flavor / texture / moisture, and the refusal to be sweetened up) (see Dyer 1997, 80–81).

In contrast to his parents' fear of the Other and their food, Ian appreciates cultural difference. Reenacting the ethos of the colonizing travelers of a previous century, he rebels against his family, his culture, and his family's foodways.[9] If Toula desires distance from her overdetermined status as ethnic Other, Ian desires contact with that very Other. Bored with his own nonethnic, normal background, Ian unconsciously responds to his exoticizing impulses, finding himself overwhelmingly attracted not only to the exotic spices at the Greek restaurant but to Toula herself, even before her metamorphosis. To some extent, Toula demonstrates, via her joke about herself as a Greek statue, that she recognizes the fetishizing role of the ethnic restaurant and Ian's cravings in terms of culinary tourism—"the intentional, exploratory participation in the foodways of an other" (Long 2004, 21; see also Heldke 2001).

A similar dynamic of culinary tourism plays out in *Along Came Polly*, set in New York City, when Reuben Feffer (Ben Stiller)—a Jewish man obsessed with cleanliness and safety—strives awkwardly to become semifluent in the foodways of Third World cultures to win the love of the worldly Polly Prince (Jennifer Aniston). Wearing mostly suits and ties,

Reuben is a senior risk analyst for a life-insurance company, someone who makes his living by assessing the relative dangers of various activities. Claiming that his mother is responsible for making him "afraid of everything," Reuben blots the excess grease off pizza, hates spicy food, and avoids dirt of any kind. This preoccupation with cleanliness is foreshadowed in the opening scenes of the film. Amid the white, sparkling formal tables, white wedding cake, and white flowers, we see Reuben as a groom making his final inspections before the ceremony begins, for example, reminding the chef about various family members' food allergies. In spite of his careful planning and risk assessment, Reuben manages to lose his perfect wife, Lisa (Debra Messing), on their honeymoon at St. Bart's island to Claude (Hank Azaria), the sexy nudist foreigner with a heavy French accent.

Flashing forward two weeks, the film shows the depressed Reuben running headfirst into both risk and filth. Several scenes illustrate his encounters with filth, beginning with a pickup basketball game, when his opponent's flabby, sweaty, dark, and hairy body repulses Reuben—shown in a slow-motion close-up rubbing against his face. Also his best friend Sandy Lyle (Philip Seymour Hoffman), an overweight Caucasian American, whom Reuben describes as "the most disgusting person I know," is constantly doing and saying distasteful things.[10] When he meets a former junior-high classmate, Polly, Reuben unwittingly confronts risk and dirt again. A tattooed, free-spirited drifter, Polly is employed for the moment as a catering waitress. Although she is supposed to be serving the guests at an art opening, we see Polly overturn conventional ways of treating food, for example, by taking an hors d'oeuvre from a tray, putting it partially in her mouth to eat, then getting distracted and putting it back onto the tray while her female associate jokingly fondles a loaf of French bread as if it were a phallus.

These scenes signal Polly as a "big eater"—a person who has a fearless, adventurous, and unrestrained attitude toward eating, lacks proper social boundaries, and is associated with dirt. Several other incidents portray Polly as a person with blurry boundaries, for example, when she finds her keys in her freezer, when Reuben learns that her only bathroom is next to the kitchen (separated only by a thin door), and when he mistakes Polly's pet ferret for a rat, a common symbol of filth and decay. During Polly's second appearance, Reuben secretly watches her from across the street, grimacing to witness her drop food on the sidewalk, inspect it briefly, pick off a few pieces of debris, and then eat it. Later, Polly eats mixed nuts from a bar with her fingers—an act of defiance—because Reuben has just finished reciting the statistics of how many people have handled the nuts and how many people do not wash their hands after using the bathroom. "I like to live life on the edge," she explains.

Despite his fear of filth, the way his sensitive stomach may be impacted by eating unfamiliar, potentially contaminated food, and his best friend's blatant, cautionary, "Just pray to God she doesn't go ethnic," Reuben lets Polly (after she insists) pick the place for their first date. In fact, Polly does "go ethnic"—the restaurant turns out to feature Moroccan cuisine, and the couple sit on the floor and eat with their hands. Polly, showing her adeptness at eating ethnic food, scoops it into her mouth, letting some slip through her fingers and back onto the communal dish. Recounting the past years of her life, Polly explains that she has "bounced around a lot," living in many places (e.g., Morocco, Austin, Istanbul, Sri Lanka, Portland, Costa Rica, and Buffalo, to name just a few). Polly is positioned, because of her association with certain exotic places and people, as someone who has gone "ethnic."

Sweating profusely, his sensitive stomach rumbling threateningly, Reuben pretends to like the spicy food to impress Polly, but after dinner, at her messy and cluttered studio apartment, he has an embarrassing flare-up of irritable bowel syndrome in her nonsoundproof bathroom (beside the kitchen), where he spends a long time trying (unsuccessfully) to avoid passing gas aloud. To make matters worse, there is no toilet paper with which to wipe, and the toilet gets clogged, overflowing when flushed. Reuben launches into prayer: "Oh God, I beg you please, if you make this water go down, I will sit at your feet, and I will serve you for all of eternity. I'll adopt a Somalian kid, or I'll work in Calcutta, or I'll..." But in spite of his deal-making attempts, the water begins to overflow onto the floor. Desperate, Reuben uses the only objects within reach to try to unplug the toilet—a hand towel (embroidered by Polly's grandmother) wrapped around Polly's brand-new two-hundred-dollar loofa sponge (from Sweden)—soiling objects that were designed to help clean the body.

This hilarious sequence of slapstick events actually suggests a psychologically complex trajectory for Reuben. That is, he is forced to deal with the abject—to surmount his fear of filth—before he can fully develop his subjectivity. Although Reuben's culinary risk-taking has some negative consequences (e.g., diarrhea, gas, vomiting), he tries ethnic food again and again, and he even begins to like it. In the penultimate scene of the film, Polly tries to reject Reuben, saying dismissively, "You're a nice, safe, conventional guy." Reuben protests, "I don't think that's who I really am. Since we've been together, I've felt more uncomfortable, out of place, embarrassed, and just physically sick than I have in my entire life. But I couldn't have gone through all of that. I couldn't have thrown up nineteen times in forty-eight days if I wasn't in love with you." Reuben proves his love for Polly, and that he is now in touch with the abject, by eating peanuts handled by an unclean-looking street vendor and rubbing some of them on the ground to underscore his point, disgusting both Polly and the vendor. Reuben has directly confronted the abject, therefore, by handling his own feces and the Other's dirt.

Having resolved for the moment this psychological crisis, Reuben is free to pursue culinary tourism like Ian in *My Big Fat Greek Wedding*. It is no accident that both characters grow to become food adventurers and that, in both cases, this development is made possible through the mediating site of the ethnic restaurant. For many westerners, eating the Other's food is the ultimate form of *cultural capital*—the social status gained by having a sense of familiarity with the exotic, appearing worldly and well traveled. There is confusion, Heather Schell writes, "at least in the world of images, between a cuisine and the people associated with producing it" (2001, 205). Hence, food becomes a metonym for the people who make it, and we tend to believe that eating it teaches us something about the culture: "We believe that they somehow imbue the food with their ethnicity. It's their presence in the food that teaches us about the culture when we dine" (207–8).

On the one hand, Warren Belasco argues that the explosion of ethnic restaurants in the United States has resulted from young white people reacting against the middle-class, hegemonic values of a culture symbolized by American food. In this model, eating foods (especially spicy ethnic food) is a form of protest against America's cultural imperialism. Ethnic food represents an alternative set of values involving tradition, continuity, authenticity, and pluralism (1989, 2–3)—all of which contrasts with the dominant culture's bland, overly processed, unnatural foodways. On the other hand, what Belasco views as a tactic of resistance should be read instead as a strategy enacted from a dominant position, rather than a marginalized one. bell hooks specifically challenges the manner in which this sort of culinary tourism belies power relationships, stating, "When race and ethnicity become commodified as resources for pleasure, the culture of specific groups, as well as the bodies of individuals, can be seen as constituting an alternative playground where members of dominating races, genders, sexual practices affirm their power-over in intimate relation with the Other" (1998, 183).

This so-called culinary tourism or adventure eating, according to Schell, is "strongly motivated by an attitude bearing deep connections to western colonialism and imperialism" (2001, 217; see also Heldke 2001).

Read this way, incorporating colonial foods into the European/American diet becomes a method of "consuming" and containing the colony (Narayan 1995), and therefore "colonialism continues in the United States in the newly fashioned guise of neocolonialism" (Projansky and Ono 1999, 151). While a desire for new lands, goods, trade routes, Christian converts, and slave sources prompted European colonizers to explore and eventually control nine-tenths of the globe (Young 2003, 2), in our current zeitgeist, the desire to grasp human nature unadulterated by the West sends food adventurers on a parallel mission for "authentic" encounters with the Other via food. Reenacting the colonial impulse to dominate the Other, adventure eating—a form of cultural food colonialism—is motivated by a "deep desire to have contact with—to somehow own an experience of—an exotic Other as a way of making [oneself] more interesting" (Schell 2001, 217).

In *My Big Fat Greek Wedding,* Ian acknowledges this perceived transformation by encounters with the Other, telling Toula that he "came alive" when he met her: "Here's some news about my life to this point. It's boring. Then I met you...and you're interesting—you're beautiful and fun." "The commodification of otherness has been so successful," writes hooks, "because it is offered as a new delight, more intense, more satisfying than normal ways of doing and feeling. Within commodity culture, ethnicity becomes spice, seasoning that can liven up the dull dish that is mainstream white culture" (1998, 181).

How does the Other's food move so quickly from being disgusting and filthy to desirable? If the self needs the abject to feel secure, then how is this abject overcome, resulting, for example, in such a dramatic increase in ethnic restaurants in the West? In the symbolic system of American foodways, the abject frequently takes the shape of ethnic food. The ethnic restaurant's goal is to combine exotic details of the foreign culture with known ones from the dominant local culture, making the customer feel more secure, "making the unfamiliar appear familiar" (Turgeon and Pastinelli 2002, 257; see also Long 2004). In this system of "staged authenticity" (MacCannell [1976] 1989, 1), the customer plays the role of tourist, wanting to feel at home while somewhere else. To create this feeling of safety, the most "offensive" or "disgusting" traditional food items are expunged from the menu, striking a balance between what is familiar to members of the culinary mainstream and what is exotic (see Molz 2004).

In addition to the food itself, the milieu of the ethnic restaurant is saturated with symbols that reassure the Westerner, the classic example being images of beautiful native women, dressed in traditional costumes and engaged in domestic activities—the epitome of Homi Bhabha's "synchronic essentialism" (1983, 24)—fixed in time as powerful, non-threatening "signifiers of stability" (24).[12] By relegating the Other to a nostalgic, precontact time, consumers are empowered to transgress boundaries safely to satisfy their desires. Ethnic restaurants, therefore, become "interstitial spaces" (Bhabha 1994, 5), ritual mediating sites that allow the elaboration of selfhood (individual and group). It is within these interstitial spaces that the abject is surmounted—rendered safe—tipping the scales of the desired/repulsed continuum in the direction of the former, making the Other palatable and, in fact, desirable. As ritualized mediating sites, ethnic restaurants facilitate the transformation of the abject into a safely consumable Other. Put another way, the abject is abjected from the ethnic restaurant.

We see this dynamic play out in *My Big Fat Greek Wedding* when the Other's food is safely consumed in the restaurant, but within the Other's home, it threatens to become disgusting again, whereas in *Along Came Polly*, the ethnic restaurant does not really rise beyond its filthy status for Reuben; he learns, rather, to embrace that very dirt. "Filth," Kristeva reminds us, "is not a quality in itself, but it applies only to what relates to a *boundary*" (1982, 69). The ethnic restaurant becomes a safe space for hooks's "ritual of transcendence"—"a movement out into a world of difference that would transform, an acceptable rite of passage. The direct objective was...to be changed in some way by the encounter" (hooks 1998, 184). Hence, both Ian and Reuben (as well as Polly) transform themselves by consuming the Other's food/body.

If food reveals the difference between Reuben and Polly in *Along Came Polly* and especially the initial polarity dividing the two families in *My Big Fat Greek Wedding*, food, finally, becomes the means by which the families find themselves able to come together at the wedding banquet. Mr. Portokalos's knowledge of the Greek etiology of words succeeds in establishing a connection. He compares the families to the difference between apples and oranges. The root of the word *Miller* is the Greek word *milo* (apple), he explains, and *Portokalos* comes from the Greek word *portokali* (orange). "So, here tonight," he declares, "we have apple and orange. We all different...but, in the end, we all fruit." With this speech, the intercultural conflicts appear to dissolve, and a happy-ever-after ending ensues.

Food in the comedies *My Big Fat Greek Wedding* and *Along Came Polly*, as with the drama *American History X*, expresses distrust about other cultures and the fear of being contaminated/soiled, while these films also depict the simultaneous impulse to consume the Other.

Because food events in such popular cultural "texts" negotiate gender, culture, and race, as well as familial dynamics, we can employ film to work out theories—showing how processes of othering, abjecting, and colonizing are enacted through food traditions. Such analyses of food behavior forge promising new directions for further research into the interrelationship among food, identity, and power dynamics—in ways that move beyond food traditions creating communitas— toward a theory of the ways food behavior and ideology can also negotiate power, belonging, and exclusion.

Notes

My thanks to Elaine Lawless and Elisa Glick for encouraging me to apply Kristeva's theory of abjection to ethnic food, and to Shelley Ingram, who helped develop my understanding of the intersections of psychoanalytic and postcolonial theory. I am also grateful to Joanna Hearne and Karen Piper for their suggestions on an earlier draft of this article.

1. See the Web site, www.lib.berkeley.edu/MRC/foodmovies.html, for a fairly recent filmography and bibliography of food in the movies. See also Zimmerman and Weiss 2005.

2. See hooks 1998; McAfee 1993; Moruzzi 1993; Witt 1998; and Young 1990

3. Later in the film, a flashback to another family meal that occurred before his father was killed shows Derek being socialized to be racist within the context of a peaceful, happy-looking, nuclear-family meal—the epitome of middle-class white America. Derek, as a high school–age student, talks admiringly about Dr. Sweeney, a teacher who has assigned Richard Wright's *Native Son* for a black literature unit. The father's (William Russ) face turns sour, and he sarcastically refers to "affirmative blacktion" and asks, "Now you gotta trade in *great* books for *black* books?" His father's critique of affirmative action sets the stage for Derek to scapegoat minorities for his father's murder (by a black man) while on the job as a firefighter in Compton, a predominantly black area.

4. Laurier Turgeon and Madeleine Pastinelli's definition of an ethnic restaurant as "a restaurant whose sign board or publicity clearly promises the national or regional cuisine of another land" (2002, 252) suggests that the label is self-applied. Ethnic restaurants are not simply places to eat but become symbolically and politically charged: "The term 'ethnic' refers to outsiders, people who come from far away and who are foreign to the mainstream culture. Groups in control are never ethnicities; they use ethnic distinctions to organize social and spatial marginalities...and to legitimize a sort of negative integration of minority groups" (252). Hence, restaurants such as Denny's, Country Kitchen, Cracker Barrel, Perkins, and McDonald's are unproblematically presumed to be all-American-style restaurants although they are not marked as Anglo or ethnic in any way (see Dyer 1997). That ethnic distinction is almost invariably reserved for the category of other, usually nonwhite groups of people.

5. Toula's voice-over provides a context for interpreting the scope of her family's "weirdness." They live in a "normal, middle-class Chicago neighborhood of tasteful, modest homes." The Portokalos house, however, is "modeled after the Parthenon, complete with Corinthian columns and guarded by statues of the gods."

6. Dan Georgakas's review "My Big Fat Greek Gripes" criticizes *My Big Fat Greek Wedding* on a number of levels: "The Greek Americans offered in the film, even allowing considerable latitude for satire, are at best fifty years out of date. The major plot element, the cultural shock of outmarriage, is actually now the cultural norm as more than seventy percent of all Greek Americans outmarry....The notion of insular and culturally naïve Greek Americans is belied by the reality that the percent of Greek Americans who graduate from college is consistently among the highest of all ethnic groups in America" (2003, 37).

7. It is also significant that, following the flashback scenes from her childhood, we never see Toula eating in the remainder of the film, which functions as a sort of female competence, according to feminist scholars (e.g., Bordo 1998).

8. H. David Dalquest designed the aluminum bundt pan in 1950. It is derived from the German word *bund* (a group of people); the *t* was added for copyright purposes. At the height of its popularity, the culinary mainstream of white America considered the bundt cake (a moist cake baked in the fluted tube pan) to be the sophisticated dessert of choice for birthdays, weddings, and other special occasions. "The beautiful, easy cakes," however, "quietly fell from fashion" several decades later (Wolf 2005).

9. As the Millers' only child, Ian is a vegetarian, in opposition to both the dominant American meat-eating culture and probably also the Miller family foodways. It seems safe to assume this based on the tendency for film to treat vegetarianism (like ethnicity) as different, whereas meat eating (like whiteness) is considered to be the norm. A number of scholars have noted how the choice to become vegetarian in the West is often seen as a sign of resistance against the family system and the dominant meat-eating culture (see Belasco 1989; Roth 2005; and Twigg 1983).

10. For example, Sandy eats frosting (intended for the wedding cake) directly from the decorating tube, squeezes the excess grease from Reuben's pizza— "the best part"—onto his own piece, advises Reuben to spank women during sex, and reports that he just "sharted" ("I tried to fart, but shitted").

11. Although I have not sufficiently theorized gender into my analysis, it is important to note Aihwa Ong's 2003 discussion of the way the non-Western woman becomes the "vehicle for misplaced western nostalgia" in relation to the way ethnic restaurants use images of women to portray ethnicity. I am reminded, for instance, of Gayatri Spivak's discussion of how the Third World subject is represented within Western discourse (1988), the mechanics of how the Other is constituted, and Edward Said's discussion of the way the Other is often portrayed as female ([1978] 1994).

Filmography

Along Came Polly (2004). 91min. John Hamburg.
American History X (1998). 119 min. Tony Kaye.
My Big Fat Greek Wedding (2002). 95 min. Joel Zwick.

Works Cited

Adams, Carol J. 1994. The sexual politics of meat. In *Living with contradictions: Controversies in feminist social ethics,* ed. Alison M. Jaggar, 548–57. Boulder, CO: Westview Press.

Angyal, A. 1941. Disgust and related aversions. *Journal of Abnormal and Social Psychology* 36: 393–412.

Belasco, Warren. 1989. *Appetite for change: How the counterculture took on the food industry, 1966–1988.* New York: Pantheon Books.

Bhabha, Homi. 1983. The other question. *Screen* 24 (6): 18–36.

———. 1994. *The Location of Culture.* London: Routledge.

Bordo, Susan. 1998. Hunger as ideology. In *Eating culture,* ed. Ron Scapp and Brian Seitz, 11–35. Albany: State University of New York Press.

Bossard, James H. 1943. Family table talk—An area for sociological study. *American Sociological Review* 18: 295–301.

Boswell, Parley Ann. 1993. Hungry in the land of plenty: Food in Hollywood films. In *Beyond the stars III: The material world in American popular film,* ed. Paul Loukides and Linda K. Fuller, 7–23. Bowling Green, OH: Popular Press.

Douglas, Mary. 1966. *Purity and danger: An analysis of concepts of pollution and taboo.* London: Routledge.

Dyer, Richard. 1997. *White.* New York: Routledge.

Fanon, Frantz. [1952] 1967. The fact of blackness. In *Black skin, white masks,* trans. Charles Lam Markmann, 109–40. Repr., New York: Grove Press.

Georgakas, Dan. 2003. My big fat Greek gripes. *Cineaste* 28 (4): 36–37.

Heldke, Lisa. 2001. Let's cook Thai: Recipes for colonialism. In *Pilaf, pozole, and pad Thai: American women and ethnic foods,* ed. Sherrie A. Inness, 175–97. Amherst: University of Massachusetts Press.

hooks, bell. 1998. Eating the other: Desire and resistance. In *Eating culture,* ed. Ron Scapp and Brian Seitz, 181–200. Albany: State University of New York Press.

Humphrey, Theodore C., and Lin T. Humphrey, eds. 1988. *"We gather together": Food and festival in American life.* Logan: Utah State University Press.

Internet Movie Database. 2005. (accessed July 19, 2005).

Kalčik, Susan. 1984. Ethnic foodways in America: Symbol and the performance of identity. In *Ethnic and regional foodways in the United States,* ed. Linda Keller Brown and Kay Mussell, 37–65. Knoxville: University of Tennessee Press.

Kovel, Joel. [1970] 1988. *White racism: A psychohistory.* Repr., London: Free Association Books.

Kristeva, Julia. 1982. *Powers of horror: An essay on abjection.* New York: Columbia University Press.

———. 1991. *Strangers to ourselves.* Trans. Leon S. Roudiez. New York: Columbia University Press.

Long, Lucy M., ed. 2004. *Culinary tourism*. Lexington: University Press of Kentucky.

MacCannell, Dean. [1976] 1989. *The tourist: A new theory of the leisure class*. Repr., New York: Schocken Books.

McAfee, Nöelle. 1993. Abject strangers: Towards an ethics of respect. In *Ethics, politics, and difference in Julia Kristeva's writing*, ed. Kelly Oliver, 116–34. New York: Routledge.

Molz, Jennie Germann. 2004. Tasting an imagined Thailand: Authenticity and culinary tourism in Thai restaurants. In *Culinary tourism*, ed. Lucy M. Long, 53–75.

Moruzzi, Norma Claire. 1993. National abjects: Julia Kristeva on the process of political self-identification. In *Ethics, politics, and difference in Julia Kristeva's writing*, ed. Kelly Oliver, 135–49.

Narayan, Uma.1995. Eating cultures: Incorporation, identity, and Indian food. *Social Identities* 1(1): 63–86.

Nichols, Michael P., and Richard C. Schwartz. [1984] 1998. *Family therapy: Concepts and methods*. Repr., Boston: Allyn and Bacon.

Ong, Aihwa. 2003. Cyberpublics and diaspora politics among transnational Chinese. *Interventions: International Journal of Postcolonial Studies* 5 (1): 82–100.

Pratt, Mary Louise. [1992] 1998. *Imperial eyes: Travel writing and transculturation*. Repr., London: Routledge.

Projansky, Sarah, and Kent A. Ono. 1999. Strategic whiteness as cinematic racial politics. In *Whiteness: The communication of social identity*, ed. Thomas Nakayama and Judith N. Martin, 149–74. Thousand Oaks, CA: Sage.

Radner, Joan Newlon, and Susan Lanser. 1993. Strategies of coding in women's cultures. In *Feminist messages: Coding in women's folk culture*, ed. Joan Newlon Radner, 1–29. Urbana: University of Illinois Press.

Roth, LuAnne. 2005. "Beef. It's what's for dinner": Vegetarians, meat-eaters, and the negotiation of familial relationships. *Food, Culture, and Society* 8 (2): 45–69.

Said, Edward. [1978] 1994. *Orientalism*. Repr., New York: Vintage Books.

Schell, Heather. 2001. Gendered feasts: A feminist reflects on dining in New Orleans. In *Pilaf, pozole, and pad Thai: American women and ethnic foods*, ed. Sherrie A. Inness, 199–221.

Spivak, Gayatri. 1988. Can the subaltern speak? In *Marxism and the interpretation of culture*, ed. Cary Nelson and Lawrence Grossberg, 271–313. Urbana: University of Illinois Press.

Spurr, David. 1993. *The rhetoric of empire: Colonial discourse in journalism, travel writing, and imperial administration*. Durham, NC: Duke University Press.

Todorov, Tzvetan. 1984. *The conquest of America: The question of the other*. Trans. Richard Howard. New York: Harper and Row.

Turgeon, Laurier, and Madeleine Pastinelli. 2002. "Eat the world": Postcolonial encounters in Québec City's ethnic restaurants. *Journal of American Folklore* 115 (456): 247–68.

Turner, Patricia A. 1987. Church's fried chicken and the Klan: A rhetorical analysis of rumor in the black community. *Western Folklore* 46: 294–306.

———. 1993. Cannibalism: "They doe eat each other alive." In *I heard it through the grapevine: Rumor in African-American culture*, 9–32. Berkeley: University of California Press.

Twigg, Julia. 1983. Vegetarianism and the meanings of meat. In *The sociology of food and eating: Essays on the sociological significance of food,* ed. Anne Murcott, 18–30. England: Gower Publishing Company, Ltd.

Witt, Doris. 1998. Soul food: Where the chitterlings hits the (primal) pan. In *Eating Culture,* ed. Ron Scapp and Brian Seitz, 258–87.

Wolf, Bonny. 2005. Remembering the era of the bundt cake. *Weekend Edition,* National Public Radio, January 16. (accessed July 19, 2005).

Yamamoto, Traise. 1999. Masking selves, making subjects: Japanese-American women, identity, and the body. Berkeley: University of California Press.

Young, Iris Marion. 1990. *Justice and the politics of difference.* Princeton, NJ: Princeton University Press.

Young, Robert J.C. 2003. *Postcolonialism.* Oxford: Oxford University Press.

Zimmerman, Steve, and Ken Weiss. 2005. *Food in the movies.* London: McFarland & Company, Inc.

Contributors

HOLLY BLACKFORD IS assistant professor of English at Rutgers University-Camden. She teaches and publishes literary criticism on American, children's, and adolescent literature, as well as literatures in English. She has recently published articles on Louisa May Alcott's *Little Women*, Emily Bronte's *Wuthering Heights*, J. M. Barrie's *Peter and Wendy*, Carlo Collodi's *Pinocchio*, Anita Diamont's *The Red Tent*, Julia Alvarez's *In the Time of the Butterflies*, Shirley Jackson's *Haunting at Hill House*, and Margaret Atwood's *Alias Grace*. Her book *Out of This World: Why Literature Matters to Girls* (Teachers College Press, education division of Columbia, 2004) analyzes the empirical reader-responses of girls to literature. She currently holds an International Reading Association research award for the study of responses to *Huck Finn* and *To Kill A Mockingbird*.

GILLIAN HELFIELD IS a film scholar and lecturer specializing in Canadian and Québec cinema. She wrote her Ph.D. dissertation on the cinéma vérité movement at the NFB, and has written articles on this subject for *Topia*, the *Encyclopedia of Documentary Film* and *Western Folklore*. Other areas of academic interest include genre studies, television studies, and national cinemas, which Dr. Helfield has taught at the University of Toronto, Trent, McMaster, the University of Warwick, and the University of Buckingham (UK). Her book on rural cinema, *Representing the Rural: Space, Place and Identity in Films about the Land* was published by Wayne State University Press in October 2006.

CAROL E. HENDERSON is associate professor of English and Black American studies at the University of Delaware, Newark campus, and teaches a number of courses on literature, popular culture, and art. She has edited and published *James Baldwin's Go Tell It on the Mountain: Historical and Critical Essays* (Peter Lang Publishers 2006), as well as her own study *Scarring the Black Body: Race and Representation in African American Literature* (U of Missouri Press 2002). In addition to numerous articles in professional journals and critical volumes, she has a forthcoming essay "King Kong Ain't Got Sh** On Me: Allegories, Anxieties, and the Performance of Race in Mass Media" in *The Journal of Popular Culture*. She is currently at work on an edited collection entitled *Imag(in)ing America: The African American Body in Literature and Culture*, and a monograph entitled *The Hottentot Venus Revisited: Visions, Revisions, and Literary Responses*.

Mikel J. Koven is a folklorist and ethnologist with a specialization in film and television studies, as well as in urban legends. He is senior lecturer at the University of Worcester and head of the Film Studies Unit. He has published *Blaxploitation Films* (Pocket Essentials, 2001), *La Dolce Morte: Vernacular Cinema and the Italian* Giallo *Film* (Scarecrow Press, 2006), co-edited a special issue of *Western Folklore* on the topic of "Film & Folklore," a special issue of *Shofar* on the topic "Cool Jewz: Contemporary Jewish Identity in Popular Culture," and his forthcoming monograph, *Film, Folklore and Urban Legends* should be out early in 2008.

K. A. Laity currently holds the position of assistant professor in the Department of English at the College of St. Rose in Albany, NY, where she teaches medieval literature and culture, film, popular culture and creative writing. She received a Ph.D. in medieval studies from the University of Connecticut in 2003. A multifaceted scholar and writer, Laity has recently won the Eureka Short Story Fellowship and a Finlandia Foundation grant. Her stories and essays have appeared in various academic journals and literary magazines. Her novel *Pelzmantel: A Medieval Tale* was nominated for several awards. Visit her website www.kalaity.com for up to date information.

Margarete Johanna Landwehr is associate professor in German and the German Program coordinator at West Chester University near Philadelphia. She received her B.A. in German from Georgetown University and her M.A. and Ph.D. degrees in German language and literature from Harvard University. Her areas of expertise include postwar German and Austrian literature and film, psychology and literature, and turn-of-the-century Viennese literature. She has published articles on Heinrich von Kleist, Arthur Schnitzler, Josef Roth, and postwar German writers and filmmakers. Her present book project deals with the trauma narrative in postwar German literature and film.

Julie M-A LeBlanc is a doctoral candidate in folklore at Memorial University of Newfoundland and a graduate student in management of cultural organizations at the École des hautes études commerciales (Montréal). Her thesis focuses on the commercialization of Québécois folklore as distributed by the micro-brewing industry. Other interests and works include the use of folklore in various media, the marketing of tradition, Québécois identity and folklore, Celtic studies, political and independence movements, popular culture, film studies, customs, legends, folklore in the tourism industry, and traditional storytelling events.

Jᴀᴍᴇs A. Mɪʟʟᴇʀ is assistant professor of film and cultural studies at Purdue University-Calumet in Indiana. He received his degree from the University of Missouri-Columbia. Research interests include religion and folklore in film and popular media, the aesthetics and politics of popular and experimental musics, and the impact of the new media on public discourse about ethics and community.

Rᴇʙᴇᴄᴄᴀ Pʀɪᴍᴇ is a doctoral candidate in the Department of Film, Television, and Digital Media at the University of California, Los Angeles, where she is writing a dissertation on blacklisted American filmmakers in Europe. Her other research interests include early ethnographic cinema and transnational cinema. Her work has appeared in the journals *Post Script* and *Film Quarterly* and will be included in the forthcoming publication *The Blacklist: Reviewing the Films of the Hollywood Left* (Rutgers University Press).

Lᴜᴀɴɴᴇ Rᴏᴛʜ teaches American folklore and film studies in the English Department at the University of Missouri, Columbia, where she also serves as associate editor for the Center for eResearch and SyndicateMizzou (SyndicateMizzou.org). Roth's research has primarily focused on foodways and material culture, her work appearing in *Western Folklore* and *Food, Culture and Society* as well as in *The Greenwood Encyclopedia of African American Folklore* (2005) and *Of Corpse: Death and Humor in Folklore and Popular Culture* (2003). Particularly interested in how food is used to negotiate ethnicity, gender, and power, her present study interrogates cinematic representations of the Thanksgiving meal through a postcolonial lens.

Mᴀʀᴋ Aʟʟᴇɴ Pᴇᴛᴇʀsᴏɴ holds a joint appointment in anthropology and international studies at Miami University (Ohio). A former political journalist, his research centers around semiotic and ethnographic analysis of media and consumer culture, particularly the diverse ways in which media texts and consumer goods become part of people's everyday experience and practice. Peterson's interests also include political rhetoric about nation and language, modernity and global-local relations, and computer pedagogy. He has conducted fieldwork in Egypt, India, and the United States. Peterson is the author of *Anthropology and Mass Communication* (Berghahn 2003). He has published articles in *Anthropology Today*, *Anthropological Quarterly*, *Childhood*, *The New Review of Hypermedia and Multimedia*, *M/C: A Journal of Media and Culture*, *Teaching Anthropology*, and *Alif: the Journal of Contemporary Poetics*. He has authored chapters in several books, including the *Encyclopedia of Anthropology* (Sage 2005), *At War With Words* (Walter de Gruyter 2003), and *Media Anthropology* (Sage 2005). He is currently working on a book entitled *Connected in Cairo: Transnational Popular Culture and the Making of the Cosmopolitan Class.*

SHARON R. SHERMAN is a folklorist and independent filmmaker. She is professor of English and former director of the Folklore Program at the University of Oregon where she teaches courses on film, folklore, fieldwork, video production, and popular culture. Her films and videos address the interconnection between tradition and the creative process. They include: *Inti Raymi*, an indigenous Andean celebration; *Kid Shoes*, on young men and music; *Tales of the Supernatural*, an analysis of story-telling events and urban legends; *Passover, A Celebration*; *Kathleen Ware, Quiltmaker*; and *Spirits in the Wood*. Sherman also served as a camera-woman for portions of Jorge Preloran's series, *Patagonia*. Most of Sher-man's published work has concentrated on the relationship between film and folklore, and perceptions about traditional expressive behavior as revealed by filmmakers. In addition to numerous articles, she is the author of *Chainsaw Sculptor: The Art of J. Chester Armstrong* (1995) and *Documenting Ourselves: Film, Video, and Culture* (1998), the first in-depth study of folkloristic films as a genre of documentary film. She and Mikel Koven co-edited "Film and Folklore," a special issue of *Western Folklore*. Sherman has served on the Executive Board of the American Folklore Society and as the film and videotape review editor for *Western Folklore* and the *Journal of American Folklore*, and is on the board of Folkstreams (www.folkstreams.net), a website devoted to streaming folklore films.

TARSHIA L. STANLEY is an associate professor in the English Department at Spelman College in Atlanta, Georgia. She teaches courses in film studies and visual imagery particularly as it pertains to images of women. She has authored several articles critiquing black women in African Ameri-can, African, and Caribbean cinema as well as black female iconography in American popular culture. She received the A.B. from Duke Univer-sity and the M.A. and Ph.D. from the University of Florida where she was a McKnight Doctoral Fellow. She is at work on a book examining the black female body in Hollywood film and editing an encyclopedia of hip hop literature for Greenwood Press.

Index